Chicago on foot

Chicago

on foot AN ARCHITECTURAL WALKING TOUR

by Ira J. Bach

President, Urban Associates, Inc.

PHOTOGRAPHS BY PHILIP A. TURNER

FOLLETT PUBLISHING COMPANY   Chicago   New York

Picture credits

Photographs © 1969 by Philip A. Turner unless otherwise noted.
Cover photo by Arthur Siegel.
Orlando R. Cabanban, 74-75, 116; Chicago Department of Urban Renewal,
89, 158; Chicago Municipal Reference Library, 98; Chicago Park District,
123, 205; Chicago Plan Commission, 33 top left, 57; Bill Engdahl,
Hedrich-Blessing, 51 left; © 1969 by Follett Publishing Company, 6, 8 right,
11 left, 19, 20 left, 26 left, top & center, 30 top left, 36-37, 40, 42, 43 left top,
middle, bottom, 45, 59, 64, 79, 84, 86, 87 left, bottom right, 90, 97 top right,
bottom, 105, 117, 122, 124, 144-145, 148, 150, 153, 187, 208, 215, 225, 226, 227,
229, 231, 235, 236, 237, 242, 243, 244, 265, 268, 269, 270-271, 274, 290-291,
294, 313; Hube Henry, Hedrich-Blessing, 11 right; Balthazar Korab, 26
bottom; Mart Studios, Inc. 76 top left.

Standard Book Number 695-81125-8   cloth binding
Standard Book Number 695-81126-6   paper binding

Library of Congress Catalog Card Number: 69-20278

First printing E

To Muriel

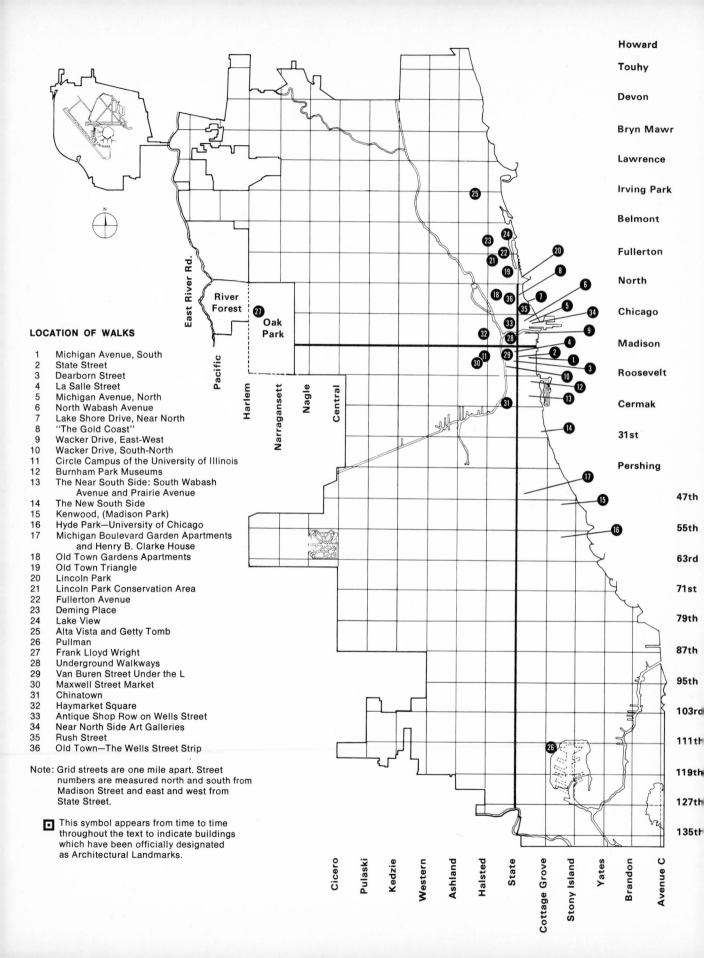

Howard
Touhy
Devon
Bryn Mawr
Lawrence
Irving Park
Belmont
Fullerton
North
Chicago
Madison
Roosevelt
Cermak
31st
Pershing
47th
55th
63rd
71st
79th
87th
95th
103rd
111th
119th
127th
135th

East River Rd.
River Forest
Oak Park
Pacific
Harlem
Narragansett
Nagle
Central

Cicero
Pulaski
Kedzie
Western
Ashland
Halsted
State
Cottage Grove
Stony Island
Yates
Brandon
Avenue C

LOCATION OF WALKS

1 Michigan Avenue, South
2 State Street
3 Dearborn Street
4 La Salle Street
5 Michigan Avenue, North
6 North Wabash Avenue
7 Lake Shore Drive, Near North
8 "The Gold Coast"
9 Wacker Drive, East-West
10 Wacker Drive, South-North
11 Circle Campus of the University of Illinois
12 Burnham Park Museums
13 The Near South Side: South Wabash
        Avenue and Prairie Avenue
14 The New South Side
15 Kenwood, (Madison Park)
16 Hyde Park—University of Chicago
17 Michigan Boulevard Garden Apartments
        and Henry B. Clarke House
18 Old Town Gardens Apartments
19 Old Town Triangle
20 Lincoln Park
21 Lincoln Park Conservation Area
22 Fullerton Avenue
23 Deming Place
24 Lake View
25 Alta Vista and Getty Tomb
26 Pullman
27 Frank Lloyd Wright
28 Underground Walkways
29 Van Buren Street Under the L
30 Maxwell Street Market
31 Chinatown
32 Haymarket Square
33 Antique Shop Row on Wells Street
34 Near North Side Art Galleries
35 Rush Street
36 Old Town—The Wells Street Strip

Note: Grid streets are one mile apart. Street
        numbers are measured north and south from
        Madison Street and east and west from
        State Street.

☐ This symbol appears from time to time
    throughout the text to indicate buildings
    which have been officially designated
    as Architectural Landmarks.

Introduction   xi

Part I: Architectural Walks

Contents

PART II. EYE LEVEL WALKS

Introduction

The walks proposed here have been selected to present Chicago as a great cosmopolitan city as well as a collection of local community areas, all tied together by an intricate web of transportation that makes them accessible to the pedestrian for a closer view.

Since Chicago is a vast outdoor museum of great architecture created in about one hundred years, the major focus of the walks is architectural. From 1883 to 1893 the "Chicago School of Architecture" came into being. During that decade a whole galaxy of buildings appeared, reaching the unprecedented heights of twelve, fourteen, sixteen, and twenty-three stories. The architects of the Chicago school employed a new type of construction: *the iron skeleton,* at that time called quite simply "Chicago Construction." They invented a new kind of foundation to cope with the problems of the muddy ground of Chicago: *the floating foundation.* They introduced the horizontally elongated window: *the "Chicago window."* They created the modern business and administration building. And around the turn of the century, the so-called Prairie House came into being here.

Of equal significance is the current work of Chicago architects, often characterized as a continuation of the "Chicago school." The pure forms, horizontally elongated windows, and rugged strength and force are still to be seen in many of today's buildings. Architects of the present, however, have not hesitated to experiment with their own designs and materials. Though Mies van der Rohe's "Glass Houses" on North Lake Shore Drive may be considered the ultimate development of certain trends of the Chicago school, the cylindrical towers of Marina City bear little resemblance. Their concrete slab construction, circular balconies, and pie-shaped rooms hardly follow the tradition of the "Chicago school" of architects. Nor does the facade of the new Geophysical Sciences Building at the

University of Chicago—though the older school of architects would approve the functional origin of the new features.

Complete coverage of buildings worth noting in Chicago can not possibly be attempted, especially in view of the tremendous pace at which construction is going on. While following the routes proposed here, the pedestrian will many times come across other interesting or beautiful buildings. The frequency with which this may happen is only another tribute to the endless vitality of this tremendous city.

Chicago is famous too for one of the first comprehensive city plans produced on this continent. The pedestrian will become aware of the planning, especially on the lake front. In 1909 Daniel H. Burnham and Edward H. Bennett enunciated policies that have been instrumental in shaping the city of today. They established, among other things, the city's shoreline for public use only, by recommending the extension of lake-front parks, and set the pattern for the city's system of forest preserves, linked by highways.

Chicago's street system is the conventional grid, laid out with major streets at mile and one-half mile spacing. There are also a number of diagonal streets, some of them tracing old Indian trails, which bisect the junctions of major streets of the grid pattern, forming six-spoked intersections—creating some of the city's most difficult traffic problems.

More recently, a number of expressways have been built in Chicago. These carry traffic to and from the central business district and also serve large volumes of north-south and east-west crosstown traffic. The new roads have considerably shortened travel time within the city and have tied the various parts of the metropolitan area more tightly together. They have also helped to improve public transportation by the installation of rapid transit lines in the median strip of the Eisenhower, Dan Ryan and Kennedy expressways.

The street numbering system in Chicago follows the compass, with the east-west division marked by State street, and the north-south directions divided by Madison street. The city is about 25 miles north and south, and about 15 miles east and west.

xiv

Since all of the city's topography is flat, walking—which is said to be one of the best forms of exercise—will not be strenuous. The routes outlined here are well lighted and well patrolled at night, although most of them are designed for daytime.

Instructions for each walk on "How to get there" assume that downtown Chicago—the Loop—is the starting place. Since bus-routes and bus numbers change from time to time, the safest way will be to phone the CTA for precise instructions before starting out—or at least ask the bus driver whether the number you are here told to take will still carry you to your destination.

This book makes no attempt to advise on places to stay or eat. The city abounds with good hotels and restaurants, lists of which can be obtained from the Chicago Convention Bureau (332 South Michigan) or the Chicago tourist office in the Civic Center (118 North Clark). Any references to eating places are given purely for information rather than recommendation.

In the preparation of this book I particularly want to acknowledge and thank Cora Barron for her editorial guidance; Lewis W. Hill, Commissioner of the Department of Development and Planning for the base maps used in the text; Robert Dishon for assistance in reviewing the text; Carl W. Condit, Hugh Duncan and J. Carson Webster for their critical statements in *Chicago's Famous Buildings* (University of Chicago Press, 1965), which have set a pattern of excellence in reviewing the Chicago School of Architecture; and Marshall Holleb, without whose companionship and wit I might have given up walking long ago.

IRA J. BACH
Chicago, March, 1969

Architectural walks

Walk-1

Buckingham
Memorial Fountain.

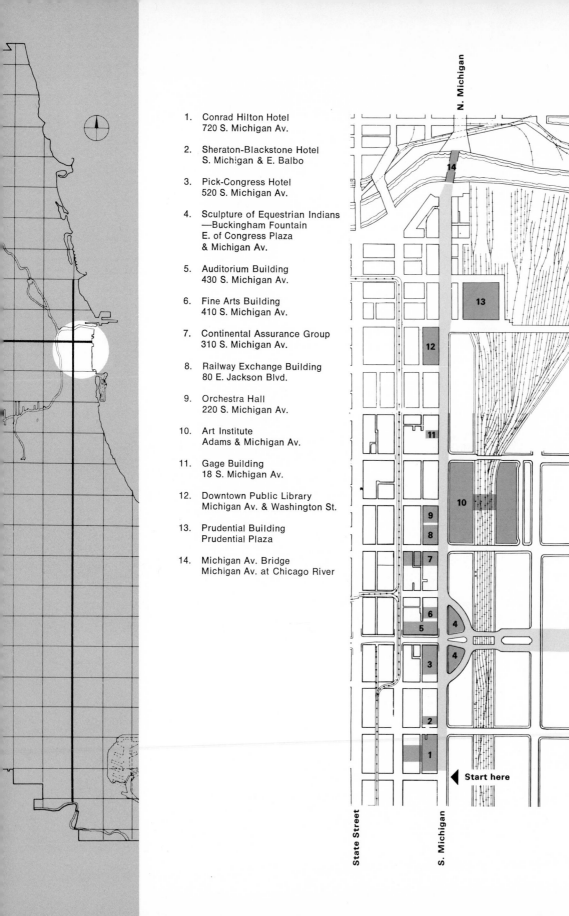

1. Conrad Hilton Hotel
    720 S. Michigan Av.

2. Sheraton-Blackstone Hotel
    S. Michigan & E. Balbo

3. Pick-Congress Hotel
    520 S. Michigan Av.

4. Sculpture of Equestrian Indians
    —Buckingham Fountain
    E. of Congress Plaza
    & Michigan Av.

5. Auditorium Building
    430 S. Michigan Av.

6. Fine Arts Building
    410 S. Michigan Av.

7. Continental Assurance Group
    310 S. Michigan Av.

8. Railway Exchange Building
    80 E. Jackson Blvd.

9. Orchestra Hall
    220 S. Michigan Av.

10. Art Institute
    Adams & Michigan Av.

11. Gage Building
    18 S. Michigan Av.

12. Downtown Public Library
    Michigan Av. & Washington St.

13. Prudential Building
    Prudential Plaza

14. Michigan Av. Bridge
    Michigan Av. at Chicago River

N. Michigan

Chicago River

Madison

Balbo

State Street

S. Michigan

Start here

Walk · 1

MICHIGAN AVENUE : SOUTH

WALKING TIME: About 2 hours.   HOW TO GET THERE: Take a southbound CTA "shuttle"
bus, No. 149 (Michigan-State-Wacker—reduced fare service) on State Street (2 blocks west of
Michigan). Get off at Balbo Street (700 S). Cross Michigan Avenue, and you are in Grant Park.

Chicago's skyline is one of the most exhilarating sights in the
world. Day or night the view is magnificent—from an airplane
approaching the city, from a boat on Lake Michigan, from a car
on the Outer Drive, or from the footpaths in Grant Park.
It is always impressive.

Michigan Avenue stretches along Lake Michigan from the ancient
Illinois Central railroad station, several blocks south of Balbo,
to the recently constructed 40-story Prudential Building, at
Randolph Street to the north, before other streets intervene to
bar the view of the lake. From the Conrad Hilton Hotel, just
south of Balbo, to the Chicago River, three blocks north of the
Prudential—the distance covered by this walk—Michigan
Avenue is rich with sculpture, gardens, and fountains.

Grant Park—Extending from Roosevelt Road (12th Street) to Monroe Street (100 S).

Grant Park was no accident. Daniel Burnham designed it as part
of the Chicago Plan of 1909. First, the lake was filled from
Michigan Avenue out to what is now the Outer Drive, to provide
the necessary land space. The park was planned as an immense
green expanse following loosely the pattern of Versailles. In
the spring, when the park's hundreds of small trees and shrubs
are in bloom, this is a place of incomparable beauty.

And in the midst is the magnificent seated Lincoln, last work of
Augustus St. Gaudens. Chicago is the fortunate possessor of
this monument because of a $100,000 bequest for a Lincoln statue
from John Crerar, the man who also willed the city the John
Crerar Library. (St. Gaudens was also the sculptor of the standing
Lincoln statue at the entrance to Lincoln Park. See Walk No. 20,

5

Lincoln Park. Don't look for a statue of *Grant* in Grant Park; that's in Lincoln Park instead!)

The area that now is occupied by the Monroe Street parking lot and the Illinois Central railroad tracks, between Monroe and Randolph, will eventually be decked over and landscaped, thus completing Burnham's original plan for the park.

Conrad Hilton Hotel—720 South Michigan.
Architects: Holabird and Roche (1927)

Start your walk from the Conrad Hilton Hotel, on the southwest corner of Balbo and Michigan. Here you will be in the world's largest hotel (previously the Stevens), which contains about 3,000 rooms. With its many restaurants, grills, bars, meeting rooms, and spacious ballroom, the Conrad Hilton is almost continuously being used throughout the year as headquarters for national conventions and conferences. (Hotel tours can be arranged by advance reservation with the service manager. For information phone WA-2-4400, and ask for the bell captain.)

Sheraton-Blackstone Hotel—Michigan and Balbo.
Architects: Marshall and Fox (1910)

Just north of the Hilton, on the *northwest* corner of Michigan and Balbo, is the Sheraton-Blackstone Hotel, many times a political headquarters during national nominating conventions. It offers a rather pleasing exterior of French Renaissance architecture. At the time it was built, in fact, it won a gold medal for excellence of design.

Congress Hotel (now the Pick-Congress)—
520 South Michigan.
Architects: Clinton J. Warren (1893);
Holabird and Roche (1902 and 1907);
Holabird and Root (1956)

The Pick-Congress Hotel stands opposite the Congress Plaza Drive. In contrast with the Sheraton-Blackstone's exterior, it has a facade of rugged gray limestone suggesting the influence of Henry Richardson. Its "Peacock Alley" off the main lobby was once one of the city's gathering places for outstanding social events. In the most recent renovation a section of the first floor, on the north side, was opened up and arcaded, to allow the

Congress Hotel.

6

widening of Congress Street into Congress Parkway. (The south side of the Auditorium Building, across the street to the north, underwent the same kind of change.)

Buckingham Memorial Fountain—Designed by Bennett, Parsons, and Frost of Chicago and Jacques Lambert of Paris (1926)

Flanking Congress Plaza—across Michigan Avenue in Grant Park —are two American Indian equestrians with drawn bows, created by the Yugoslavian sculptor Ivan Mestrovic. Of heroic scale, they make a sweeping entrance to the enormous Buckingham Fountain, just to the east. This fountain, modeled from one of the Versailles fountains, is said to be the largest in the world—about twice as large as its model. It has a great central stream with 133 jets of water, some of which reach about two hundred feet in the air. Each night from 9:00 to 9:30 during its active season (May through September) the Fountain is illuminated, with shifting colors played on it throughout the half hour. It has become a popular rendezvous day and night for visitors to Chicago.

The Buckingham Fountain was donated to the city of Chicago in 1927 by Miss Kate Buckingham in memory of her brother Clarence.

⊡ Auditorium Building—430 South Michigan. Architects: Adler and Sullivan (1889); Architect for Restoration of Auditorium Theatre: Harry Weese (1967)

The Auditorium Building, on the northwest corner of Michigan Avenue and Congress Parkway—now owned by Roosevelt University—is one of Chicago's most famous cultural and architectural landmarks. Its construction was a triumph of the partnership of Louis Sullivan, with his inspired architectural imagination, and Dankmar Adler, with his extraordinary engineering genius.

The Auditorium Theatre, originally surrounded by hotel and office space, has long been justifiably renowned for its large, well-equipped stage and its perfect acoustics.

The Chicago Landmarks Commission citation reads:

> In recognition of the community spirit which here joined commercial and artistic ends, uniting hotel, office building, and

theatre in one structure; the inventiveness of the engineer displayed from foundations to the perfect acoustics; and the genius of the architect which gave form and, with the aid of the original ornament, expressed the spirit of festivity in rooms of great splendor.

Disaster threatened the building in 1929, however, when the Chicago Opera Company, which had used the Auditorium Theatre for many years, moved to the newly completed Civic Opera Building; and it became a certainty with the economic depression of the 1930's. By 1940 the Auditorium Building was bankrupt and the theatre was closed. From 1942 to 1945 the building was used as Chicago headquarters for the United Service Organization. In 1946 it was purchased by Roosevelt University (then Roosevelt College), and hotel rooms and offices were converted as needed for its new purpose.

Left, Auditorium building. *Right,* Fine Arts building.

8

The Auditorium Theatre was fortunately left untouched at this time, though all movable contents had been sold at auction soon after bankruptcy was declared. Unable to raise the enormous amount of money needed to restore the theatre, Roosevelt University nevertheless appreciated its value. In 1958 the University established a nonprofit organization, the Auditorium Theatre Council, which in nine years succeeded in raising the $2,250,000 required for restoration. After 26 years of darkness, the Auditorium Theatre opened once again on October 31, 1967, with the New York City Ballet performing to an audience of 4,200.

Tours of the Auditorium Theatre may be arranged by contacting the Council at 922-2110.

Fine Arts Building—410 South Michigan.
Architect: S. S. Beman (1884)

Next to the Auditorium is the Fine Arts Building, for years a center of musical and dramatic events and at one time—along with the Auditorium and Orchestra Hall—the performing arts center of Chicago. The facade is obviously less distinguished than that of the Auditorium. The interior contains two theatres and high-ceilinged upper floors with studios and recital halls—from which sounds of hopeful artists can be heard scaling the heights.

Continental National American Building—
55 East Jackson.
Architect: C. F. Murphy Associates (1962)

Of the two Continental Insurance buildings on Jackson Boulevard, the one facing Michigan, which was constructed in 1925, is inconsequential in design. The newer building, facing Jackson Boulevard and Wabash Avenue, is far superior. This is a design of the highest quality—a building that expresses tremendous strength, especially through the use of steel in vertical supports and horizontal spandrels.

As you turn back to Michigan Avenue, note the *Railway Exchange Building* on the corner (80 East Jackson), famous chiefly because Daniel Burnham had his office there while preparing the Plan of 1909 for Chicago. *Orchestra Hall*, next door, at 220 South Michigan, is the home of the Chicago Symphony Orchestra. The building has been recently rehabilitated throughout.

Art Institute of Chicago—Michigan Avenue at Adams.
Architects: Shepley, Rutan, and Coolidge (1892);
For McKinlock Court: Coolidge and Hodgson (1924);
For Morton Wing: Shaw, Metz, and Associates (1962)

Now cross Michigan to view one of Chicago's most prized
possessions, its Art Institute—the entrance guarded by two large
sculptured lions. So overpowering, in fact, are the lions that
most people fail to see the statue of George Washington
that is standing in the central arch at the top of
the entrance steps.

The original part of the building is French Renaissance in spirit,
a style considered appropriate for art museums at the time but
quite at variance with the trend of the Chicago School. In the center
of McKinlock Court, which is classical rather than Renaissance,
is a fountain with sea creatures sculptured by Carl Milles—a
duplicate of one in his native Sweden. Here in the open air,
lunch is served on clear summer days.

The Art Institute houses a theatre and an art and drama school,
in addition to its art collections. A section of special interest
to architects is the Burnham Library of Architecture Gallery,
created to provide space for exhibits from the Burnham Library
Collection—established in 1912 in memory of the great
architect and city planner, Daniel H. Burnham.

Among the Institute's especially noted art treasures are an
unusually large collection of French impressionist paintings, a
superb variety of works by the Spanish master El Greco and his
fellow countryman Goya, a room of paintings by Rembrandt,
and an extensive collection of Oriental art. The building's latest
addition, Morton Wing, contains a permanent exhibit of
contemporary painting and sculpture.

Open daily 10:00 A.M. to 5:00 P.M. Sundays, 1:00-6:00 P.M.
General admission always free. For special, temporary exhibits a
small fee is usually charged.

Under Michigan Avenue, north and south of the Art Institute,
are 2 of the city's largest underground parking facilities,
with space for 4,000 cars.

Top left, Bronze lion in front of the Art Institute. *Bottom left,* Entrance to the main reading room of the Chicago Public Library with its elaborate mosaics and coffered ceiling. *Right,* Continental National American building.

10

◘ **Gage Building**—18 South Michigan.
Architects: Holabird and Roche; architect for the
decorative facade: Louis Sullivan (1898)

Back on the west side of Michigan, just beyond Monroe Street,
you come to the Gage Building. Referring to Louis Sullivan's
facade on this building—the only part of the structure that he
designed—the Architectural Landmarks Commission in its citation
speaks of "the imaginative use of original ornament." Although
the 2 buildings to the south of it, at 30 and 24 South Michigan,
which were completely the work of Holabird and Roche,
seem more modern in their lack of ornament, they do not equal
the high quality of design in the Gage Building.

The entire citation from the Architectural Landmarks
Commission reads:

> In recognition of the fine relations established between piers,
> windows, and wall surfaces; the excellence of proportions
> throughout; and the imaginative use of original ornament.

Chicago Public Library—78 East Washington.
Architects: Shepley, Rutan, and Coolidge (1897)

Extending a full block along Michigan Avenue, from Washington
to Randolph, is the main building of the Chicago Public Library.
Though not at all in the style of the Chicago School of that time,
it is an impressive example of revivalist architecture, not only
on the outside but throughout the interior as well. The broad
marble staircases and the many beautifully colored mosaics that
decorate both the walls and the ceilings are a magnificent
sight for any period.

Here are the central stacks and reading rooms of the city's entire
library system, which consists of more than 50 branches and a
total of over 3 million items—phonograph records, musical scores,
pictures, and slides, as well as books and periodicals.

Open daily 9:00 A.M. to 9:00 P.M.; closed Sundays and holidays.

North of Randolph

Cross Michigan Avenue at Randolph to visit the observation
tower—and restaurant if you choose—at the top of the
Prudential Building, a 40-story skyscraper on the northeast side

of this intersection. If the day is clear, you will be rewarded with a magnificent panoramic view of the city.

End the walk 3 blocks farther north, at the Michigan Avenue bridge over the Chicago River, and read the commemoratative markers about Fort Dearborn and the Fort Dearborn massacre. This is the spot where it all began for Chicago. In good weather, boat trips on the river and lake are available at the bridge. For those who decide to take one, another excellent view of the city's skyline is one of the rewards.

This area east of Michigan and north of Randolph is about to be developed into a city within a city, comprised of high-rise buildings with apartments, offices, and cultural facilities—all constructed on railroad air rights. It is estimated that the apartments alone will house about 25,000 people. Included in the plans are three horizontal decks over the tracks: (1) for express traffic, (2) for parking and pedestrians, and (3) for local traffic and landscaping. In this development, known as the Illinois Central Air Rights Project, the railroad and the developers have agreed to follow the city's plan and guidelines for the area.

1. Sears, Roebuck and Co.
   403 S. State St.

2. Home Federal Savings and
   Loan Association of Chicago
   201 S. State St.

3. Montgomery Ward and Co.
   140 S. State St.

4. Palmer House
   State and Monroe Sts.

5. Carson Pirie Scott and Co.
   1 S. State St.

6. 32 N. State (previously the
   Reliance Building)

7. Marshall Field and Co.
   111 N. State St.

8. United of America Building
   1 East Wacker Dr.

State St.

Wacker Drive

Madison

Congress

Start here

State St.

Walk · 2

STATE STREET

WALKING TIME: About 1 hour.   HOW TO GET THERE: Walk to Congress Parkway, 7 blocks
south of Randolph; or take any southbound CTA bus on State Street south of Randolph,
and get off at Congress (500 S). (Check with the driver to be sure the bus will not leave
State before it reaches Congress.)

State Street—"That Great Street," as the city's commercial
promoters enjoy calling it!—boasts the biggest strip of major
department stores of any street in America. As a part of Chicago's
central business district, State Street offers economic advantages
provided nowhere else in the entire Midwest. It is a market for
buyers and sellers from all over the nation and the world, and this
fact alone would give it special distinction. But, in addition,
State Street displays some architectural gems along the way as it
stretches through the Loop from the Congress Parkway to
Wacker Drive—the extent of this walk.

Although State Street itself is not predominantly a theatre
and entertainment strip, it becomes at night Chicago's Great White
Way, as a result of its unusually large and brilliant lights.

◱ Sears Roebuck Store—403 South State Street. Architect: William LeBaron Jenney (1891)

Starting the walk at Congress, you come first to the Sears
Roebuck Store, located on the east side of State and extending a
whole block—from Congress north to Van Buren. In its early
days this was known as the Leiter Building II. Levi Z. Leiter, once
a partner of Marshall Field, had already done business on his
own at another location. The first Leiter Building, also designed by
Jenney, stood at the corner of Wells and Monroe streets and
later became the Morris Building. Although the present Sears
Roebuck store was originally constructed for still another
company, Leiter took it over after a very short time. Just under

15

the cornice of the State Street facade remains this inscription:
L. Z. LEITER, MDCCCXCI.

This 8-story building, with 3 facades of white Maine granite,
was designed by one of the pioneers in the Chicago school
of architecture, William LeBaron Jenney. He had produced the
first example of typical Chicago construction in his Home
Insurance Building of 1885 (no longer standing), and he continued
the development of the Chicago school in the second Leiter
Building. Jenney allowed the steel skeleton, only recently
introduced at that time, to determine the outward characteristics
of the building—its division into enormous square sections,
each filled with many large windows.

A plaque attached to the building on the State Street side quotes
a citation from the "Chicago Dynamic Commission," dated
October 27, 1957 (two months before the Architectural Landmarks
Commission was formed):

> Bold, vigorous and original design expresses the light and
> open character of this building. One of the nation's most
> impressive early works of commercial architecture.

Home Federal Savings and Loan Building—
201 South State Street.
Architects: Skidmore, Owings, and Merrill (1966)

State Street has few new buildings or skyscrapers. It remains
principally a street lined with multistory buildings of moderate
height, occupied by stores of long-established companies selling
wearing apparel, jewelry, and the endless assortment of the
department stores.

The principal exception is the Home Federal Savings and Loan
Building, on the southeast corner of Adams and State. In this
handsome new structure the vertical lines are accented by the
stainless steel mullions. The entire building is enveloped
in dark glass panels.

To make way for this building, the Home Federal Savings and
Loan Association demolished an earlier one of considerable
architectural merit—the Republic Building designed by Holabird
and Roche, dating back to 1905.

Opposite, The Sears, Roebuck
store, formerly the Leiter Building
II.

16

Montgomery Ward Store—Adams and State.
Architects: William LeBaron Jenney (1890-91);
Perkins and Will Partnership (1963)

Montgomery Ward and Company now occupy the building at the
northwest corner of Adams and State, previously known as the
Fair Store. This 11-story structure, extending along Adams from
State to Dearborn, is the largest of 3 large buildings designed
by Jenney and completed in 1891. Even larger than the Sears
Roebuck store, it covers a floor space of some 55,000 square feet.
Again Jenney used the principle of the steel skeleton as his
design, although here he used more ornamentation than in the
Sears building. In 1963 the whole store was remodeled from plans
by the Perkins and Will Partnership. The rehabilitation work is
well designed and appropriately sympathetic with the original
building; the result is a pleasant exterior and an efficient, warm
interior. (See also comments on Walk No. 3, Dearborn Street.)

Palmer House—State and Monroe.
Architects: J. M. Van Osdel (1875);
Holabird and Roche (1925)

The building on the east side of State at Monroe is the Palmer
House, long one of the most distinguished hotels in Chicago, with
a popular shopping arcade running through the building from
State to Wabash. The Palmer House preceding this building was a
real Chicago pioneer, for it was erected only a few years after
the Great Fire of 1871—a still earlier Palmer House having been
opened just two weeks before the fire and then completely
destroyed. The 1875 building is said to have been the first fireproof
hotel and the first to provide its residents with electric lights,
telephones, and elevators. It was built at a time when the Chicago
school of architects was making great strides in improving the
construction and facilities of hotels and apartment buildings.

◘ **Carson Pirie Scott Store**—1 South State Street.
Architects: Louis Sullivan (1899, 1904);
Daniel H. Burnham and Company (1906);
Holabird and Root (1960)

At State and Madison, the intersection that is famed as the
"World's Busiest Corner," stands the most *notable* of Chicago's

18

department stores architecturally, and the one always most *noticed* by the infrequent visitor to State Street—the Carson Pirie Scott Store.

What you see today is the result of several stages of construction, so that the total building is probably less unified than it would otherwise have been. Fortunately, however, the architects of 1906 and 1960 had such deep respect for Sullivan's original design that they followed the pattern closely in their additions. Here you have one of the best illustrations of the effectiveness of the horizontally elongated "Chicago window." The ornamentation decorating the windows of the first 2 stories is in pleasant contrast with the clean, unadorned precision of the window lines above them.

Originally occupied by the Schlesinger and Mayer Company, for whom it had been constructed in 1899 and enlarged in 1904, it was purchased later in 1904 by Carson Pirie Scott. The first and easternmost section, of only 3 bays and 9 stories, faced only Madison. The 1904 enlargement was made possible by the demolition of two older buildings next to this site. The addition, which rose 12 stories instead of 9, included 3 more bays on Madison and extended around the corner, with 7 bays on State Street. Sullivan was the architect for both the original building and the extension. His love of incorporating ornamentation even in the designs of commercial buildings is expressed here in the intricate intermingling of leaf and flower designs that decorate the main entrance at the corner, as well as the windows of the lower stories. This rich but delicate pattern gives an unusually luxurious effect to an entrance already distinguished by its semicircular shape and its location at the corner of the building.

The third unit, extending the building still farther on State Street, was designed by Burnham in 1906; and the most recent extension of that long facade, by Holabird and Root in 1960, still following Sullivan's original plan. The result is therefore a true Sullivan masterpiece, no matter what other architects were involved before the building reached its present proportions.

In *Space, Time and Architecture*[1] Sigfried Giedion says of this building:

Ornamental cast iron detail, Carson Pirie Scott building.

19

The front is designed to fulfill its indispensable function, the admission of light. Its basic elements are the horizontally elongated "Chicago windows," admirably homogeneous and treated to coincide with the framework of the skeleton. The whole front is executed with a strength and precision that is matched by no other building of the period.

And Frederick Koeper remarks, "In this design Sullivan has afforded us those dual pleasures of architecture: an involvement with decoration as well as the satisfaction of discipline and order."[2]

◘ 32 North State Street (previously the Reliance Building)
Architect: Charles Atwood, of Daniel H. Burnham and Company (1894-95)

In the next block, on the northwest corner of State and Washington, is an Architectural Landmark once known as the Reliance Building. The dark limestone base contrasts markedly with the glass and white terra-cotta of the towering, 15-story structure above.

Speaking of the Reliance Building, Giedion comments that ".... although its glazed white tiles have become encrusted with dirt, its airiness and pure proportions make it a symbol of the Chicago school." And pointing out that the Reliance was built nearly 3 decades before Mies van der Rohe envisioned his glass-and-iron skyscraper as a kind of fantasy, in 1921, he continues: "But it may be that this Chicago building is something more than an incentive for fantasy: an architectonic anticipation of the future."[3]

The citation by the Architectural Landmarks Commission reads:

> In recognition of the early and complete expression, through slender piers, small spandrels, and the skillfully restrained use of terra-cotta with large areas of glass, of the structural cage, of steel that alone supports such buildings.

Marshall Field Store—111 North State Street.
Architects: Daniel H. Burnham & Company (1892, 1904, and 1907)

The walk up State Street should include the interior of the Marshall Field and Company Store. You can walk through from State to Wabash or from Washington to Randolph, for the building occupies the entire block. At the Washington and Randolph ends of the store are open courts, surrounded by grilled railings at each floor and covered by skylights. The skylight at the south end of the store (Washington Street) is a slightly arched dome of colored mosaic at the level of the fifth floor ceiling. The other (Randolph Street) is a plain glass skylight at the top of the building. The Randolph Street court is a perfect setting for the enormous Christmas tree that delighted Marshall Field customers for years.

Opposite left, Entrance, Carson Pirie Scott. *Right*, the Marshall Field clock at the corner of State and Randolph.

21

The original Marshall Field store was built at the corner of State and Washington. This was the site of 3 previous buildings that had been used by the Field and Leiter partnership—the first of which had been destroyed by the Chicago fire a few years after it was erected. The rest of this famous store was constructed in two sections—in 1904 and 1907; and the Marshall Field men's store, at the southwest corner of Wabash and Washington was added in 1914.

United of America Building—1 East Wacker Drive. Architects: Shaw Metz and Associates (1962)

Continuing the State Street walk, you cross Randolph, the movie theatre section of the Loop, and come to the last building of this tour—the marble-faced tower of the United Insurance Company of America, which is said to be the tallest marble-faced commercial structure in the world. The strongly vertical lines of this 41-story structure contrast sharply with the circular towers of Marina City just across the river. (Marina City is featured as the last stop of Walk Number 3, Dearborn Street.) From a restaurant at the top of the United of America building, diners have a panoramic view of the city.

Marina Towers.

1. Manhattan Building
   431 S. Dearborn

2. Fisher Building
   343 S. Dearborn

3. Monadnock Building
   53 W. Jackson

4. Federal Government Center
   & Plaza
   219 S. Dearborn

5. Marquette Building
   140 S. Dearborn

6. Montgomery Ward
   Department Store
   140 S. State

7. Inland Steel Building
   30 W. Monroe

8. First National Bank
   Building & Plaza
   38 S. Dearborn

9. Civic Center, Plaza—
   Picasso Sculpture
   Dearborn, Clark, Washington,
   Randolph

10. City Hall—County Building
    121 N. LaSalle—118 N. Clark

11. Chicago Temple Building
    77 W. Washington

12. Brunswick Building
    69 W. Washington

13. Connecticut Mutual Building
    33 N. Dearborn

14. Blue Cross - Blue Shield
    Building
    S.W. Corner Dearborn
    & Wacker

15. Dearborn St. Bridge
    Dearborn St. at Chicago River

16. Marina City
    300 N. State

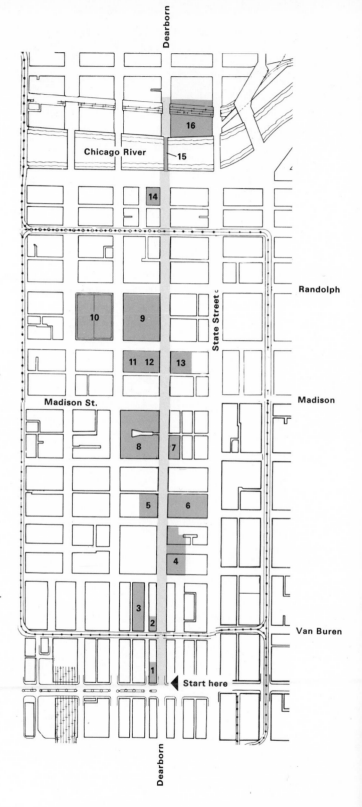

Walk · 3

DEARBORN STREET

WALKING TIME: About 1½ hours.   HOW TO GET THERE: Take any southbound CTA bus on State Street south of Randolph, and get off at Van Buren (400 S). Walk west across Plymouth Court, to Dearborn (36 W), which runs parallel to State Street.

Manhattan Building—431 South Dearborn. Architect: William LeBaron Jenney (1890)

This walk offers a virtual history of the modern skyscraper, which had its beginnings here in Chicago—one of the results of the tremendous architectural development that rebuilt the city after its almost total destruction by fire in 1871.

Located at the south end of the walk—in fact one block farther south than Van Buren—is the Manhattan Building, famed as the first 16-story building in the world. (Though only 12 stories when first built, 4 more were added a few years later.) Designed by the man who has often been called the father of the steel skyscraper, William LeBaron Jenney, the Manhattan is now the oldest tall office building to have used skeleton construction throughout. The second Rand McNally building, designed by Burnham and Root in the same year, also used skeleton construction throughout but was demolished in 1911.

Although the design of the Manhattan Building is not first-rate, it gives a not unpleasing effect.

⊡ Fisher Building—343 South Dearborn. Architects: Daniel H. Burnham and Company (1896)

North of Van Buren, on the same side of Dearborn, stands the Fisher Building, an Architectural Landmark. The steel frame skeleton, which was also used here, is by no means disguised by the rather elaborate Gothic ornamentation. The architect for this building was the Burnham who is world-famous for his Chicago city plan. His frequently quoted admonition, "Make no little plans; they have no magic to stir men's minds," seems to have been heeded by Chicago architects, and Dearborn Street is one of the results.

☐ Monadnock Building—53 West Jackson.
Architects: North half, Burnham and Root (1891);
south half, Holabird and Roche (1893)

Across the street from the Fisher Building, between Van Buren
Street and Jackson Boulevard, is another Architectural Landmark,
the Monadnock, internationally famed as the world's largest
office building at the time of construction and still known as the
highest commercial building (16 stories rising 197 feet high)
with outside walls of wall-bearing construction. Some of the walls
at the base are said to be 15 feet thick to support the tremendous
weight. Even the north half of the building, however—the only
part that has outside walls of masonry only—did use steel
for the interior columns and floor supports; and the south half,
built two years later, used some vertical steel in the outer walls.

Originally this building had 4 separate entrances to 4 separate
sections, each named after a New England mountain, according to
the fancy of the 4 branches of the New England family that
owned it. The main entrance, still the most impressive, was at 54
West Van Buren, but when construction of the elevated railroad
tracks and station darkened Van Burean, Jackson became the
more desirable street. Following these changes, the Monadnock's
management transformed its "back door," at 53 West Jackson,
into the main entrance. In the late 1890's it was decided to call the
entire building merely the Monadnock, dropping the other 3
mountain names, though continuing to operate the four sections
separately as A, B, C, and D. Finally, in the 1920's, all
division into 4 parts was abandoned.

The Monadnock's files tell of an early test of the building's
ability to withstand Chicago's winds despite its unusual height and
lack of wind braces. When a near-hurricane, with winds reaching
the velocity of 88 miles an hour, struck Chicago a few years
after the Monadnock was completed, experts in engineering
rushed to the building with some trepidation and conducted a
pendulum experiment from the top floor. A plumb bob that was
swung down through the stairwell to the lobby floor, to measure
the structure's vibrations at the height of the storm, marked a
small pattern not more than ⅝″ by ⅜″—an experiment
that reassured everyone who had feared what high winds
might do to this building!

Left, top and center, The Fisher
building, details. *Bottom,* Arcade
of U.S. Courthouse. *Right,* Monadnock building.

The citation of the Monadnock Building as an Architectural Landmark reads:

> In recognition of its original design and its historical interest as the highest wall-bearing structure in Chicago. Restrained use of brick, soaring massive walls, omission of ornamental forms, unite in a building simple yet majestic.

U.S. Courthouse and Office Building—
219 South Dearborn. Architects for the Federal Center, of which this is the first building completed: Ludwig Mies van der Rohe; Schmidt, Garden, and Erikson; C. F. Murphy Associates; A. Epstein and Sons. (1964)

Crossing Jackson Boulevard on Dearborn, going north, means jumping from the late nineteenth century to the middle twentieth. On the east side of Dearborn stands a spectacularly modern 27-story structure of steel and glass, the U.S. Courthouse and Office Building. This is the first of three buildings already planned for Chicago's new Federal Center. When completed, the Center will extend from Jackson Boulevard north to Adams Street, occupying both sides of Dearborn to Clark. An office building of over 40 stories will follow the Courthouse, and then a new post office in a low-rise building. All 3 structures will face a large open plaza—the entire design being a strong statement of the genius and influence of the great architect Mies van der Rohe.

As you continue north on this walk, you will see two more great plazas surrounded by first-rate buildings. This current trend toward more open space around city skyscrapers is in marked contrast with the canyon effect so often developed in the past. Dearborn Street is indeed a street of overwhelming architecture, in space as well as in time.

Marquette Building—140 South Dearborn.
Architects: Holabird and Roche (1894)

At the northwest corner of Dearborn and Adams is the Marquette Building. The influence of Louis Sullivan can be noted in the ornamental design, which marks off the bottom 2 stories and the top 3, distinguishing these clearly from the rest. The wide windows and the obvious response of the pattern to the skeleton structure are characteristic of the Chicago school.

You will want to go inside this building to see the mosaics of scenes from Chicago history that decorate the mezzanine balcony.

Montgomery Ward Store—Adams and Dearborn.
Architects: William LeBaron Jenney (1890-91);
Perkins and Will Partnership (1963)

Directly across the street from the Marquette is the recently remodeled Montgomery Ward Store (previously the Fair Store), seen from its State Street side on Walk Number 2. (See also comments for that walk.) In the remodeling, the original wide-span windows so characteristic of the Chicago school of architecture have been retained, but the old facade has been completely covered with a new skin of attractive light-colored stone. The interior is most inviting, with all the advantages of a modern structure.

◘ **Inland Steel Building**—30 West Monroe.
Architects: Skidmore, Owings, and Merrill (1957)

One block to the north, at the northeast corner of Dearborn and Monroe Streets, is the Inland Steel Building, appropriately constructed of stainless steel and glass. In the lobby is a stunningly unique piece of wire sculpture by Richard Lippold.

This 19-story building was one of the first to use only *external* steel columns for support, also one of the first to build a separate structure (to the east) for elevators and stairs, and to use steel and glass as the chief building materials. The result is a striking, first-rate design.

First National Bank Building—Madison at Dearborn and Clark streets.
Architects: Perkins and Will Partnership and Charles F. Murphy Associates, 1969

One block farther north and directly to the west are the sweeping lines of the new First National Bank Building. This "A" shaped, 60-story structure, its steel frame covered with white granite, is an exhilarating sight. It is the tallest building in the Loop, surpassing even the Prudential Building. The only taller building in Chicago is the John Hancock Building being constructed north of the Loop on Michigan Avenue.
(See Walk No. 5.)

When this building is ready for occupancy, the space now used by the *old* bank building, at 38 South Dearborn, will be cleared and converted into another great plaza.

On this site once stood the 50-story Morrison Hotel, the tallest building ever to be demolished.

Chicago Civic Center—between Washington and Randolph, Dearborn and Clark.
Architects: C. F. Murphy Associates;
Loebl, Schlossman, and Bennett; Skidmore, Owings and Merrill (1964)

One block north, on the same side of Dearborn, is the great plaza of the Chicago Civic Center, a focal point of city and county government activity. This immense open space offers the visitor an exciting visual treat and a chance to sit and rest in the midst of otherwise crowded city streets. With fountain, flags, and trees, the plaza is dominated overwhelmingly by the huge Picasso sculpture in Cor-Ten steel. The design of "Chicago's Picasso" was a gift to the city from the sculptor himself, and the original model is in Chicago's Art Institute. Like most of Picasso's creations for many years, this was the subject of much controversy. There was disagreement about whether it represents the great head of a woman, the soaring wings of an enormous bird, a strange composite animal, or—as one facetious newspaper columnist would have it—the head of Picasso's pet basset hound! Controversy aside, however, this is a powerful work of art. It has been erected in an especially appropriate setting, which allows viewers to walk around it freely and consider it from all angles and various distances—from each of which it presents a different effect.

The *Civic Center Building,* 31 stories of offices and courtrooms, covers the north half of the plaza. This too was highly controversial at first, especially before the steel of its walls had oxidized to its present russet brown. Cor-Ten steel was chosen as the material for the building, as well as for the Picasso, because it requires no upkeep and becomes more beautiful as it ages. (A special virtue of Cor-Ten steel is its resistance to *atmospheric* corrosion, so that it is not worn away by weathering, even though its color is changed.)

Left top, Inland Steel building. *Bottom,* Chicago Civic Center plaza and Picasso sculpture. *Right,* First National Bank Building.

31

The power and the scale of this contemporary structure are overwhelming; the older, smaller buildings around the plaza come into focus only later, though many were most impressive when erected. They are a phenomenon of contrasts, one with another. The horizontal bays are 89 feet wide which makes this distinguished building one of great strength and vigor.

City Hall-County Building—121 North LaSalle. Architects: Holabird and Roche (1907, 1911)

One of these older buildings, dating back more than half a century, is the City Hall-County Building—really 2 duplicate buildings, the county building on the east having been completed several years before its city twin. They are built on sturdy classic revivalist lines with heavy Corinthian columns across the facade. Together they cover an entire block to the west of the Civic Center. Tours may be arranged in advance by calling the Mayor's Office of Inquiry and Information (744-3370).

Chicago Temple Building—77 West Washington. Architects: Holabird and Roche (1923)

To the south, across Washington, is the Chicago Temple Building, standing 550 feet high, in Gothic revival style, including an elaborate spire. This provides space for offices and a downtown Methodist church. Except for a short time after the Great Fire of 1871, this site has been occupied continuously by a downtown church for more than 100 years.

Brunswick Building—69 West Washington. Architects: Skidmore, Owings, and Merrill (1964)

Next to the Chicago Temple is the massive Brunswick Building. Though only recently constructed, the heavy concrete wall surfaces of the Brunswick are reminiscent of the Monadnock Building. From the lower concourse of this building you can reach other downtown buildings by an underground walkway. (See Walk No. 28.)

Connecticut Mutual Life Building—33 North Dearborn. Architects: Skidmore, Owings, and Merrill (1966)

Left top, Brunswick building. *Bottom*, City Hall-County building. *Right*, Connecticut Mutual Life building.

Just across Dearborn Street from the Brunswick is an utterly different type of building, the Connecticut Mutual, a glass

32

structure standing light and lean on its steel frame. Though this was designed by the same firm of architects as the Brunswick, the two buildings are in striking contrast with each other. They are a tribute to the versatility of the architects' inventiveness and illustrate the wide variety of modern building materials and forms.

Blue Cross - Blue Shield Building—222 North Dearborn. Architects: C. F. Murphy Associates (1969)

As you leave the Civic Center, continue north across Randolph and Lake streets. On the west side of Dearborn is the new building erected for the Blue Cross - Blue Shield groups. This all-beige-colored concrete structure has a rugged, heavy quality; it gives an effect of tremendous mass, especially in the upper section extending by cantilever construction beyond the lower part.

Marina City—300 North State Street. Architects: Bertrand Goldberg Associates (1964)

Although the official address of Marina City is State Street, you have an excellent view of these twin towers from Dearborn and Wacker Drive. This exciting, world-famous complex has included its many functions in a highly concentrated space— apartments, garages, restaurants, offices, bank, television theatre, ice-skating rink, and marina. The parking space is a continuously rising circular slab throughout the first 18 stories of each tower, the apartments taking up the rest of the 62 stories of each. The cantilevered balconies of the apartments give these cylindrical towers their scalloped forms. Apartments are pie-shaped.

Marina City marks a departure from the glass-and-steel skeletons that have been so popular in recent years. This tallest concrete building in Chicago, 62 stories rising more than 580 feet in the air, uses virtually no structural steel. These are towers of slab construction, circular discs resting on columns. Marina City also demonstrates excellent application of core-and-cantilever construction, which was first used by Frank Lloyd Wright.

A model apartment may always be seen at Marina City, and a trip to the open-air observatory at the top is available Saturdays and Sundays when the weather permits. (Since the observatory

34

is not roofed or glassed in, no visits are permitted after the first snowfall of the year.)

To enter Marina City, you cross the Dearborn Street drawbridge, with plaques worth reading. They summarize the history of the bridge and quote the citation presented to it as the "Most beautiful steel bridge movable span," by the American Institute of Steel Construction in 1963-64.

NGE BUILDING

'89

30
NORTH LA SALLE
BUILDING

Walk-4

Entrance to 30
North LaSalle (old
Chicago Stock
Exchange).

1. State of Illinois Building
   160 N. LaSalle

2. Bismarck Hotel
   171 W. Randolph

3. Sherman House
   Clark & Randolph St.

4. City Hall & County Building
   121 N. LaSalle

5. 30 N. LaSalle Building
   Old Stock Exchange

6. St. Peter's Church
   110 W. Madison

7. Loop Synagogue
   16 S. Clark

8. Northern Trust Building
   50 S. LaSalle

9. Harris Trust Building
   111 W. Monroe

10. Midwest Stock Exchange
    Central National Bank Building
    120 S. LaSalle

11. Field Building &
    LaSalle National Building
    185 S. LaSalle

12. The Rookery
    209 S. LaSalle

13. Continental Illinois
    National Bank &
    Trust Co. of Chicago
    231 S. LaSalle

14. Board of Trade Building
    141 W. Jackson

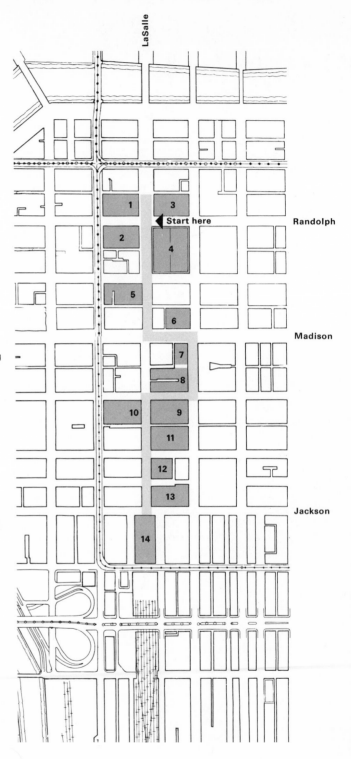

Walk · 4

LA SALLE STREET

WALKING TIME: 1 to 1½ hours.　　HOW TO GET THERE:　Walk west on Randolph to
La Salle Street (140 W), 3 blocks west of State Street.

Be sure to take this walk on a weekday during business hours,
when the rhythm of Chicago at work is best felt.
LaSalle Street in the Loop is the Wall Street of the Midwest.
From Randolph, the street looks like a canyon, with skyscraper
office buildings and banks along each side and the 45-story
Board of Trade Building like a towering mountain at the south.
Here, in the 4-block area between Madison and Jackson, are
clustered Chicago's major banks; here are found both old and
new stock exchange buildings; and here, at the end of the 4
blocks, stands the overpowering Board of Trade Building with
the statue of Ceres at its top. Activities inside some of these
buildings send political and economic waves across the country,
affecting in fact the world economy.

The best place to start a stroll through the financial district of
Chicago is Randolph Street, at LaSalle. Here on the northwest
corner, at 160 North LaSalle, stands the *State of Illinois Building*.
And on the southwest corner is the *Bismarck Hotel,* where
politicians often meet over meals. At the northeast corner of
this intersection is another popular meeting place for politicians,
the *Sherman House,* where the headquarters of the Democratic
party is located.

On the east side of LaSalle, between Randolph and Washington,
looms the bulky, massive *City Hall-County Building* with its
heavy pillars, designed under the old belief that government
buildings should be monumental in size and style. (See Walk
No. 3.) The interior is presently being renovated and modernized.
Tours are available through the Mayor's Office of Inquiry and
Information, Room 100. (Telephone: 744-3370)

◻ 30 North LaSalle Building (the old Stock Exchange Building)—
Architects: Adler and Sullivan (1894)

Diagonally across the intersection of LaSalle and Washington from the City Hall-County Building stands the *old* Chicago Stock Exchange, now devoted only to offices and known merely as the 30 North LaSalle Building. Its exterior shows without question that it is the work of architects Louis Sullivan and Dankmar Adler. The tall arches that link the second and third floors, creating a 3-story base, have been criticized as of undue proportions, but Sullivan doubtless designed them to follow the interior structure, where a 2-story trading room starts from the second floor. The ornamentation above these arches is outstanding, and the projecting bays in the upper stories contrast well with the rest of the facade, which is characterized by flat planes and large windows. The magnificent 2-story arched entrance, comparable to the broad, ornamented arches that Sullivan used in his famous Auditorium Building (see Walk No. 1, Michigan Avenue—South), are flanked by two circular plaques—one showing the house of P. F. W. Peck, a Chicago pioneer, as it looked when it stood on this site in 1873; the other a seal bearing the date the present structure was started—1893. In this building, for the first time in Chicago, engineers used caissons as part of the foundation.

The original iron grilles around the elevator shafts, characteristic of Sullivan's delicate ornamental designs, have now been removed, but a sample panel is preserved inside the building in a special Louis Sullivan room.

St. Peter's Church and Friary—110 West Madison.
Architects: K. M. Vitzthum and J. J. Burns (1953)

At Madison, a side trip to two recently constructed places of worship is well worth while. The first is St. Peter's Church in Chicago, a 5-story, marble-covered Roman basilica, consisting of the main church, two chapels on the second floor, and living quarters on the other 3 floors for the Franciscan Fathers in charge. The facade is overwhelmingly dominated—as the designers intended it to be—by a gigantic crucifix, Christ of the Loop, 18 feet high, weighing 26 tons. This extraordinarily expressive figure of Christ, the work of the Latvian sculptor Arvid Strauss, hangs above the entrance in front of the only window of the building—a Gothic arch of stained glass. The church, built on the site of the old LaSalle Theatre, was planned as a religious center for Catholic visitors to the city and the many thousands of Catholics who work in the Loop.

The Chicago Loop Synagogue—16 South Clark Street.
Architects: Loebl, Schlossman, and Bennett, 1957

As you approach the Loop Synagogue, just a few doors south of Madison, on Clark Street, you will be struck by the unique metal sculpture above the entrance—"The Hands of Peace," by the Israeli sculptor Henri Azaz. Symbolic outstretched hands are surrounded by irregularly spaced letters, in both English and Hebrew, spelling out a Biblical benediction.

From the visitors' balcony inside you can see the interesting, well-conceived plan of this structure, which has made optimum use of the narrow city lot on which it is constructed. The seating arrangement, running at right angles with what is expected, achieves a special effect of spaciousness. And the entire wall opposite the street entrance is composed of a gloriously colored stained-glass design on the theme "Let there be light!"—the work of Abraham Rattner, of New York.

Northern Trust Company—50 South LaSalle.
Architects: Frost and Granger, 1906, 1930
Architects for newest section:
C. F. Murphy Associates (1967)

Back on La Salle, at the northwest corner of Monroe and La Salle is the Northern Trust Company and its new, adjoining structure to the west, which extends almost to Wells Street. At Wells there is a refreshing change from La Salle's city canyon—an open space landscaped with fountains, providing a drive-in section for hurried or late customers.

Harris Trust and Savings Bank—
111 West Monroe Street.
Architects for eastern part of buildings:
Skidmore, Owings, and Merrill (1957)

At the southeast corner of this intersection is the Harris Trust and Savings Bank, in a structure that is really a series of four buildings, all facing Monroe, which are connected with each other at the ground floor.

An unusual feature of the building farthest east is its recessed floor halfway up, which holds all the mechanical equipment usually found on the roof or in the basement. The stainless steel mullions and the tall, narrow glazing pattern are especially effective in this first-rate building.

Midwest Stock Exchange and Central National Bank—120 South LaSalle Building.
Architects: Graham, Anderson, Probst, and White (1926-29)

In the second block beyond Madison is the building now used by the Midwest Stock Exchange, the financial center of the Midwest—second only to New York's in size and economic significance. More than 500 members of the Exchange represent security firms doing business in all parts of the country. The Central National Bank, however, occupies most of the lower floors of this building.

The building, which also provides space for various other financial concerns, faced many difficulties in its early years, for it was completed just at the beginning of the depression of the '30's.

Visitors' gallery open daily 9:00 A.M. to 2:30 P.M. Closed Saturdays and Sundays.

Field Building—135 South LaSalle Street.
Architects: Graham, Anderson, Probst, and White (1934)

At the end of the same block comes the Field Building, at the northeast corner of LaSalle and Adams, which represents a sound business investment by the Marshall Field Estate. One of it's major tenants is another of the street's many banks—the LaSalle National Bank. This is the site of the famous *Home Insurance Building* (demolished in 1931), which was the world's first skeleton steel and iron building, designed in 1884 by the father of such construction, William LeBaron Jenney.

Field building. *Opposite,* overall view and details of the Rookery.

42

◘ The Rookery—209 South LaSalle Street.
Architects: Burnham and Root (1886);
Frank Lloyd Wright (1905)

Just across Adams Street is an Architectural Landmark—an extraordinary building called The Rookery. This quaint name is a heritage from the temporary city hall located here from 1872 to 1884, which had been nicknamed The Rookery because it seemed to be the favorite gathering place of downtown pigeons! The city hall had been built around an iron water tank, the only remnant of the previous occupant of this site—a city reservoir building serving the south side of Chicago, which was destroyed in the Fire of 1871. While the temporary city hall was here, Chicago's first public library stored its books in the old water tank—surely the only library in the world to have been housed in such a container.

The present Rookery, one of the oldest precursors of the modern skyscraper, is distinguished in its own right. Its sturdy yet ornamental exterior is partly of skeleton structure, partly wall-bearing, and the building as a whole has the appearance of enormous vitality. The powerful columns, alternating with piers, arches, and stonework, which characterize the exterior, make a dramatic contrast with the lobby inside, which is unique in its elaborate but delicate ornamentation. The glass-and-iron tracery of the domed skylight above the second floor of the lobby court (though now painted over) harmonizes with the extensive grille work used below around the first- and second-floor balconies and along the sides of the two-part suspended stairway at the west side. The main stairway, unconnected with this one, starts at the second floor and runs to the top of the building. A cylindrical staircase, it projects beyond the west wall of the building, requiring an additional, semicircular tower to enclose it. With elevators for regular upward travel, this main stairway is still considered useful as a possible fire escape.

The gold-and-ivory decorations of the court are the work of Frank Lloyd Wright, who remodeled this part of the building in 1905.

Lower LaSalle Street and the Board of Trade building.

The citation from the Landmarks Commission reads:

44

In recognition of its pioneering plan in providing shops and offices around a graceful and semi-private square and further development of the skeleton structural frame using cast iron columns, wrought iron spandrel beams, and steel beams to support party walls and interior floors.

Continental Illinois National Bank and Trust Building—231 South LaSalle Street. Architects: Graham, Anderson, Probst, and White (1923)

In the giant, block-square building of the Continental Illinois National Bank and Trust Company, you have revivalist architecture again. The "classic" design is said to have been taken from some early Roman baths. Inside, you take an escalator to the enormous open banking floor, where tall Ionic columns stress again the pseudo-classic style.

The Continental Illinois claims to be Chicago's oldest bank, the result of many mergers and changes of name dating back to 1857. It became officially the Continental Illinois National Bank and Trust Company, with a national charter, in 1932.

Across the street from the Continental Illinois, at 230 South LaSalle, is the Federal Reserve Bank of Chicago, ornamented with Corinthian columns (architects, Frost and Granger, 1922). A second tower to the west was designed by C. F. Murphy and Associates, 1960.

Board of Trade Building—141 West Jackson Boulevard. Architects: Holabird and Root (1929)

The focal point of this entire walk has been the Board of Trade Building, with its commanding location at the foot of LaSalle Street, on Jackson Boulevard. From Randolph this towering structure seems to block LaSalle Street at its southern end, but at Jackson you discover that LaSalle merely jogs a bit to the left and continues southward beyond the Board of Trade. At the top of the 45 stories in this building stands—appropriately—a statue of Ceres, Greek goddess of grain, a 32-foot figure topping the 526-foot skyscraper.

The enormous room of the grain exchange, which is the largest in the world, is on the second floor. Since this "Pit" rises for several floors, it can be well observed from the visitors' gallery

on the fifth floor. (Open daily 9:30 A.M. to 1:15 P.M. Closed Saturdays, Sundays, and holidays.) To the uninitiated, the sights and sounds of trading in this Pit seem like bedlam. Fortunately, however, visitors are given a leaflet explaining the rules of the game, which indeed is a game full of economic consequences everywhere. Here are several "pits," each a circle of traders interested in buying or selling a particular commodity—wheat, soybeans, soybean oil and meal, oats, rye, and several other commodities, such as cotton, lard, and beef. Shouts and hand signals in the bidding are clear to those involved, and the constantly changing prices are recorded on a big board immediately for all to see. Messengers run back and forth between the bidders with messages telephoned or wired from firms or individual customers from all parts of the world. The men trading here represent more than 1400 members of the Board of Trade. Traders, messengers, and staff of the exchange are distinguished by the color of the jackets they wear. The Board of Trade is indeed a tremendous marketplace, although the actual commodities that change hands here are miles away.

The Board of Trade Observatory, at the top of the building, provides one of the highest viewpoints in Chicago. (Open daily 9:00 A.M. to 5:00 P.M. Adults, 50¢, children, 25¢)

Chicago Water
Tower.

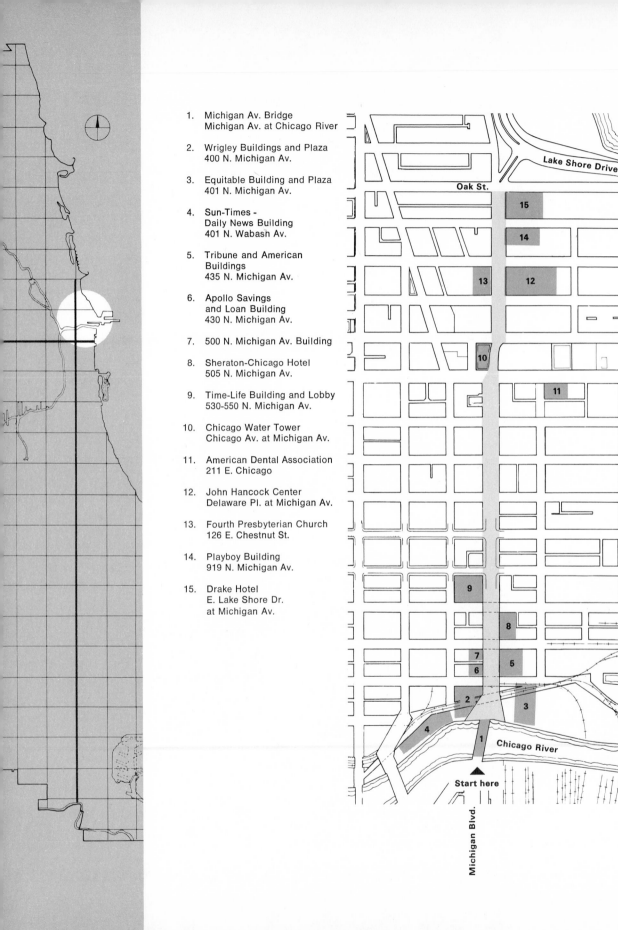

1. Michigan Av. Bridge
   Michigan Av. at Chicago River

2. Wrigley Buildings and Plaza
   400 N. Michigan Av.

3. Equitable Building and Plaza
   401 N. Michigan Av.

4. Sun-Times -
   Daily News Building
   401 N. Wabash Av.

5. Tribune and American
   Buildings
   435 N. Michigan Av.

6. Apollo Savings
   and Loan Building
   430 N. Michigan Av.

7. 500 N. Michigan Av. Building

8. Sheraton-Chicago Hotel
   505 N. Michigan Av.

9. Time-Life Building and Lobby
   530-550 N. Michigan Av.

10. Chicago Water Tower
    Chicago Av. at Michigan Av.

11. American Dental Association
    211 E. Chicago

12. John Hancock Center
    Delaware Pl. at Michigan Av.

13. Fourth Presbyterian Church
    126 E. Chestnut St.

14. Playboy Building
    919 N. Michigan Av.

15. Drake Hotel
    E. Lake Shore Dr.
    at Michigan Av.

Lake Shore Drive

Oak St.

Lake Shore Dr

Chicago Ave.

Chicago River

Start here

Michigan Blvd.

Walk · 5

MICHIGAN AVENUE : NORTH ("THE MAGNIFICENT MILE")

WALKING TIME: About 1½ hours.   HOW TO GET THERE: Take any of the following northbound CTA buses—No. 151 (Sheridan), No. 152 (Addison), or No. 153 (Wilson-Michigan) on State Street; or a No. 76 (Diversey) on Wabash. Get off at the Michigan Avenue bridge, Michigan and Wacker (300 N).

Where Chicago's "Magnificent Mile" begins, just north of the Chicago River, are buildings of contrasting architecture. The development of this part of Michigan Avenue, featuring both revivalist and contemporary styles, might be said to date from the 1920's, when both the street and underground levels of the Michigan Avenue bridge were completed.

Wrigley Building—400 North Michigan.
Architects: Graham, Anderson, Probst, and White (1921; annex 1924)

The gleaming white Wrigley Building (named for the family of chewing-gum fame) with its finger-like clock tower rises from the northern edge of the Chicago River. The white terra-cotta with which the building is covered and the powerful floodlights focused on it every night make this always a conspicuous part of the Chicago skyline. Featuring baroque terra-corra ornamentation, the building is an architectural link to Chicago's earlier days. Between the main building and its annex is an attractive small plaza.

Equitable Building—401 North Michigan.
Architects: Skidmore, Owings, and Merrill; Alfred Shaw & Associates (1965)

The Equitable Building, representing the architecture of the present, stands like another sentinel on the east side of the Avenue. Set far back from the street, it is approached through a spacious plaza called Pioneer Court, which includes an attractive fountain with the names of early Chicago leaders—

its pioneers—inscribed around the base. From Pioneer Court a descending stairway leads to a restaurant and shops below, directly on the river bank.

The building itself, a 40-story structure of metal and glass, is clearly a product of the twentieth century, with a variation in the window arrangement that gives it special character. The slender external "piers" that separate the regular groups of 4 windows each have no supportive value, but they are more than ornamental. Within these "piers" are pipes for pumping hot or cold air into the offices as needed—from machinery located at the top and bottom of the building.

Together the Equitable and Wrigley buildings offer an appropriate gateway to what has been called the Champs Élysées of Chicago—North Michigan Avenue, famous throughout the country for its shops of great prestige, along with distinguished art galleries, restaurants, and clubs.

Sun Times-Daily News Building—401 North Wabash. Architects: Naess and Murphy (1957) (See also Walk No. 6, North Wabash Avenue.)

The gateway to the Avenue is also the newspaper center of Chicago. The Field Enterprise Inc., of the Marshall Field family, operates the *Sun Times-Daily News*. The building, though not actually on Michigan but along the north bank of the river, presents a striking view to the pedestrian crossing the Michigan Avenue bridge. It is connected with the famous avenue by a plaza located between the towers of the Wrigley building.

For tours through this busy, modern newspaper plant, call 321-3005.

Tribune Tower—435 North Michigan. Architects: Hood and Howells (1925)

The Tribune Tower, a Gothic revival skyscraper that has long been the citadel of the *Chicago Tribune* and the McCormick family's newspaper empire, stands on the east side of Michigan, just north of the Equitable building. Its sister paper, *Chicago's American,* is housed in an annex just north of the Tower.

In 1922 the Tribune held an international competition for the design of its building. The choice of Hood and Howells as the

Left, Wrigley building. *Right,* Equitable building.

50

winners was far from popular among architects of the time. The Gothic revival proposal had little or no relation to contemporary steel skeleton construction. The winning architects, however, did succeed in producing a truly impressive building.

Along the south side of the Tribune Tower are displayed page ones of various issues of the *Tribune,* with headlines of great national events back into the last century.

A more astonishing feature of this building, especially noticeable to the pedestrian, is the incorporation in its facade of numerous unmatching chunks of material purported to be souvenirs of the publisher's travels or those brought here by his newpaper's correspondents abroad—pieces of such buildings as Westminster Abbey, Cologne Cathedral, the Arch of Triumph in Paris, the Holy Door of St. Peter's in Rome, and even the Taj Mahal! Whether Mr. McCormick really succeeded in securing architectural samples from all the places named or was playing a game with the public, the incongruous scheme can hardly be said to enhance the beauty of his building.

Three Recent Neighbors of the Tribune Tower

Across the street from the Tribune Tower are two new buildings that show the changing face of the Avenue—the *Apollo Savings and Loan, at 430 (1964),* and the *500 North Michigan Building (1968).* The first of these is especially distinguished by the Plaza of the Americas, built alongside to the south, which is decorated with flags of all the nations of the western hemisphere, with the exception of Cuba. The 500 North Michigan Avenue Building is characterized by a travertine marble facade, which offsets some of the boxlike appearance of this structure. Across from those, at *505 North Michigan* are the two towers of the *Sheraton-Chicago Hotel.* Only one tower—the north one—is a new neighbor (1961). The south tower, which once was the Medinah Temple, still carries the signs of its earlier function in the Oriental turret and onion-shaped dome at the top.

Standing in front of any of these structures, you can see near the north end of the Avenue the biggest of them all—"Big John," the 100-story John Hancock Center, still in construction in

1968. It draws the attention of any northbound stroller on Michigan Avenue. But there are other things to see before you reach Big John. Inside the *old Time-Life building,* for instance, *at 540 North Michigan,* you can see *Diana Court,* with a fountain and sculpture by the Swedish sculptor Carl Milles.

During the growing season, trees, flowers, and shrubbery give this part of North Michigan Avenue color, texture, and beauty. It is a real pleasure to stroll here and view these outdoor attractions, as well as the enticing window displays of jewelry, books, and exclusive wearing apparel. At Christmas time, tiny Italian lights strung through all the trees down the Avenue create an air of enchantment.

Water Tower—800 North Michigan, at Chicago Avenue. Architect: W. W. Boyington (1867-1869)

At Chicago Avenue, on Michigan, stands one of Chicago's most famous—though by no means its most beautiful—landmarks, the Water Tower. Now closed and empty, this elaborate tower symbolizes Chicago's historic growth. When it was built, 2 years before the Great Fire, this fantastic, pseudo-Gothic creation, with its many turrets rising around the central tower like a section of a medieval castle, was considered a most artistically satisfactory disguise of the standpipe that it concealed.

Its design is far removed from what was developed later in the century by the Chicago school of architects—except that in a sense its form did follow function (or at least originated in function) as those later builders insisted that it should. Within the tower was an iron standpipe 3 feet in diameter and nearly 150 feet high that stored the water supply for the Near North Side. Across the street is the pumping station—still in use!—built of the same material (Joliet limestone) but with less elaborate ornamentation. In 1867 it was noteworthy that the "new" station could pump as much as 18 million gallons a day. Historic notes on the back of a menu for the Water Tower Cornerstone Centennial Luncheon in March 1967 (sponsored by the Greater North Michigan Avenue Association) pointed out that the 1967 capacity of Chicago's water system was then 3 *billion* gallons a day.

Left, Tribune Tower.

54

John Hancock building.

Though long ago the Water Tower ceased to be of any use as a standpipe, the city cherishes its presence in the midst of Michigan Avenue traffic. For all its antiquated style of architecture, it seems strangely appropriate here among the more beautiful modern structures around it. By its very contrast in style it is a reminder of Chicago's triumph over the Great Fire of 1871, which destroyed practically everything else in this part of Chicago but was followed by a period of unprecedented building and architectural progress.

American Dental Association Building—
211 East Chicago Avenue.
Architects: Graham, Anderson, Probst, and White (1966)

In marked contrast with the curiously squatty effect of the historic Water Tower is the slender, stately structure now used as the headquarters of the American Dental Association, a 23-story building just across Michigan on Chicago Avenue.

John Hancock Center—875 North Michigan Avenue.
Architects: Skidmore, Owings, and Merrill, 1969

Returning to Michigan Avenue, you will be overwhelmed by the 100-story John Hancock Building, towering more than 1,000 feet in the air. This dominates the vicinity and the skyline much as the Eiffel Tower does in Paris. This characteristic, however, is the only one the two structures have in common. The modern steel building of the John Hancock, surrounded by much open space at its base, is a combination commercial-residential project, with apartments limited to the uppermost 50 stories. Black anodized aluminum and tinted glass are the materials used in the exterior. To cope with Chicago's winds (it is said that the top of the building may sway anywhere from 10 to 15 feet— though those inside would not be aware of it!) the John Hancock has huge cross-bracing steel members that make several giant X's on each side. These produce an interesting ornamental effect as the X's become gradually smaller with the tapering of the building from foundation to top.

The tallest building in Chicago, the John Hancock Building is to date the second tallest in the world.

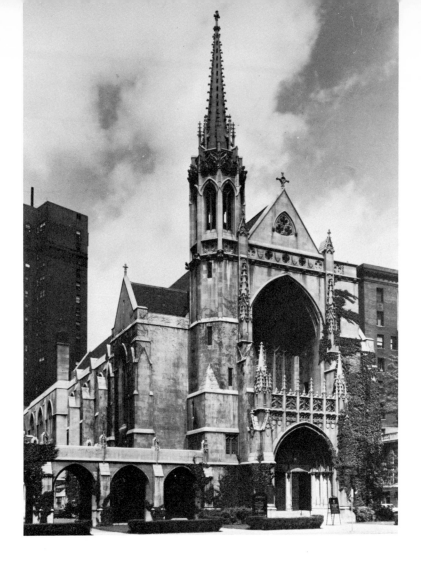

Fourth Presbyterian Church—
126 East Chestnut (860 N).
Architects: Ralph Adams Cram (1912);
Parish House: Howard V. Shaw (1925)

Directly across the street, providing a diametric contrast, is the
Fourth Presbyterian Church, which is famed for its modified
Gothic style. The architect designed many other Gothic revival
buildings at that time. The modifications executed here can be
seen in such things as the narrowness of the side aisles and the
placement of a balcony in the transept space. The buildings,
of carved Bedford stone, surround on 3 sides a grass plot, with
the 4th side an arcade. The stained glass windows were
designed by Charles Connick.

Fourth Presbyterian Church.

Playboy Building—919 North Michigan.
Architects: Holabird and Root (1929)

Formerly the Palmolive Building, this is now a part of the Hugh Hefner empire. A 38-story building, it was one of Chicago's first skyscrapers to use the simplified vertical style. The architects also made effective use of setbacks in this building. To most Chicagoans the Playboy Building is best known by the tremendously powerful, revolving Lindbergh Beacon at its top, which both airplanes and sailing vessels recognize from far away. With the advent of the John Hancock apartments high in the air, it has become necessary to build a shield shutting off the revolving light as it shines in that direction.

When the Palmolive Building was constructed, more than a generation ago, it was the first substantial building to go up in the 12 blocks between this spot and the Chicago River. The builders were considered mad to erect it at this preposterous location, but their vision resulted ultimately in the "Magnificent Mile."

End of the "Magnificent Mile"

The "Magnificent Mile" comes to an end just beyond the Drake Hotel, where Michigan Avenue loses its identity by merging with North Lake Shore Drive. Here, at Oak Street beach, is a glorious view of Lake Michigan and the beginning of one of the most glamorous boulevards in the world. North Lake Shore Drive is lined with sumptuous apartment buildings for miles along the lake. (See walk No. 7, Lake Shore Drive: Near North.) The Drake Hotel was the work of Marshall and Fox, Architects, 1922.

Walk-6

Courtyard in the
Tree Studio building.

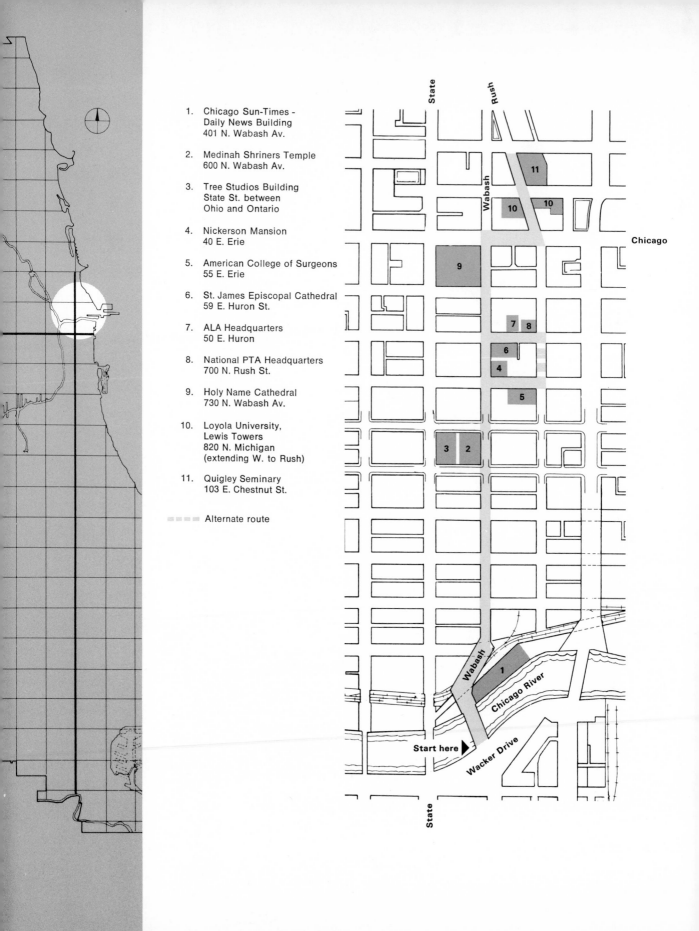

1. Chicago Sun-Times -
   Daily News Building
   401 N. Wabash Av.

2. Medinah Shriners Temple
   600 N. Wabash Av.

3. Tree Studios Building
   State St. between
   Ohio and Ontario

4. Nickerson Mansion
   40 E. Erie

5. American College of Surgeons
   55 E. Erie

6. St. James Episcopal Cathedral
   59 E. Huron St.

7. ALA Headquarters
   50 E. Huron

8. National PTA Headquarters
   700 N. Rush St.

9. Holy Name Cathedral
   730 N. Wabash Av.

10. Loyola University,
    Lewis Towers
    820 N. Michigan
    (extending W. to Rush)

11. Quigley Seminary
    103 E. Chestnut St.

▪▪▪▪▪ Alternate route

Walk · 6

NORTH WABASH AVENUE

WALKING TIME: 45 minutes.   HOW TO GET THERE: Walk 1 block west of Michigan at Randolph, then turn right on Wabash and walk 3 blocks north, crossing the Wabash Avenue bridge over the Chicago River.

If you are a lucky sightseer, you may arrive at the Chicago River just in time to see one or more of the bridges split in two and rise, permitting tall boats to pass by. These are bascule bridges, or—as they are sometimes called—"jackknife" bridges. Don't be in a hurry; both bridge and boats move slowly!

Chicago Sun-Times - Daily News Building—
401 North Wabash Avenue.
Architects: Naess and Murphy (1957)
(See also Walk No. 5, Michigan Avenue: North.)

This walk starts at the Chicago Sun-Times - Daily News Building on the north bank of the Chicago River at Wabash Avenue. This modern newspaper plant is housed in a long, low building that faces the river the full length of its facade. The horizontal emphasis in the building's architecture is accentuated by this location as well as by contrast with so many skyscrapers on all sides. A pleasant open effect is achieved by the river beside it and the Wrigley Building plaza, which gives it easy access to Michigan Avenue. This landscaped plaza on the east and a pedestrian walkway on the riverside contribute to making the building and its environs a pedestrian's delight.

As you walk inside into the main corridor, you will see the enclosed presses on one side of the building. Through the glass partition you can generally watch one of the many newspaper editions going to press—a fascinating process to the uninitiated.

Guided tours throughout the building are offered. For hours call the public service office (321-3005).

61

Medinah Shriners Temple—600 North Wabash Avenue.
Architects: Huehl and Schmid (1912)

Now walk north 3 blocks to Ohio Street, and note the very large
Medinah Shriners Temple at the northwest corner of Ohio and
Wabash. The building with its Moorish style of architecture
resembles a mosque, as of course the designer intended. Inside
are drill halls, offices, and an auditorium seating about 2,000,
which is used for circus performances and other spectaculars
as well as for the Medinah drill teams and Shriners band.

Tree Studios Building—State Street, between Ohio and Ontario streets.

Walk west on Ohio to the other half of this block for a glimpse of the Tree Studios building. Though rather drab in outward appearance, this is nevertheless a unique structure, devoted to spacious artists' studios with high ceilings and large window areas. Judge Tree, whose wife was an artist, donated the building. Be sure to walk through the Ohio Street entrance, marked rather oddly "4 - Tree Studios - 6" for a pleasant surprise: on the other side of a small vestibule a door leads you again outdoors, into a delightful, hidden bit of park—with trees, flowers, and benches—which runs the length of the building. Since the park is enclosed on all sides, this gives a special privacy to the studio entrances.

Nickerson Mansion—40 East Erie.
Architects: Burling and Whitehouse (1883)

Return to Wabash and walk north 2 blocks to Erie. The building on the northeast corner, now carrying the dignified commercial sign "Pinnn [sic] Productions," was once one of the most opulent homes in Chicago, the Nickerson residence. This 3-story stone mansion of some 30 rooms was built for the Nickerson family more than 10 years after their previous home on the North Side had been destroyed by the Great Fire of 1871.

For more than 40 years the building was occupied by the American College of Surgeons (see the next stopping place). Nickerson himself, an active financier and one of the founders of the first bank in Chicago to become a national bank, enjoyed it for many years, selling it only in his last years, when he returned east. In his day it was referred to as "Nickerson's Marble Palace," and the richness of the interior certainly merits the name. As you enter the building (visitors are allowed on the first floor), you find yourself in an enormous hall with marble floors and pillars, onyx wall panels, and an alabaster staircase. Handcarved woodwork decorates the entire building. Since Nickerson was an art collector, he used one large room as an art gallery, the contents of which he gave largely to the Art Institute of Chicago when he sold the house.

Fortunately, those who have used the building since Nickerson's

Boats carrying newsprint paper dock alongside the Sun-Times/Daily News building.

63

day have cherished its original elegance and kept it in good condition. Pinnn Productions, makers of audio-visual materials, distributes an attractive brochure. The soot-begrimed exterior, they say, is irreparable, because the porous building material makes sandblasting useless.

American College of Surgeons Headquarters—55 East Erie. Architects: Skidmore, Owings, and Merrill (1963)

One block farther east, on the southwest corner of Rush and Erie, with main entrance on Erie, is the new building of the American College of Surgeons. From 1919 until the completion of this building in 1963, the College of Surgeons occupied the Nickerson Mansion just described. At 50 East Erie, across the street immediately east of the Nickerson Mansion is the Auditorium used by the American College of Surgeons, the John B. Murphy Memorial. The ground on which the Memorial Auditorium stands was once the side yard of the Nickerson Mansion.

Episcopal Cathedral of St. James—Huron and Wabash. (In the 1870's) Parish House by architect James Hammond (1968)

One block farther north, at Huron, is the Episcopal Cathedral of St. James. This structure is typical of a number of churches built shortly before and after the Great Fire of 1871, for which architects followed the Gothic style in a free, somewhat inventive manner. These churches were often built of local limestone, called Joliet stone or Lemont limestone, which is seen in this building. To the east is a parish house of contemporary design, just completed.

Headquarters of the American Library Association and the National PTA

On the north side of Huron are 2 buildings dedicated to educational purposes. At *50 East Huron* is the headquarters of the *American Library Association (architects: Holabird and Root, 1961-63)*, built on the site of a much older structure, which had been used by the ALA since 1945. The earlier building was once known as the McCormick House. Cyrus H. McCormick II, of the family that won both fame and fortune—as well as occasional

Detail of massive ornamental facade of the John B. Murphy Memorial.

64

labor problems—through the McCormick Harvester plant, is said to have been still living in the house in 1889.

Immediately to the east, at *700 North Rush Street*, is the headquarters of the *National PTA—National Congress of Parents and Teachers (architects: Holabird and Root, 1954)*. Funds to meet the expenses of constructing the National PTA building came largely from individual or PTA donations of anywhere from 10 cents to 10 dollars. "Quarters for Headquarters" was the slogan, and PTA members all across the country contributed whatever they could to provide a home of their own, where the national staff might work in more convenient space and better conditions than had been possible previously in their rented offices. PTA's may well be proud of the result, for the building was cited for excellence of design soon after it was completed.

The sculptured figures on the face of the building, by Chicagoan Milton Horn, symbolize parents' and teachers' responsibilities in educating children. Father, mother, and teacher—each is represented with a child.

Both the ALA and the PTA have recently expanded their quarters by the purchase of property on Rush Street. The PTA now owns the building just north of its 700 North Rush headquarters. And the ALA is already at work in a building at 716 North Rush.

Buildings Related to the Roman Catholic Archdiocese of Chicago

In the next few blocks you will come to a variety of buildings representing the Roman Catholic faith and its Archdiocese in Chicago. (For the Archbishop's residence see Walk No. 8, "The Gold Coast.")

The Catholic *Cathedral of the Holy Name (architects: P. C. Kelly, 1874; Henry J. Schlacks, 1915)* and immediately related buildings occupy the entire block between Wabash and State, Superior Street (732 N) and Chicago Avenue (800 N). School buildings, parish houses, and convent share the block with the church, all built in a similar style—the neo-Gothic used so widely for places of worship. The Cathedral is closed for renovation until mid-1969.

Cathedral of the Holy Name.

To the north, on the other side of Wabash, is *Loyola University's Downtown Center, Lewis Towers Campus.* The structure that gives this complex of buildings its name is a converted office building on Rush Street (official address, 820 North Michigan Avenue) donated by the late Frank Lewis, Chicago philanthropist (*architects: Schmidt, Garden, and Erikson, 1925*). A newer building on the west side of Rush, connected with Lewis Towers at the 2nd floor by a covered walkway over the street, carries the name "Pere Marquette Campus."

And to the north of Lewis Towers are the imposing buildings of *Quigley Preparatory Seminary*, where youngsters start their training for the priesthood (*architect: Gustav Steinbeck of New York, 1918*). Archbishop James E. Quigley in 1905 had established what was then called Cathedral College. He died before his plans for an expanded school could be carried out, but his successor— Cardinal George Mundelein—fulfilled his aims. Many of the funds came as gifts from children of the Archdiocese, and the school's name was changed to make it a memorial to the man who had originally planned it.

At Quigley Seminary you feel that you are standing before a great French Gothic municipal hall of the 12th century. Various Gothic features combine to give the effect of an authentic medieval structure: the rose window over the chapel entrance, the sculpture on either side, the high-pitched roofs, the buttresses on the Chestnut Street side, and the medieval courtyard. They almost make you expect to see knights in armor ride in on horseback—until you catch a glimpse of the 20th century cars parked inside the courtyard! Whatever Louis Sullivan might have thought of the architecture, this is a most impressive complex of buildings.

Walk-7

North Lake Shore
Drive from the Chess
pavilion in the
foreground to Oak
Street beach.

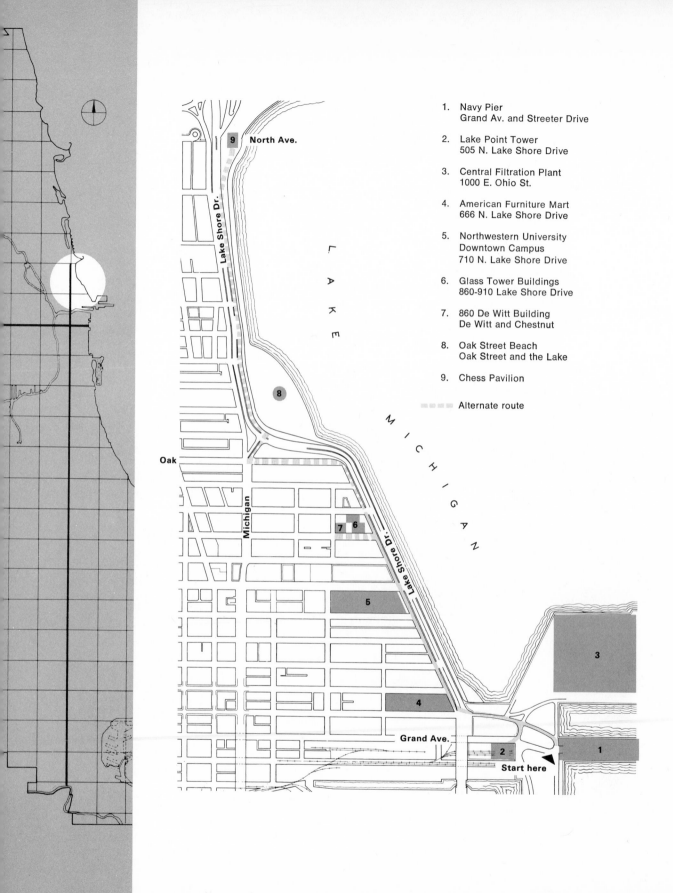

1. Navy Pier
   Grand Av. and Streeter Drive

2. Lake Point Tower
   505 N. Lake Shore Drive

3. Central Filtration Plant
   1000 E. Ohio St.

4. American Furniture Mart
   666 N. Lake Shore Drive

5. Northwestern University
   Downtown Campus
   710 N. Lake Shore Drive

6. Glass Tower Buildings
   860-910 Lake Shore Drive

7. 860 De Witt Building
   De Witt and Chestnut

8. Oak Street Beach
   Oak Street and the Lake

9. Chess Pavilion

▬ ▬ ▬ ▬ Alternate route

North Ave.

L A K E

M I C H I G A N

Lake Shore Dr.

Oak

Michigan

Grand Ave.

Start here

Walk · 7

LAKE SHORE DRIVE : NEAR NORTH

WALKING TIME: 1½ hours.   HOW TO GET THERE: Take any of the following northbound
CTA buses—No. 151 (Sheridan), No. 152 (Addison), or No. 153 (Wilson-Michigan) on State
Street; or a No. 76 (Diversey) on Wabash. Get off at Michigan and Grand Avenue (530 N), and
transfer to an eastbound bus No. 65 (Grand Avenue), which will take you to Navy Pier,
which is the end of the line.

This walk starts at *Navy Pier*, just one block to the east and
one block to the north of the Outer Drive/Lake Shore Drive bridge
(which crosses the Chicago River, a strip of land at North Water
Street, and then a strip of water called Ogden Slip).

Navy Pier links Chicago, an international port without a seacoast,
with the rest of the world. Since the opening of the St.
Lawrence Seaway, ships from faraway places change cargo here
during the shipping season—an activity that many find fascinating
to watch. The Pier, stretching nearly a mile out into Lake
Michigan, was built in 1916 as a storage and shipping facility for
lake traffic. In its life of more than half a century it has served
various purposes. During both world wars it was a training center
for the U.S. Navy, and for several years it was the home of the
Chicago branch of the University of Illinois—surely unique
among campuses! Since the University's construction of its new
Circle Campus in Chicago (see Walk No. 11) and its subsequent
departure from Navy Pier, the space here has been used
for convention exhibits and trade shows.

For the sightseer Navy Pier offers unparalleled views of
Chicago's "marine" activity and its spectacular skylines—
both to the south and to the north.

Streeter Drive, a short, curving street at the foot of Navy Pier,
is a reminder that you are on the border of what was once widely
known as *Streeterville*, named after a controversial figure of the
1880's. Just to the north (between Grand and Chicago avenues, St.
Clair and Lake Michigan) lies the part of the city to which
George Wellington Streeter and his wife for more than 30 years
claimed squatters' rights. They called their 180-acre shantytown

the District of Lake Michigan and claimed that neither the laws of Chicago nor those of Illinois had any jurisdiction over it. Other "squatters" whom Streeter persuaded to buy real estate from him gave him substantial backing in his many lawsuits with the city of Chicago. Not until 1918 was this notorious character actually removed from the lakefront land, which had multiplied its value many times during the years of Streeter's occupation.

Though the structures of Streeterville could never have been called architectural achievements, this sea "captain" turned real estate con man deserves more than passing mention. He seems to have been the first to redeem land from Lake Michigan and make a profit on it—a procedure that literally underlies many lakefront skyscrapers today!

The story goes that Streeter and his wife, Maria, started this fantastic real estate project in 1886 after running their excursion boat aground on a sandbar in Lake Michigan somewhat south of Chicago Avenue. Instead of freeing the boat, which they found difficult, they decided to fill up the lake around it instead. And— with the assistance of nearby residents who contributed dirt from construction sites, trash, garbage, and whatever lay at hand —this is exactly what they did. Despite protests from mansion-owners across the Drive, Streeter defied all attempts by the law to oust him from "his" property until someone was killed in one of the numerous confrontations with police. He was then sent to Joliet Penitentiary on a charge of manslaughter. Out on parole 9 months later, he returned to his battle with law and order. Finally, in 1918, court orders were actually carried out: Streeter was removed and the shanties of Streeterville burned to make way for later development.

For all his early success with real estate, Streeter could never have dreamed of the skyline that today has replaced his controversial territory!

Lake Point Tower—505 North Lake Shore Drive. Architects: Schipporeit-Heinrich; Graham, Anderson, Probst, and White (1968)

Opposite, Four foreign vessels docked at Navy Pier.

The most prominent building on the shoreline to the north is Lake Point Tower. This 70-story, cloverleaf-shaped,

72

glass-sheathed apartment building is indeed a beautiful sight.
Nearly 50 years ago (in 1921) a similar building was *designed* by
Ludwig Mies van der Rohe in Berlin, but it was never built.
The young architects who designed Lake Point Tower, former
colleagues of Mies, were obviously influenced by the master.
Much of the building's sweep and fluidity, its even sensuous
quality, has to do with its hidden columns, all enclosed by the
bronze-tinted glass. It is almost mirror-like at times, and in
the setting sun's reflection it looks like a golden shaft.

The owners of this 900-apartment skyscraper own also the
warehouses to the south and west; they plan to construct several
additional apartment and office buildings, to be connected
with Michigan Avenue by pedestrian walks.

Central District Filtration Plant of Chicago— 1000 East Ohio Street. Architects: C. F. Murphy Associates and the City Architect (1966)

Out in the lake, just north of Navy Pier, spreads the Central
District Filtration Plant of Chicago, largest facility of its kind in
the United States—with landscaped grounds and many illuminated
fountains. The sculpture in the lobby of the main building,
by the Chicagoan Milton Horn, represents the history
of the various uses of water.

Above, Central District Filtration
Plant and Park.

Visitors to this plant are permitted by appointment only.
Call City Hall 744-4000.

74

American Furniture Mart—666 North Lake Shore Drive.
Architect: N. Max Dunning.
(East portion, 1923; West portion, 1926)

Across Lake Shore Drive you pass two modern hotels—Lake
Tower Inn, at 600 Lake Shore Drive, and Holiday Inn, at 644—and
come to the renowned American Furniture Mart, at 666. This is
one of the two major marts used by leading furniture
manufacturers to display their latest creations, especially during
"market" weeks. (The other of course, is the Merchandise Mart,
also in Chicago. See Walk No. 9, Wacker Drive: East-West.)

Unlike the Merchandise Mart, the American Furniture Mart is
restricted to dealers in furniture—a condition that makes it the
world's largest building given to a single business. Displays by
practically every wholesale furniture dealer in the country
are shown here, and only furniture buyers are
permitted in the building.

Northwestern University Chicago Campus—
710 North Lake Shore Drive.
Architects: Holabird and Root (From 1925 on)

An activity center of a completely different kind lies one block
north of the Mart—the Chicago campus of Northwestern
University (which has most of its buildings in Evanston). Here are
the graduate schools of medicine, dentistry, business, and law—
in various buildings along the 300 block of East Chicago Avenue,

75

with administrative offices at 710 North Lake Shore Drive. The large medical center serves 7 hospitals, including 3 in the immediate area—Passavant, Wesley Memorial, and the Veterans Administration Research Hospital—and the Rehabilitation Institute of Chicago, only a few blocks away.

Construction has been going on since 1925, with many new buildings in recent years. The campus plan lacks unity, for the earlier structures have a collegiate Gothic design whereas those completed in recent years are contemporary in spirit. The lack of adequate spatial relationships among the various buildings is the result of enormous expansions that have over-taxed the original plans.

◨ 860-88 Lake Shore Drive Apartment Buildings.
Architect: Ludwig Mies van der Rohe, with associate architects P A C E (Planners, Architects, Consulting Engineers) and Holsman, Holsman, Klekamp, and Taylor (1952)

Two blocks north, beyond a city playground, the Armory, and the headquarters of the American Hospital Association, stand four apartment buildings designed by Mies van der Rohe. The first pair of these to be constructed (860-888) have been cited by the Architectural Landmarks Commission in these words:

> In recognition of an open plan in a multistory apartment building where the steel cage becomes expressive of the potentialities of steel and glass in architectural design.

The second pair, at 900-910 Lake Shore Drive, were built four years later, in 1956. These buildings reflect the skill of a great architect, engineer, and innovator. Nicknamed "The Glass Houses" because they seem to be made almost entirely of glass, they have been the inspiration for many buildings all over the world.

860 DeWitt Building—860 North DeWitt.
Architects: Skidmore, Owings, and Merrill (1966)

Directly west of the 860-880 Lake Shore apartment buildings, at DeWitt and Chestnut streets, is the 860 DeWitt apartment building—a handsome structure of reinforced concrete covered with travertine marble. The contrast between this and "The Glass

Top left, Lake Point Tower. *Right*, Mies van der Rohe apartments with 860 DeWitt building just behind. *Bottom*, Lake Shore Drive from Pearson to Oak Street.

77

Houses" is a reminder that modern builders can use old-time building materials—as well as new—with effective results. Always present in the background of this walk is the imposing John Hancock Building with its 100 stories, 2 blocks to the west on Michigan Avenue. (See Walk No. 5, Michigan Avenue: North.)

Chess Pavilion—North End of Oak Street Beach. Architect: Morris Webster (1956)

Around the corner on Lake Shore Drive, as it bends westward after meeting Oak Street, are several palatial apartment buildings that mark the beginning of that section of Chicago referred to as the "Gold Coast." (Walk No. 8 is devoted entirely to the "Gold Coast.") The Drake, a luxury hotel, stands at the spot where Lake Shore Drive joins Michigan Avenue.

If the weather (and your endurance!) permits, stroll along Oak Street Beach, which you can reach through a pedestrian tunnel at the corner. Such a walk can be exhilarating, with Lake Michigan on one side and the prestigious apartment buildings on the other. The heavy automobile traffic along Lake Shore Drive is in direct contrast with the quiet of the water—or even with its ocean-like turbulence on windy days, which is refreshingly different from the mechanical noises of the city it borders.

The Chess Pavilion at the north end of Oak Street (the south end of Lincoln Park) is a fitting terminal to this walk. This small building is beautiful in its unusual and simple design. The reinforced concrete roof appears to be floating in the air.

Walk-8

Bateman School.

North Ave.

Clark

State

Astor

Division

Start here

Walk · 8

THE GOLD COAST

WALKING TIME: About 1 hour.   HOW TO GET THERE: Take a northbound CTA bus No. 36 (Broadway) on State Street, and get off at Division Street (1200 N).

In Chicago the term "Gold Coast" applies to the area bounded by Lake Michigan on the east, LaSalle Street on the west, Oak Street (1000 N) on the south, and North Avenue (1600 N) on the north. The name was given many years ago, indicating of course that this section of the city was peopled by those with most of the city's gold. (Suburbs and country houses were still a thing of the future.)

On the face of the 1000 Lake Shore Drive Building is sculpture —by Bernard Rosenthal, of New York, formerly of Chicago— literally depicting the Gold Coast of Africa.

This walk, however, covers another part of the Gold Coast, starting at State and Division, and moving through Scott Street, Astor Street, and Burton Place. (It seems especially appropriate that the Gold Coast should include a street that carries the glittering name of John Jacob Astor!)

You will be struck by the beauty and tranquillity of this residential area. What is unseen is the struggle to preserve these qualities in the face of change. At one time the section was zoned for single-family residences only, but as land values increased, zoning was changed to accommodate the economic forces. As in Kenwood (see Walk No. 15), most people could no longer afford to maintain such establishments—with rising taxes, increased cost of operation, and the dearth of household help. The choice for many was selling the property to high-rise developers or converting the interior into apartments. Wherever feasible, the latter was attempted. Fortunately, some of the home-owners have been able to keep their property as single-family dwellings.

1209 State Parkway—Just north of Division on the east side of the street is a brick apartment building painted white with glass block windows and small terra-cotta figures in the brickwork. This was built around the time of the 1933-34 Century of Progress in the Art Moderne style of the time. High ceilings, balconies, and terraces give this structure a handsome appearance.

17-19-21 East Scott Street—At Scott Street (1240 N) turn east and stop at 17, 19, and 21. Note the delightful limestone-and-brick facades. The bay windows and individual entrances give each house a bit of Old World charm.

23 East Scott—An old townhouse handsomely remodeled. The below-grade entrance with the white limestone wall and black columns behind a black iron picket fence give it a modernized 1890 look. The yellow-painted facade of the upper 3 stories is quite striking.

1240-42-44 Astor—Turn north from Scott Street onto Astor (50 E). Here are 3 charming townhouses built around 1890, delightful 3-story structures with bay windows. At 44, the below-grade entrance and curved facade give an 18th-century character to the house.

1250 Astor—A 3-story 1890 townhouse, with limestone facade, imitating an Italian Renaissance design.

1260 and 1301 Astor—At 1260 a 10-story, limestone-faced apartment building in the Art Moderne style of about 1936, and across the street, at 1301, a similar structure. These are 2 of the elegant cooperative apartment buildings that have replaced some of the earlier one-family residences, and they were designed for very much the same kind of home-owner. The Potter Palmers, for instance, took the top 3 floors of 1301 Astor as their Chicago home.

Hotels Ambassador—East and West. At Goethe—pronounced "go-thee" with the "th" as in "thin," which may be necessary guidance if you come from outside Chicago—(1300 N) make a short side trip to State Parkway once more. At the corner of Goethe and State Parkway are the Ambassador hotels, home of the noted Pump Room, where so many famous people have dined and danced—or entertained those dining and dancing there.

Astor Tower Hotel—1300 North Astor. And back on Astor is the Astor Tower Hotel, designed by Bertrand Goldberg

Opposite, Astor Tower Hotel.

82

Associates, 1963—architects for Marina City (see the end of Walk No. 3, Dearborn Street). The Astor Tower Hotel is particularly famous for its French restaurant, Maxim's de Paris, a branch of the celebrated restaurant by that name in Paris, France. Interior design of the restaurant reproduces the original, and so— is it claimed—do the service and cuisine.

1308-10-12 Astor—Three delightful townhouses in sandstone and red brick, with beautiful bay windows at 2nd and 3rd stories.

Playboy Mansion—1340 North State. The famous multimillionaire owner of the Playboy empire, Hugh Hefner, lives just around the corner. Make another short side trip for a view of the outside. (Inside views are more difficult, though in odd-numbered years you may visit the first floor if you find out the exact date of the Inurbia Tour of the Francis W. Parker School—to raise funds for the school.) Hefner's "pad" is a large Georgian mansion complete with swimming pool, art collections, and of course Bunnies!

Court of the Golden Hands—1349-53 Astor. Back on Astor you will see, on the east side of the street, the "Court of the Golden Hands," a charming apartment complex with a delightful courtyard. Each of the 2 golden hands at the entrance seems to be holding an apple. The Georgian facade and marble figure set in a niche make this a memorable sight.

1355 Astor—A well-designed, large-scale English Georgian mansion, constructed about 1910, copied from 18th-century originals.

◘ Charnley House—1365 Astor.
Architects: Adler and Sullivan (1892)

This 11-room, 3-story, 1-family residence has fortunately been maintained as such. Although the official architects were Adler and Sullivan, this is understood to be a Frank Lloyd Wright design, drawn up by him for the famous partnership of architects, for whom he was then working as a young draftsman. The building's compactness contrasts with Wright's later rambling "Prairie House" style but is similar to other early works. Some see Sullivan's touch in the wooden balcony and copper cornice.

What is obviously an extension to the south was built at a later

84

date, to bring the kitchen up from the basement and make the original dumbwaiter service unnecessary. It detracts from the original symmetry of the design.

36-48 Schiller (1400 N)—At Schiller, walk east past the row of townhouses numbered 36 to 48—red brick, 3-story, vine-covered houses, some with bay windows and each with a distinctive subtle design of its own.

1412 Astor—Back at Astor, on the west side, you come to a combination limestone and yellow-brick house. A pediment at the roof line and ornament on the facade give it a Dutch quality.

1416 and 1430 Astor—Here are two handsome Georgian houses— one of which has been remodeled into very fine apartments. The buildings are separated by a large garden with a unique wall: a series of brick columns, each topped by a stone ball, is held together by a brick wall of inverted arches filled with iron picket work. These are known as the Blair and the Bowen houses— homes of the William McCormick Blairs and Joseph T. Bowens, prominent in Chicago society. The Blairs, who still occupy 1416, are said to have lived on Astor Street longer than any other residents there. Mrs. Blair was a Bowen from next door before her marriage.

1427 Astor—Across the street, a 4-story brick house, painted gray, has a handsome, pristine look.

1431 Astor—A curved facade embraces the gray brick of this building, with white Ionic columns supporting a pediment over the porch. This was once the home of Edward L. Ryerson, former chairman of Inland Steel's board of directors.

1435 Astor—Another facsimile of a great Georgian mansion, a style so popular here at the turn of the century. The pilasters at the corners with their Ionic caps give the facade a somewhat heavy appearance. The pleasant ornamentation below the cornice somehow lends an air of authenticity. Black iron picket fences enclose the grounds.

1432 Astor—Back on the west side of the street is a stunning remodeling of a townhouse, converting it into 3 apartments. Limestone and large horizontal glass areas give this daring design a contemporary look. (*Architect, James Eppenstein, 1936*)

Opposite, Charnley House.

85

1444 Astor—An interesting 4-story apartment building with a limestone facade and bay windows, having some of the appearance of Art Moderne. (Architects, Holabird and Root, 1936)

1450 Astor—At 1450, facing Burton Place, is another handsome Georgian townhouse, with limestone base and red brick facade.

20 East Burton Place, now the Bateman School—
Architects: Stanford White (1900); David Adler (1927)

At 20 East Burton Place stands another landmark, now used by a private elementary and high school. The building's historical associations are with Chicago's society life. It was built for Mrs. Robert W. Patterson, daughter of Joseph Medill (once mayor of Chicago and *Chicago Tribune* editor), by the ill-fated architect Stanford White. The next owner— Cyrus McCormick—had extensive alterations made in 1927.

This red brick building with marble columns—a mansion of some 40 to 90 rooms (the count varies)—was the scene of some of Chicago's most sumptuous social functions. Here, it is said, slept visiting kings and queens as guests.

The gracious director of the Bateman School, its present tenant, allows visitors the opportunity to enjoy the splendor within— the graceful winding staircase, the 3-inch-thick doors, and the marble bathrooms. A visit inside 20 East Burton Place is a step into the glittering past.

Office of the Greek Orthodox Archdiocese is not far away— in the building at the corner of Astor and Burton Place (1500 N), 40 East Burton.

1518 Astor—A red brick Georgian design with bay windows and a well-proportioned entrance.

1525 Astor—On the east side of the street is the headquarters of the Polish Consulate of Chicago, housed in a handsome red brick Georgian structure, once a townhouse.

1529 and 1539 Astor—Two more charming Georgian houses, of delightful design, with a beautiful garden between them.

Roman Catholic Archbishop's Residence, 1555 North State Parkway—Architect: Alfred F. Pashley (1880)—At the very north end of Astor, facing Lincoln Park, is a large 19th-century,

Wrought iron gate in front of the Bateman School. *Opposite,* exterior view and details of Madlener House.

86

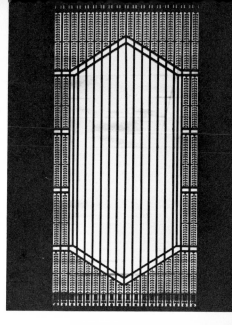

3-story, red brick, electric mid-Victorian mansion. Many chimneys (you will count 19 if you see them all!), several roof peaks, and impressive facades make this building a distinctive landmark, This has been the home of Chicago's Archbishop since the 1880's.

◨ **Madlener House**—4 West Burton Place, now the Graham Foundation for Advanced Studies in the Fine Arts. Architects: Richard E. Schmidt (1902); for interior remodeling: Brenner, Danforth, and Rockwell (1963)

Walk west on North Avenue to North State Parkway, then south one block to Burton Place to the home of the Graham Foundation for Advanced Studies in the Fine Arts, at 4 *West Burton Place*. This is the noted Madlener House, an Architectural Landmark, which has been compared with Florentine palaces. Note the Sullivan-like ornamentation around the door, relieving somewhat the severity of the design as a whole. Open to the public by arrangement 9:30 A.M. to 5:00 P.M., Monday through Friday. Call SU-7-4071.

Carl Sandburg Village, between Clark and LaSalle, extending from Division to North Avenue. Architects: L. R. Solomon and J. D. Cordwell and Associates (1960 on)

Now walk 2 blocks west of State to Clark Street, along the western border of the old Gold Coast, for a view of Carl Sandburg Village. This "village," named of course for Chicago's famous and well-loved poet Carl Sandburg, consists of high-rise apartment buildings, townhouses for sale or rent, studios, gardens, fountains, and shops. A central pedestrian mall covers the parking areas.

An urban renewal plan referred to as the Clark-LaSalle Redevelopment Project cleared the slums to which the area had deteriorated. It is expected that more buildings will eventually be erected here.

Red Star Inn, Germania Club, and Latin School of Chicago— Before ending this walk, note the Red Star Inn, *1528 North Clark*, a restaurant popular since the early part of the century,

Opposite, Carl Sandburg Village.

88

which boasts of its excellent German chefs; the Germania Club, *108 West Germania (1536 N)*; and the building for the younger students of the Latin School of Chicago, at *1531 North Dearborn*. (The upper school of this historic Chicago institution is now at 59 East Scott. A new building for these older students is already under construction at North and Clark.)

The Red Star Inn.

Executive House
and Lincoln Tower.

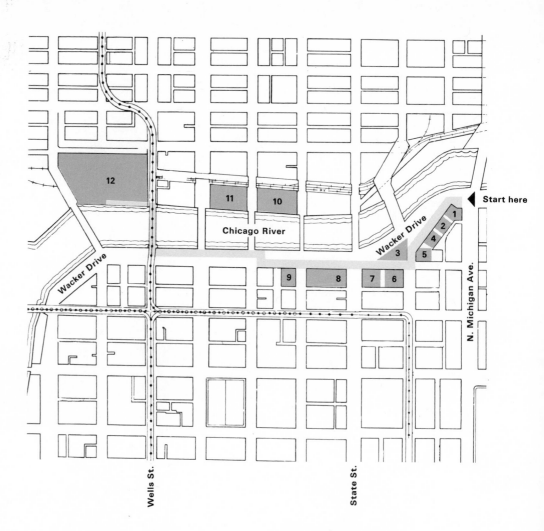

Start here

Chicago River

Wacker Drive

Wacker Drive

N. Michigan Ave.

Wells St.

State St.

1. Stone Container Building
   360 N. Michigan

2. Lincoln Tower Building
   75 E. Wacker Dr.

3. Heald Square—Sculpture:
   George Washington—Salomon—Morris
   State & Wacker & Wabash

4. Executive House
   71 E. Wacker Dr.

5. 17th Church of Christ Scientist
   Wabash—Wacker Dr.—South Water

6. North American Life Insurance Bldg.
   35 E. Wacker Dr.

7. United of America Building
   One E. Wacker

8. "Bird Cage" City Garage
   11 W. Wacker Dr.

9. Blue Cross - Blue Shield Bldg.
   Dearborn & Wacker Dr.

10. Central Cold Storage Warehouse
    315 N. Clark St.

11. City of Chicago Central Office Building
    (formerly Reid Murdoch)
    325 N. LaSalle St.

12. Merchandise Mart
    Chicago River - Orleans St.

Walk · 9

WACKER DRIVE : EAST-WEST

WALKING TIME: 1½ hours.   HOW TO GET THERE: Take any of the following northbound CTA buses—No. 151 (Sheridan), No. 152 (Addision), or No. 153 (Wilson-Michigan) on State Street; or a No. 76 (Diversey) on Wabash. Get off at Michigan Avenue and Wacker Drive (300 N).

This walk begins at the intersection of East Wacker Drive and North Michigan Avenue, the spot where once stood Fort Dearborn, one of the military outposts established by President Thomas Jefferson. Plaques on both sides of the street are the only things to remind you of this historic fact. If you stand near the Michigan Avenue bridge and look west, you can see an exciting panorama of today's Chicago along the banks of the Chicago River, where that primitive fort was once the only settlement. The array of contemporary architecture—vertical, horizontal, round, and square—would surely have astonished those early settlers, no matter how ambitious their visions for the future may have been.

The Chicago River, along which you walk, is famed as the river that runs backwards. In order to make it serve more adequately the commercial and sanitary needs of metropolitan Chicago, engineers reversed its current more than 50 years ago, so that it now flows *from* Lake Michigan to the Mississippi River, rather than *into* Lake Michigan as it used to flow. With the recent opening of the St. Lawrence Seaway, the character of the boats seen on the river has changed. In addition to the barges and pleasure boats that always used it, seagoing vessels from distant ports are sometimes anchored here—from England, Denmark, Sweden, Italy, and other far countries.

Wacker Drive, named for Charles Wacker, first chairman of the Chicago Plan Commission, was constructed in 1925, following up the Burnham Plan of 1909. The cluttered old South Water produce market was demolished to make way for this vast improvement.

Wacker Drive and North Michigan Avenue, along with the Michigan Avenue bridge, are double-decked, with a seemingly different life going on at the lower level. A double-decked ring road around the Loop had been proposed as part of the Burnham Plan of 1909. But the Wacker Drive segment was the only portion to be completed. (The other two segments—the Eisenhower Expressway and the Outer Drive—have been finished only as upper-level roads.) Traffic on this lower level moves freely.

Stone Container Building—360 North Michigan Avenue. Architect: Alfred S. Alschuler (1923)

The Stone Container Building, at the southwest corner of Wacker Drive and Michigan Avenue, is the first building to be noted on this walk. Formerly the London Guarantee Building, it is especially well known for the replica of a Greek temple on its roof. Obviously, the designers were not following the standards of indigenous art that were developed by the late nineteenth century architects of the Chicago school.

Lincoln Tower Building—75 East Wacker Drive. Architect: Herbert H. Riddle (1928) (Formerly the Mather Tower)

A few hundred feet west is the 24-story Lincoln Tower Building, with its pseudo-Gothic ornamentation in terra-cotta. This narrow structure is distinguished primarily by the fact that it has the *smallest* floor space per story of any commercial building in Chicago!

Heald Square—East Wacker Drive, West of Michigan.

A block west of Michigan Avenue lies Heald Square, with sculptured figures of American Revolutionary War heroes in the center—George Washington, Haym Salomon, and Robert Morris. The square was named for Captain Nathan Heald, ill-fated commandant of Fort Dearborn at the time it was ordered evacuated. He was advised that the Indians would permit safe passage of the soldiers and their families. But as the group of 95 left the fort on August 15, 1812, they were attacked. Only 45 survived.

Revolutionary War Heroes in Heald Square.

Incidentally, this is an excellent place from which to view the area—and take pictures if you are a camera fan.

94

Executive House—71 East Wacker Drive.
Architects: Milton M. Schwartz and Associates (1960)

Just to the east of Heald Square you will see the stainless
steel balconies of the striking high-rise Executive House,
designed as a high-quality hotel with special appeal to
businessmen—an appeal that has proved highly successful.

Seventeenth Church of Christ Scientist—
55 East Wacker Drive.
Architects: Harry M. Weese and Associates (1968)

To the west of Executive House is a handsome, travertine
marble church—semicircular-shaped and topped by a dome.
This is the Seventeenth Church of Christ Scientist, constructed
in 1968. Entrance to the main auditorium, which has arena-type
seating, is through a lower-level foyer.

North American Life Insurance—35 East Wacker Drive.
Architects: Giaver and Dinkelberg, with Thielbar
and Fugard as Associates (1926)

South of Heald Square is the former Jewelers Building, now the
North American Life Insurance Building. It is topped with a
neoclassical temple on each of the four corners, surrounding
a huge central tower. Not following any single architectural
style, the designers may be said to have used here an
eclectic design.

United of America Building—1 East Wacker Drive.
Architects: Shaw, Metz, and Associates (1964)

Next to the North American Building is the glistening white
marble tower of the United of America Insurance Building.
This 41-story structure is said to be the tallest marble-faced
commercial building in the world. It is featured as the last
stop of another walk—No. 2, State Street.

City Parking Facility, "The Bird Cage"—
11 West Wacker Drive.
Architects: Shaw, Metz, and Dolio (1954)

Just across State Street, at the southwest corner of State and
Wacker, is one of the city's parking structures, known to most
Chicagoans as "The Bird Cage." Your first view will convince

you that the nickname is appropriate. The cables used in the construction give the building its bird-cage appearance. There is a strong contrast between the windowless center portion shielding the elevators (which emphasizes the vertical) and the open wing for parked cars on each side (which strongly emphasize the horizontal). The only ornamentation on the windowless facade is a piece of sculpture by Milton Horn, "Chicago Rising from the Lake." The dark metal of the sculpture contrasts dramatically with the plain white expanse that it decorates. Its sudden projection from the wall may well suggest Chicago's rapid growth.

Blue Cross - Blue Shield Building—222 North Dearborn.
Architects: C. F. Murphy Associates
(still in construction 1968)

Next, at Dearborn Street, is the Blue Cross-Blue Shield Building. This heavy, beige-colored concrete structure, with its cantilevered floors, is described in Walk No. 3, Dearborn Street.

Central Cold Storage Warehouse—
315 North Clark Street.
Architect: George H. Edbrooke (1883)

Across the river, on its north bank, is one of the city's old river-front warehouses, the Central Cold Storage Warehouse (formerly the Hiram Sibley Warehouse), which has been cited as an Architectural Landmark. Not only does this building represent the first use in Chicago of deep piles under the wall of a structure (the wall on the river side is supported by 3 rows of 30-foot oak piles); it was also among the first to establish the Chicago school of architecture style with horizontal spans for the windows.

▣ **City of Chicago Central Office Building (formerly Reid, Murdoch and Company Building)**—
325 North LaSalle Street.
Architect: George C. Nimmons (1913)

Opposite, top left, Milton Horn sculpture on facade of parking facility. *Right*, Blue Cross-Blue Shield building. *Below*, Seventeenth Church of Christ, Scientist.

West of Clark Street, still on the river front, is the City of Chicago Central Office Building, operated by the city of Chicago as a Traffic Court, with offices for city departments. Formerly the Reid Murdoch and Company Building, it was bought by the

Monarch Foods Company, who leased it to the city. This is a clean, straightforward structure in red brick—its 320-foot-long facade of 8 stories topped off at the center with a prominent clock tower of 4 more stories. The brick work and contrasting terra-cotta accents give this structure a pleasing effect.

Merchandise Mart—Merchandise Mart Plaza (about 350 North Wells).
Architects: Graham, Anderson, Probst, and White (1930)

One block west of the Central Office Building, between Wells and Orleans, where the CTA elevated lines cross the river, looms the massive Merchandise Mart. Although its architectural design is hardly as distinguished or praiseworthy as it was thought to be at the time of construction, this building is nevertheless not to be passed by. For many years the largest building in the world, the Merchandise Mart is still the world's largest wholesale marketing center and one of its 5 largest commercial buildings. Its floor space amounts to about 4 million square feet, where more than 5,000 manufacturers and designers display their products, chiefly furniture and other home furnishings. Twice a year wholesale buyers from all across the country come to Chicago to the home furnishings show that is held here.

Opposite the entrance to the Merchandise Mart on the river side of the plaza stand 6 tall columns with the busts of those who have been selected as the "Merchandise Mart Hall of Fame": Julius Rosenwald, Frank Winfield Woolworth, Marshall Field, John Wanamaker, George Huntington Hartford, and Edward A. Filene.

The Mart is owned by Joseph P. Kennedy, who bought it in 1945 from the Marshall Field family.

Though not open to the public, the Merchandise Mart offers a 1½ hour guided tour daily, leaving the lobby every 30 minutes, between 9:30 a.m. and 3:30 p.m. Adults, 50¢; children under 12, free. (Closed Saturdays and Sundays.)

By crossing the Wells Street bridge you can reach the Merchandise Mart Plaza, with a close-up of this enormous building, the last to be noted on Walk 9.

Left, Merchandise Mart.

1. Union Station
   210 S. Canal St.

2. Gateway Center Buildings
   10 S. Riverside Plaza

3. Chicago &
   North Western Station
   Madison and Canal Sts.

4. Riverside Plaza Building
   2 N. Riverside Plaza

5. Kemper Insurance
   (formerly Civic Opera)
   20 N. Wacker Dr.

6. Morton Salt Building
   110 N. Wacker Dr.

7. Illinois Bell Telephone Building
   311 W. Washington

8. Hartford Plaza
   100 S. Wacker Dr.

9. U.S. Gypsum Building
   101 S. Wacker Dr.

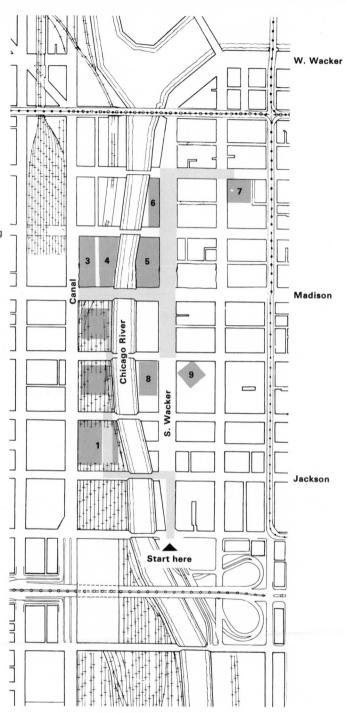

Walk · 10

WACKER DRIVE : SOUTH-NORTH

WALKING TIME: About 1 hour.   HOW TO GET THERE: Walk south to Van Buren Street
(400 S), and take a westbound CTA bus No. 126 (Jackson). Get off at Wacker Drive (348 W).

Wacker Drive, which here runs north and south, intersecting
Van Buren (and continuing south 2 blocks as far as Harrison) is the
same street you followed from east to west in Walk No. 9. The
change in direction took place just after the end of that walk,
where Wacker Drive follows a bend in the Chicago River and
then turns directly south, at Lake Street, to follow the South
Branch of the river.

Daniel Burnham, in his plan for Chicago back in 1909, saw
Wacker Drive as part of a ring road system surrounding the Loop.
Incidentally, Burnham also, in his plans nearly 60 years ago,
anticipated the need for a highway comparable to the Eisenhower
Expressway. With this plan in mind, the architects constructed
the Central Post Office—2 blocks south and across the river
from where this walk starts—with a large opening in the center
at ground level. Consequently, the Eisenhower Expressway
passed through and under the building with a minimum of
inconvenience to the Post Office.

This section of the city is sometimes referred to as the Gateway
area, since Wacker Drive and the South Branch of the Chicago
River are in fact a gateway to the near west. South Wacker Drive,
formerly the wholesale garment section of the city, lost hundreds
of tenants to the Merchandise Mart when that building was
constructed, in 1930 (see Walk No. 9). This change forecast in a
way the Drive's redevelopment. The city government and area
businessmen are now carrying out a gigantic urban renewal
program in this area, extending to the Kennedy Expressway
on the west.

Union Station—210 South Canal Street.
Architects: Graham, Anderson, Probst, and White (1925)

If you walk down the steps in the structure at the northwest corner of Jackson and Canal—the first street the other side of the river—you will reach the cavernous, high-pillared waiting room of Union Station, one of the few enormous railroad stations left from the grand old days of railroading. Thousands of suburban commuters still plow through the waiting room and the iron-pillared train concourse daily for the Milwaukee Road and Burlington commuter trains.

The main waiting room of Union Station covers one entire city block. The 6-story-high, barreled and vaulted ceiling is said to have been patterned after an early Roman bath.

Gateway Center—10 South Riverside Plaza.
Architects: Skidmore, Owings, and Merrill
(still under construction, 1969)

Eventually, Union Station and its concourse may give way to further development of nearby Gateway Center. The first two buildings, just north of the station's concourse exit ramp at West Adams Street, were built on air rights over the tracks leading to Union Station. They were the first buildings in the continuing style of the Chicago school of architecture to extend the Loop business center west of the Chicago River. The tinted glass and russet beams used in the buildings give them the functional exterior framework of the old school.

Surrounded by wide plazas, these two buildings look somewhat squat and bulky, despite their 20-story height—a characteristic dictated by construction over the tracks. The wide architectural spans, similar to those used by the same architects in the Chicago Civic Center, were made possible by the omission of any columns between the center service core and the exterior columns.

From Gateway Center Plaza along the river bank you have a distant view of two markedly different architectural neighbors back on the east side of the river—the Hartford Plaza Building, a contemporary expression of the still vibrant Chicago school of architecture, and its sculptured neighbor, the U.S. Gypsum Building, sitting gracefully askew on its site at Wacker and Monroe. You will have a close-up view of the two buildings later in the walk.

Opposite, Union Station.

102

103

Chicago and North Western Railway Station—
500 West Madison Street.
Architects: Frost and Granger (1911)

At the north end of Gateway Center Plaza, the massive columns of the Chicago and North Western Railway Station stand stolidly in their classic revival past. The station is one of the busiest commuter centers outside of New York City, and the management has converted the vast waiting room interior into a bright, attractive, and well-planned shopping gallery. A pedestrian way connects the station to the Riverside Plaza Building, which houses the railroad's offices and those of the Northeastern Illinois Planning Commission.

Riverside Plaza Building (formerly Chicago Daily News Building)—2 North Riverside Plaza.
Architects: Holabird and Root (1928)

As you cross the bridge over the river at West Madison Street, you can see the Riverside Plaza Building more fully, sitting sphinx-like as it was designed. With its setbacks and angles, the building is an excellent example of the Chicago skyscraper of that period.

Kemper Insurance Building (formerly Civic Opera House)—20 North Wacker Drive.
Architects: Graham, Anderson, Probst, and White (1929)

Another example of the Chicago skyscraper of the 1920's is the 45-story Kemper Insurance Building, an immense structure erected—at a cost of some $20 million—by Samuel Insull in 1929. Such an investment in that year by even the most sound and upright financier would have been a gamble; in this case it proved a disaster. The subsequent ruin of Insull's financial empire, to say nothing of the dubious methods he had used in building it up, unfortunately wiped out whatever pleasant associations Chicago might have had with the name of a man who loved opera. And the fact that the construction of this building led to the closing of the Auditorium Theatre (see Walk No. 1, Michigan Avenue: South) seemed to many Chicago opera-lovers a cause for resentment rather than gratitude. Herman Kogan has expressed this harsh but understandable judgment of Samuel Insull:

104

THE CIVIC OPERA HOVSE

> More than any one man, he was responsible for the abandonment of the glorious Auditorium as a center of music and opera, because he had built, in an illogical place and with inferior acoustics, his own Civic Opera House at Wacker Drive and Madison Street. [4]

Whatever may be the sentiments toward Insull, however, his building has not gone empty. The current Lyric Opera of Chicago uses its auditorium, seating 3,500 people, just as two other opera companies did before the Lyric was formed. And hundreds of offices became available in the remainder of this mammoth structure.

Morton Salt Building—110 North Wacker Drive. Architects: Shaw, Metz, and Dolio (1961)

Located on the west side of Wacker Drive is the Morton Salt Building, extending from Washington to Randolph and from Wacker Drive to the Chicago River. This Indiana limestone structure, housing the main offices of the Morton Salt Company, affords all its offices and dining rooms a splendid view of the river.

Illinois Bell Telephone Building—225 West Randolph. Architects: Holabird and Root (1967)

The new building of the Illinois Bell Telephone Company, one block east of Wacker on Randolph, makes an effective use of vertical lines of marble and glass, dramatized at night by the interior lighting. This is a first-rate modern building.

Detail: Kemper Insurance building.

105

U.S. Gypsum building.

And just one block beyond this building, at Lake Street, comes the bend in Wacker Drive, where it follows the Chicago River to become the east-west street you traveled in Walk Number 9.

Hartford Plaza Building—100 South Wacker.
Architects: Skidmore, Owings, and Merrill (1961)

At Wacker Drive and Monroe Street, back south three blocks, are the two conflicting architectural neighbors already mentioned. On the southwest corner is the Hartford Plaza Building—of the Hartford Fire Insurance Company. In this the architects exaggerated the old Chicago school belief that the facade of a building should disclose its interior structural composition. The 21-story concrete skeleton here becomes more than a framework: it serves as sunshades for the interior and gives the building a constantly changing pattern of light and shadow during the day. A second building to the south was started in 1968 by the same owners and architects.

U.S. Gypsum Building—101 South Wacker.
Architects: Perkins and Will Partnership (1961)

Directly across the street from the Hartford Fire Insurance Building, on the southeast corner, is the U.S. Gypsum Building. Its placing on the building lot—at a 45° angle from the street lines —caused some consternation among the adherents of the Chicago school of architecture. Many of them felt this departure from the usual procedure insulted the unity of the buildings that Chicago school architects had developed in the Loop over more than half a century. Many others, however, admired the arrangement and the building itself, designed as a trademark to symbolize the company and the materials the company mines. For example, the triangular character of the plazas and the shape of the building itself (note that each of the 19 stories has 8 corners!) were designed to represent the crystalline mineral in gypsum. Thus the building and its placement were intended to suggest the corporate image of the company that owns it. The soberness of the slate panels and gray glass is offset by the columns of white Vermont marble, which also give the building a sweeping vertical effect.

Walk-11

Circle Campus,
University of Illinois.

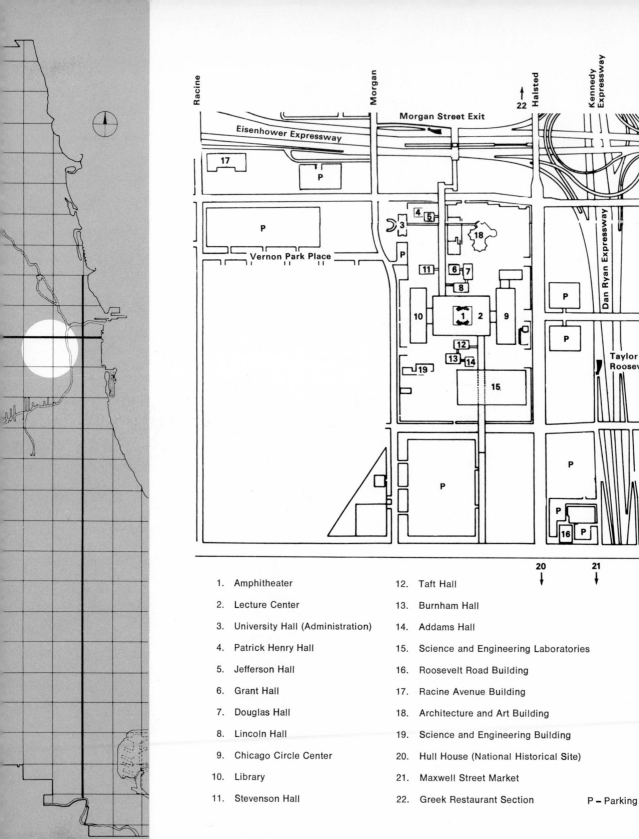

Racine

Morgan

Halsted
↑
22

Kennedy
Expressway

Eisenhower Expressway

Morgan Street Exit

17

P

Harrison

P

4
5

3

18

Vernon Park Place

P

11

6 7

8

Dan Ryan Expressway

10

1 2

9

P

Polk

P

12

13 14

Taylor Street
Roosevelt Exit

19

15

P

Taylor

P

P

P

16 P

Roosevelt

20
↓

21
↓

1. Amphitheater
2. Lecture Center
3. University Hall (Administration)
4. Patrick Henry Hall
5. Jefferson Hall
6. Grant Hall
7. Douglas Hall
8. Lincoln Hall
9. Chicago Circle Center
10. Library
11. Stevenson Hall

12. Taft Hall
13. Burnham Hall
14. Addams Hall
15. Science and Engineering Laboratories
16. Roosevelt Road Building
17. Racine Avenue Building
18. Architecture and Art Building
19. Science and Engineering Building
20. Hull House (National Historical Site)
21. Maxwell Street Market
22. Greek Restaurant Section   P – Parking

Walk · 11

CIRCLE CAMPUS OF THE UNIVERSITY OF ILLINOIS

WALKING TIME: 1 to 2 hours, depending on how much you "browse" among the buildings.
HOW TO GET THERE: Walk 3 blocks west of Michigan to Dearborn, enter the CTA Dearborn
Street subway, and board a westbound Congress Street train. Get off at the Halsted-Circle
Campus station. Or take any southbound CTA bus on Michigan, Wabash, or State that will
transfer you to a bus No. 7 (Harrison) at Harrison Street (600 S). (Inquire of the conductor.)
The Harrison Street bus will take you to Halsted Street (800 W).

Architects: Skidmore, Owings, and Merrill (Walter A. Netsch, Jr.) (Phase I, 1965; Phase II, 1967; Phase III, under construction in 1968) Architects for the Student Union Building: C. F. Murphy Associates.

The modern urban university has emerged to serve space-age students who live with speed, movement, and change. One of the newest of these is the Circle Campus of the University of Illinois, less than a mile southwest of Chicago's Loop. It has replaced the "temporary" headquarters of the University's Chicago undergraduate division, which operated for nearly 20 years (1946-1965) at Navy Pier (see Walk No. 7, Lake Shore Drive). The new location is far more accessible to students from every part of the Chicago area. Featured specifically as a "commuter college," with no resident students, Circle Campus is easily reached by every kind of transportation—commuter railroads bringing passengers to 6 different stations in Chicago, city subway and buses, and of course private cars. (The college provides extensive parking space.)

The name Circle Campus itself reflects the mood of modern traffic, for it comes from the Circle Interchange, where the

111

Eisenhower, Kennedy, and Dan Ryan expressways exchange an unending flow of moving horsepower. But the name alone was not the only contribution of the freeways to the campus. In this constant stream of vehicles the architect, Walter A. Netsch, Jr. (a partner in Skidmore, Owings, and Merrill, who had already designed the Air Force academy in Colorado) must have seen the elements of his campus design—power, dash, energy, freedom of movement, and strength. These ingredients he mixed on his drawing board and fit the entire campus plan around a centerpiece that epitomizes the university concept of all times—communications.

This centerpiece is an open amphitheatre, surrounded by a powerful grouping of buildings in concrete, glass, and brick. Netsch planned this as an open forum, to be used for drama, debate, "outside classrooms," discussions, political rallies, or just socializing. The amphitheatre is especially spectacular because it descends from the center of the Great Court, which constitutes the common roof of 6 lecture buildings. Here are open elevated walkways from which students may enter the other major buildings of the campus at the second-story level or go down to the lower-level walkways through the amphitheatre. These 2-level granite walkways give Circle Campus a character far removed from the green lawns of traditional college campuses. And so does the design of the campus buildings outside the Great Court—the Student Union, library, and engineering buildings with their strong concrete skeletons and skins of brick and glass.

The campus is constantly expanding and new construction is always visible. Graduate and undergraduate facilities being added south of Taylor Street include sciences and engineering buildings. The behavioral sciences building, directly west of University Hall, is scheduled for completion in 1969. Total completion is expected in the early 1970's. Fully developed, the University of Illinois' $200 million Chicago branch will enroll 20,000 to 30,000 students on its 106-acre campus.

Presiding over the Great Court with its forum and the surrounding group of buildings, garden courts, and lecture centers is University Hall, a 28-story administration and faculty office

University Hall.

112

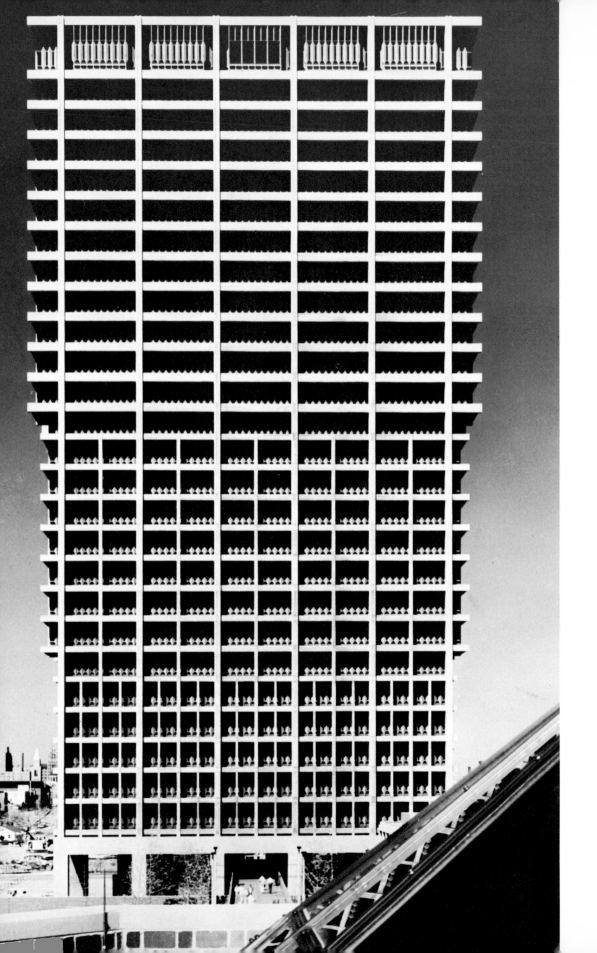

building. This high-rise structure spreads in width as it stretches skyward—it is 20 feet wider at the top than at the base—so that the upper floors provide more space. Students have already nicknamed it "Mr. Clean" after the broad-shouldered giant of TV commercials! Narrow, almost Gothic windows squeeze between concrete channels to limit distracting outside views and unnecessary exterior light.

The Circle Campus, developed on a former slum that was Chicago's "Port of Entry" for thousands of immigrants, retains an important link to the past—the 2 buildings of the original Hull House, now a National Historic Landmark, resting quietly and with dignity near the main campus entrance on Halsted Street. These buildings perpetuate the saga of Jane Addams and her dedicated aides in helping the forefathers of many of today's students adjust to their new urban environment.

The University of Illinois has rehabilitated and restored the original 2 structures. Jane Addams' furniture and fixtures are in their proper places, so that here you have a delightful example of the architecture and furnishings of a late 19th-century Chicago residence, reflecting the individual qualities of the extraordinary,

Above, Hull House.

114

indomitable woman who once lived and worked there. As a museum, they now make a fitting memorial to Jane Addams.

In some ways it is unfortunate that this beautiful restoration stands on its original site, for it is now dwarfed by the massive contemporary structures around it. But in the controversy about the siting of the University's new campus (which necessitated taking over a whole block of the Hull House complex) sentiment for keeping the original Hull House at its original location was so great that respecting this wish of the area's residents became a necessary part of the pragmatic compromise.

Although the University of Illinois now occupies the site once used by the world-renowned Hull House, Jane Addams' work goes on in other parts of the city. The programs of Hull House continue at various locations—including a Spanish Outpost at 3352 North Halsted, a community house at 500 East 67th Street, and several theater groups.

You can tour Circle Campus by yourself at any time. Or you may arrange for guided tour service (preferably on one week's advance notice) by calling 663-8686 or by writing the Campus Information and Tour Center, Box 4348, Chicago 60680. Parking lots with

coin-operated gates, on the east, south, and west edges of the
campus, are available to visitors.

Not only the architectural student will be fascinated with Circle
Campus. Any adult—or child, for that matter—will be thrilled by
the scale of this vast complex, reminiscent of the Mayan
pyramids, temples, and courtyards, yet definitely modern in
design and function.

In contrast with these contemporary buildings is the Maxwell
Street Market, only 2 blocks south of the south end of the
campus. There is an Old-World atmosphere about this outdoor
marketplace, where almost anything can be purchased,
especially on Sunday. (See Walk No. 30.)

Another contrast is at the north end of the campus, just across
the Eisenhower Expressway. A small section of shops clustered
together and known as "Greek Town" has restaurants that feature
belly dancers as well as those that provide other kinds of
atmosphere in addition to the good food.

The Great Court.

116

Walk-12

Meigs Field
Terminal looking
toward Soldier Field
across Burnham
Harbor.

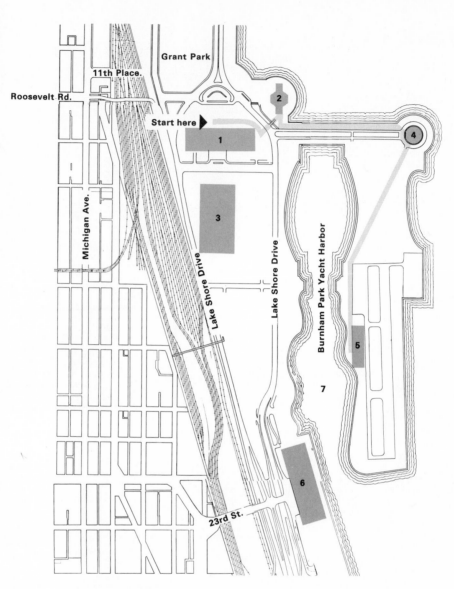

Grant Park

11th Place.

Roosevelt Rd.

Start here ▶

Michigan Ave.

Lake Shore Drive

Lake Shore Drive

Burnham Park Yacht Harbor

1

2

3

4

5

6

7

23rd St.

1. Field Museum of Natural History
   E. Roosevelt Rd. and S. Lake Shore Dr.

2. John G. Shedd Aquarium
   1200 S. Lake Shore Dr.

3. Soldier Field
   425 E. 14th St.

4. Adler Planetarium and Astronomical Museum
   900 E. Achsah Bond Dr.

5. Merrill C. Meigs Field
   Outer Drive at 14th St.

6. McCormick Place
   E. 23rd St. and Lakefront

7. Burnham Park Yacht Harbor

Walk · 12

BURNHAM PARK : MUSEUMS

WALKING TIME: 1 hour or less for outside viewing. (For inside visits each museum rates a separate trip. You will want to spend anywhere from one hour, say, at the Shedd Aquarium to whole days at the Field Museum. Hours when the museums are open vary somewhat and sometimes change from summer to winter. Between the hours 10:00 A.M. and 4:00 P.M. you will find them all open (except on holidays). It is wise, however, to consult each museum separately just before making your visit.   HOW TO GET THERE: You can reach the Burnham Park area over the foot bridges from Michigan Avenue at 11th Street, or through Grant Park along Columbus Drive and the adjacent formal gardens. Or you can take a southbound CTA "shuttle" bus, No. 149 (Michigan-State-Wacker), on State Street, which will take you directly to the Field Museum at the north end of Burnham Park. If you drive, you will find the best parking near Adler Planetarium or Soldier Field.

On Chicago's lakefront just south of Grant Park is a great concentration of museums and other public facilities. Still just a portion of Lake Michigan in 1910, it was filled with land and developed in accordance with the Burnham Plan of 1909. Construction of the Field Museum was started in 1911, Soldier Field in 1924, Shedd Aquarium in 1929, and Adler Planetarium in 1931. In 1933-34 this stretch of land reclaimed from the lake was the site of Chicago's Century of Progress exposition and a few years later of its Railroad Fair. Here too are Meigs Field airstrip and McCormick Place, once the nation's busiest convention center, now being rebuilt after destruction by fire.

On the west bank of Burnham Harbor (east of the Drive, opposite Soldier Field) is a single marble column of the Roman composite style. It commemorates the 1933 flight of several Italian amphibious airplanes flown here to honor Chicago's Century of Progress exposition. They brought the monument with them— in sections—as a gift from the Italian government. Leader of the group was Marshall Italo Balbo, for whom Balbo Drive was named.

119

Field Museum of Natural History.

Field Museum of Natural History—
Lake Shore Drive at Roosevelt Road.
Architects: Graham, Burnham, and Company;
Graham, Anderson, Probst, and White (1911-1919);
architects for the new Stanley Field Hall (interior):
Harry M. Weese and Associates (1968)

Start at the Field Museum, pausing on the long flight of steps for a glorious view of Chicago's downtown skyline. Field Museum was built—and partly maintained—with funds donated by Marshall Field I, the founder of Marshall Field and Company, then by other members of his family and other Chicago families interested in its program. The huge structure is a variation of the Fine Arts Building in Jackson Park (now the Museum of Science and Industry—See Waik No. 16), which was built in 1893 for the Columbian Exposition and used as the Field Museum from then until 1920, when the Field collections were moved to their present quarters.

Part of the celebration of the Field Museum's 75th anniversary, in 1968, has been a redesigning of Stanley Field Hall—the

120

tremendous entrance space on the first floor, named for a
nephew of Marshall Field closely identified with the
museum's development.

The Field Museum is a distinguished showcase for prehistoric
and recent cultures, with a staff of scholars behind the scenes
who are constantly extending knowledge as the result of their
investigations in the fields of anthropology, botany, geology, and
zoology. Though they are classified according to these four areas
of knowledge, the exhibits seem endless in variety—from the
enormous stuffed African elephants and dinosaur skeletons in
Stanley Field Hall, and corridor after corridor of dioramas
showing hundreds of stuffed animals in their native habitats, to
the life-sized figures of prehistoric man in *his* environment;
from one of the world's finest collections of Oceanic art and of
American Indian art and artifacts, to displays of meteorites,
rare gems, and flowers. The Museum is in fact filled with
priceless specimens.

Admission is always free to children, students, and teachers;
free to all on Thursdays, Saturdays, and Sundays; other days,
25¢ admission for adults.

John G. Shedd Aquarium—
1200 South Lake Shore Drive.
Architects: Graham, Anderson, Probst, and White (1929)

Directly east of the Field Museum, reached by a pedestrian tunnel under the Outer Drive, is the Shedd Aquarium, built with funds donated by John G. Shedd, former chairman of the board of Marshall Field and Company. Far smaller than the Field Museum, this is nevertheless the world's largest building devoted exclusively to living specimens of aquatic life. A white marble structure with bronze doors, it has a simple Doric design, another example of the neo-classical tendency that inspired the style of so many public buildings of the time.

In more than 130 tanks of water the Shedd Aquarium displays some 7,500 living specimens, representing 350 different species of marine and fresh-water creatures.

Admission is always free to children, students, and teachers; free to all on Thursdays, Saturdays, and Sundays. Other days, 25¢ for adults.

Soldier Field—425 East 14th Street.
Architects: Holabird and Root (1924).

The stadium, Soldier Field, with a seating capacity of about 106,000, was constructed as a war memorial. It is the site of the annual All-Star football game, special fireworks each Fourth of July, political rallies, and various other activities. The 100-foot Doric columns that surround Soldier Field harmonize its architecture well with that of the Field Museum, just to the north. In 1950 the north end of the stadium was closed by the Administration Building of the Chicago Park District.

Adler Planetarium and Astronomical Museum—
900 East Achsah Bond Drive (about 1300 South).
Architect: Ernest A. Grunsfeld, Jr. (1931)

Directly east, about 2 city blocks away, is the Adler Planetarium, named for its donor, Max Adler, a former vice-president of Sears Roebuck and Company. Located on the lakefront at the end of a series of reflecting pools, this small granite structure with its planetarium dome is handsome and strong, devoid of all architectural superlatives.

Opposite top, John G. Shedd Aquarium. *Bottom,* Adler Planetarium. *Below,* one of 12 zodiac ornaments on the planetarium.

122

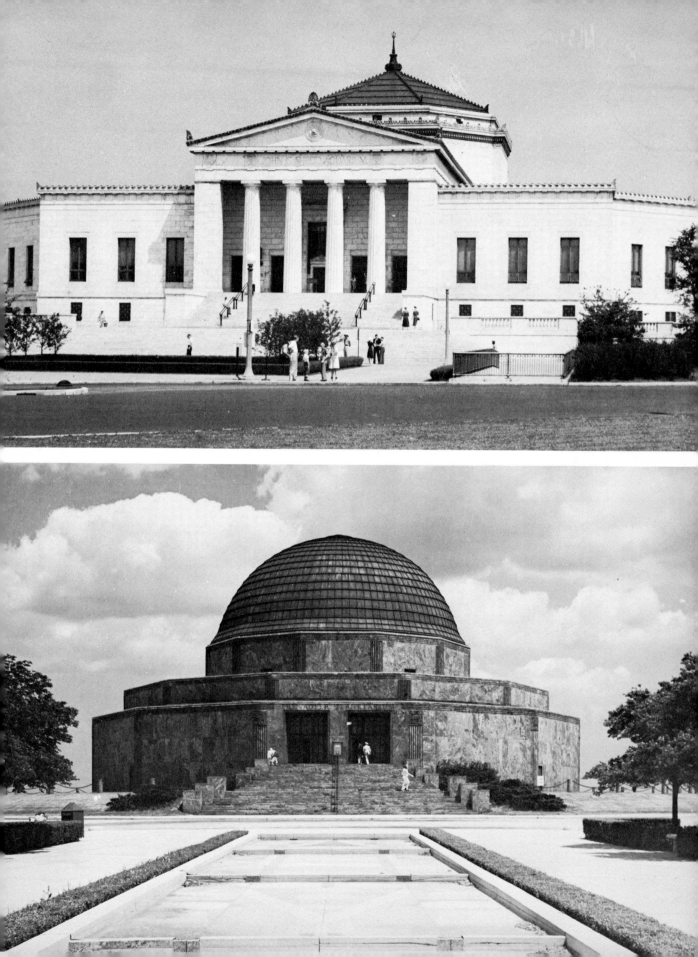

Terminal Building, Meigs Field.

The Astronomical Museum section contains one of the
finest collections in the world of antique astronomical and
mathematical instruments (second only to the collection in
Oxford, England) as well as some of the most modern. Frequent
15-minute demonstrations of how some of these
instruments work are given daily.

For anyone interested in stars and planets—and who of any
age isn't?—the chief attraction of the Planetarium lies in its daily
sky show inside the domed chamber in which the Zeiss
projection instrument, also called a "planetarium," reproduces

124

the natural night sky at any time or any place selected for fascinating explanations about what is going on up there. The lectures that accompany these projections of the sky make faraway scientific information simple and clear for anyone. For this sky show, which varies from month to month, a small fee is charged. Admission to the Planetarium itself and the other demonstrations is free.

Merrill C. Meigs Field Passenger Terminal—
Outer Drive at 14th Street. City Architect (1963)

The city architect's office produced a delicate, well-planned building to serve as the passenger terminal for Meigs Field. This lakefront airstrip for light planes and helicopters is the largest downtown space of its kind in the country.

McCormick Place—East 23rd and the Lakefront.
Architect: Gene Summers, of C. F. Murphy Associates (still in construction, 1969)

A new McCormick Place is being built on the site of the previous building, which was destroyed by fire soon after making its reputation as the world's busiest convention center. Since the architect for the new building was associated with Mies van der Rohe for many years, it is natural that this new plan bears the Mies influence. A splendid design for an extremely difficult planning problem was drawn up, giving the new McCormick Place 2 buildings separated by a great plaza with generous underground parking—one building to contain a large-scale theater, and the other to be devoted exclusively to exhibition and convention space. Although details of the original plan had to be qualified, it is hoped that the new McCormick Place, which promises to be even more impressive than its predecessor, will be ready for use by 1970.

Before ending your walk, take advantage of the delightful harbor view at what is known as the Burnham Park Yacht Harbor. Sit on the shore a while and just watch the many sail and power boats setting out into the lake or anchored there in the harbor.

1. 630 S. Wabash Av.
   Formerly Wirt Dexter Bldg.

2. Old St. Mary's Paulist Church
   901 S. Wabash Av.

3. Chicago Police Dept. HQ
   1121 S. State St.

4. The Coliseum
   1513 S. Wabash

5. Glessner House
   1800 S. Prairie Av.

6. Kimball House
   1801 S. Prairie Av.

7. Keith House
   1803 S. Prairie Av.

8. 1900 S. Prairie Av.

9. 2013 S. Prairie Av.

10. 2110 S. Prairie Av.

11. Raymond Hilliard Center, CHA
    2030 S. State St.

12. Chicago Housing Authority
    55 W. Cermak Road

Walk · 13

THE NEAR SOUTH SIDE :
South Wabash and Prairie Avenue

WALKING TIME: About 2 hours.   HOW TO GET THERE: Take a southbound CTA bus No. 4
(Cottage Grove) on Wabash Avenue, and get off at Harrison (600 S).

Just as the railroads were responsible for the original growth of
the Near South Side and again involved in its near demise, so will
the railroads play a significant role in its redevelopment.

Chicago was once the transfer point for all transcontinental
railroads. Anyone going from New York to California, for instance,
or Massachusetts to Oregon had to change trains here. The 5
rail terminals in this part of the city provided millions of
transients each year, all eager to go shopping and sightseeing
between trains. It was thus that the section prospered for many
years. With the curtailment of railroad passenger service, this
enormous outside source of patronage dropped drastically, with
inevitable deterioration of the area. Now, however, the city
has tentative plans to consolidate the rail terminals and then
revitalize the area by constructing apartment and office buildings,
as well as a sports arena, on the air rights over these old railroad
yards. When this happens, the area should again prosper.

◪ 630 South Wabash (formerly Wirt Dexter Building)
Architects: Adler and Sullivan (1887)

Once known as the Wirt Dexter Building, 630 South Wabash
is one of the simplest of Sullivan's famous structures, with none
of the elaborate ornamentation that he lavished, for instance,
on the Carson Pirie Scott building some 12 years later. The
narrow mullions in the central bay, with the slight moldings
crowning them, give a touch of distinction to the
otherwise unadorned facade.

Old St. Mary's Paulist Church—901 South Wabash. Architect: Gurdon P. Randall (1866-67)

Farther south, at the corner of Ninth and Wabash, stands Old St. Mary's Church, which in 1964 was declared an historical landmark by the City Council of Chicago. This is one of very few public buildings to have survived the Great Fire of 1871. Built originally for the Plymouth Congregational Church, it was sold in 1872 to Old St. Mary's, which has occupied it now for nearly a century.

Previously, the parish of Old St. Mary's, dating back to 1833 and the oldest in Chicago, had been located in 3 other places—first in a frame church on the south side of Lake Street, which was later moved to the corner of Michigan and Madison, where it was enlarged; then in its first brick building, both parish church and cathedral, on the corner of Wabash and Madison. Everything at this third location was destroyed by the 1871 Fire.

Architecturally, the earliest church was the most noted, for it was the first building to be constructed on a "balloon frame," so-called—at first derisively—because the light framework was so much airier than the old-time heavy construction still used in most places. Augustine D. Taylor, who is credited with having invented the "balloon frame," planned and supervised the building of that little frame church on Lake Street back in 1833.

The design of the present home of Old St. Mary's is the somewhat free and innovative pseudo-Gothic style used so frequently for churches in the late 1800's. The facade is of local limestone, called Joliet or Lemont limestone.

Chicago Police Department Headquarters—1121 South State Street. City Architect Paul Gerhardt (1963)

Still farther south and one block west, on State Street, you come to the headquarters of the Chicago Police Department. This complex of buildings contains the world's most modern police communications system and a new police data processing system, installed in 1967. Here too are the crime detection laboratory, the central lockup, women's and children's courts, and administration office. Open to the public 24 hours a day. A self-tour sheet, supplemented by a taped message prepared for visitors by Superintendent of Police James Conlisk, are provided. For guided group tours—daily from 9:00 A.M. to 4:00 P.M.—reservations must be made, preferably by letter well in advance.

The Coliseum—1513 South Wabash.
Architects: Frost and Granger; engineers: E. C. and R. M. Shankland (1900)

Return to Wabash and continue south to the Coliseum, at 1513. The Coliseum has a colorful history as the location of many political conventions, horse shows, circuses, and roller skating derbies. The architectural design is unique—to say the least! The strange fortress-like sections on the Wabash Avenue side are a grim memorial to the Civil War—remains of a wall of Libby Prison, built in 1889 in Richmond, Virginia, and re-erected here. Of considerably greater architectural significance is the fact that 12 large, 3-hinged trusses cover the immense interior without supports. The use of iron and steel for these trusses was part of the development of the structural use of these metals here in Chicago.

Across the street, at 1510 South Wabash, is a 5-story public school relic of the old days, constructed in 1884 and still in use.

◪ Glessner House—1800 South Prairie Avenue.
Architect: Henry Hobbs Richardson (1886)

Continue south to 16th Street, walk east to Indiana, south on Indiana to 18th Street, and then one block east to Prairie Avenue. This street was once so far superior to its present run-down condition that it claimed some of the city's wealthiest families as residents—including such names as the Philip Armours, Clarence and Kate Buckingham, the Marshall Fields (both I and II), the W. W. Kimballs (of piano fame), the George Pullmans, and the M. M. Rothschilds.

According to the Chicago School of Architecture Foundation, which makes its home in the Glessner House, J. J. Glessner, a founder of the International Harvester Company, in 1885, commissioned the great architect Henry Hobbs Richardson to design a fitting house for him on Prairie Avenue, referring to the street as the finest residential street in Chicago.

It is appropriate that an architectural foundation should be housed in the only remaining example in Chicago of a design by one of the earliest and greatest of American architects. The Foundation has an architectural museum, library, and information center in the building. (For information call 326-1393.) Although this 35-room, fortress-like granite house seems a far cry from the delicate atrium houses of the architect Wong in Kenwood (see Walk No. 15), they have one feature in common: window placings of both are designed for privacy and quiet. All main rooms of the Glessner house face on a private courtyard, instead of on the street.

The citation from the Architectural Landmarks Commission reads:

> In recogniion of the fine planning for an urban site, which opens the family rooms to the quiet serenity of an inner yard; the effective ornament and decoration; and the impressive Romanesque masonry, expressing dignity and power.

Kimball House—1801 South Prairie.
Architect: Solon S. Beman (1890)

Across the street, at 1801 South Prairie, is the Kimball House, designed like a Parisian mansion of the late 19th century. It is well preserved and well maintained by its present occupant, Medalist Publications, a division of Cahners Publishing Company.

Keith House—1803 South Prairie. Next door is the Keith House, also built about 1890 but unfortunately *not* well preserved or maintained.

1900 South Prairie—Farther south, a fine old mid-Victorian 3-story mansion, with mansard roof and classic columns at the 2nd-floor porch.

2013 South Prairie—A 3-story house with a classic façade of brick and stone trim. Note the Palladian motif at the 3rd-floor window and the Ionic columns at the porch level.

2110 South Prairie—A 3-story limestone facade in Romanesque style, with a large pediment at the roof, a design that suggests the influence of Richardson.

Opposite, Glessner House.

This is all that remains of the once great wealth-laden avenue

130

131

of fine houses and mansions. In 1890 one of the grandest mansions on this same Prairie Avenue was that of Marshall Field, built for the multimillionaire merchant by Richard Morris Hunt, the famous architect who had also designed the luxurious dwellings of such New York millionaires as William H. Vanderbilt and John Jacob Astor.

Nearly all the property in the area has been acquired by the Lakeside Press of R. R. Donnelly and Sons Company, who have constructed an enormous complex of buildings to print— among other things—*Life* and *Time* magazines and many telephone directories.

Raymond Hilliard Center—Chicago Housing Authority, 2030 South State Street (once the site of Chicago's infamous Levee). Architect: Bertrand Goldberg Associates (1967)

Continue south to Cermak Road (2200 S), and turn west to Michigan Avenue, where—at the northeast corner—you pass the *Michigan Hotel*, once the headquarters of Al Capone, vice lord of Chicago in the 1920's.

Now continue west 2 blocks to State Street to see the Raymond Hilliard Center of the Chicago Housing Authority: two 15-story cylindrical towers, containing 350 apartments for the elderly; and two 22-story semicircular concrete structures with open galleries, containing 350 apartments for families with children. The development also includes a community building, open-air theater, landscaped gardens, play lots, and parking areas. Apartments in the towers for the elderly are petal-shaped, extending from a central core that contains all the service facilities. This represents a breakthrough in Chicago, away from the institutional appearance commonly seen in older public housing projects. Some comparison with the Marina City design by the same architects (see walk No. 3, Dearborn Street) is inevitable and justified. Architect Bertrand Goldberg, continuing his exploration of scalloped forms (which began with Marina City) has designed a 4-building group that defies convention yet stays within the government's development costs ceiling. In all 4 buildings, major rooms are enclosed in load-bearing concrete

132

walls, their irregular spacing controlled by the needs of the Center's program rather than structural considerations.

The land on which the Raymond Hilliard Center is built was once part of Chicago's most famous red light district, known as the Levee. The center of the Levee was the 2100 block of South Dearborn one block farther west, where for more than 10 years the Everleigh Club was managed by 2 beautiful sisters from Kentucky. According to Herman Kogan, the Everleigh Club was "the most affluent, the most expensive, and the best known" of all the bordellos in the area, in fact of all the world.[5] The Everleigh sisters believed in conducting a high-class establishment, catering to the "cultured." They introduced patrons to prospective partners in library, music room, or art gallery! Reform mayor Carter Henry Harrison the Younger for years had tried to bring pressure on the entire Levee. Finally, in 1911, the Everleigh sisters caused their own downfall by publishing an illustrated booklet advertising the comforts of their "Club." The mayor became sufficiently indignant at such open defiance from the ladies that he overrode all objections and actually closed down the "Club." The Everleigh sisters, who moved to New York with more than a million dollars that they had accumulated, could hardly have been crushed by the eviction. More than their departure, however, was needed before vice could be cleaned out of the Levee. "Extending down Dearborn Street from Nos. 2131-33," says Kogan, "were such other establishments as Ed Weiss' Saratoga Club, Georgie Spencer's, French Emma Duval's, Maurice Van Bever's Sans Souci."[6]

Chicago Housing Authority—55 West Cermak Road. Before leaving the area, note the central office building of the Chicago Housing Authority, at 55 West Cermak Road. This is the nerve center for the management and operations of approximately 40,000 public housing dwelling units—and the number is constantly increasing.

Walk-14

Crown Hall, Illinois
Institute of
Technology.

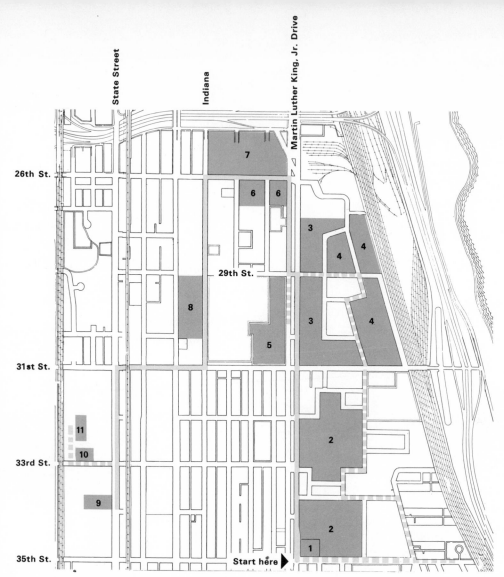

State Street

Indiana

Martin Luther King, Jr. Drive

26th St.

29th St.

31st St.

33rd St.

35th St.

Start here ▶

1. Lake Meadows Shopping Center
   N.E. Corner of S. Martin Luther King, Jr., Dr. &
   E. 35th St.

2. Lake Meadows Apartments
   S. King Dr. to S. Rhodes & 32nd St. to 33rd St.
   & 32nd St. to 33rd St.

3. Prairie Shores Apartments
   2729-3035 S. King Dr.

4. Michael Reese Hospital Campus
   29th - 32nd St. along Ellis Av.

5. Dunbar Vocational High School
   N.W. Corner of 31st St. & S. King Dr.

6. Prairie Courts
   26th, S. King Dr., & S. Prairie Av.

7. Mercy Hospital Complex
   2510 S. King Dr. & 2500 S. Prairie Av.

8. South Commons from 26th to 31st Sts.
   Between Michigan and Indiana Avs.
   Illinois Institute of Technology

9. Crown Hall
   N.W. Corner 34th & State Sts.

10. John Crerar Library
    35 W. 33rd St.

11. Herman Hall
    3215 S. Federal

▭▭▭▭ Alternate route

Walk · 14

THE NEW SOUTH SIDE :
Housing and Institutional Developments

WALKING TIME: About 2 hours.   HOW TO GET THERE: Take a southbound CTA bus No. 1
(Drexel-Hyde Park) or No. 2 (Hyde Park) on Michigan; or a No. 4 (Cottage Grove) on Wabash.
Get off at 35th Street and Martin Luther King, Jr., Drive (formerly South Parkway). If driving,
follow Lake Shore Drive south to 31st Street, then go west to King Drive and south to 35th Street.

Note the statue of a World War I Negro veteran at the
intersection of King Drive and 35th Street.

Before setting out on the main part of this walk, go east
on 35th Street to Cottage Grove (800 East) to note several items
of historical interest:
1. *Stephen Douglas Monument and Tomb*, at 35th Street just
   east of Cottage Grove.
2. *St. Joseph's Carandelet Child Center,* across the street, which
   in 1864 was a soldiers' hospital for Civil War veterans.
3. *Groveland Park and Woodland Park*, just to the north,
   which *during* the Civil War was the site of a huge prison
   camp for captured Confederate soldiers. Around 1890, the
   peripheries of both these parks became settings for residential
   developments, which still are standing—some of the houses
   in good condition. Just to the north of the parks is a cluster of
   townhouses constructed in 1963, designed by the architects
   Pyskacek-Rosenwinkel. The land for this 1963 development
   was made available by the same urban renewal project that
   made Lake Meadows possible.

Lake Meadows—31st to 35th Street, along
Martin Luther King., Jr., Drive. Architects:
Skidmore, Owings, and Merrill (1956-60)

If you have taken the suggested walk to Cottage Grove, follow
the broken line indicated on the map. The main walk starts with the
Lake Meadows shopping center at 35th Street and Martin Luther
King, Jr., Drive, from which you can continue north to the
north boundary of Lake Meadows at 31st street.

Lake Meadows was planned especially to provide much-needed housing for middle-income families, and from its beginnings it has promoted interracial living. In addition to 10 sleek high-rise apartment buildings, with more than 2,000 living units, Lake Meadows has a shopping center, elementary school, medical center, and recreational space for both children and adults. Park space between the tall, glass-encased apartment buildings gives an effect of openness and freedom that is especially welcome here in the heart of a crowded city.

Lake Meadows replaced 100 acres of slums and started the revitalization of this badly deteriorated area, which early in the city's history had been considered Chicago's "Gold Coast." Though not a public housing project (Lake Meadows was financed by the New York Life Insurance Company), it can be called the first large urban renewal project in the country. Before federal urban renewal laws had been passed, Lake Meadows was developed under provisions of Illinois laws—the result of pressure from a coalition of organizations soon after World War II.

Prairie Shores—2801-3001 Martin Luther King, Jr., Drive. Architects: Loebl, Schlossman, and Bennett (1958-62)

Before the Lake Meadows undertaking was completed, a similar housing development called Prairie Shores was in progress just north of 31st along King Drive. Prairie Shores was developed by the board of trustees of Michael Reese Hospital, though it is now managed by a Chicago real estate firm. The primary purpose was to provide good nearby housing for the hospital's own medical staff and employees. It was hoped that rents could be kept low enough to permit families of moderate income to live side by side with faculty, students, and medical staff of various institutions in the area, so that the population of Prairie Shores would be mixed sociologically as well as racially.

About half the total plan is represented by 5 stunning apartment buildings, with some 1,700 living units. These high-rise, glass-encased structures with park space between are comparable in style to the Lake Meadows apartments. The buildings are set parallel to each other but at an angle to the Drive.

138

Michael Reese Hospital Campus—
29th to 32nd Street, along Ellis Avenue.
Architects: Schmidt, Garden, and Erikson (1897);
Loebl, Schlossman, and Bennett (since 1952)

The buildings of Michael Reese Hospital stretch along the east
side of Ellis Avenue, to the east of Prairie Shores. The original
building, more than 70 years old, remains the center of the huge
complex. An entire campus of new buildings, devoted to special
uses and connected by an underground pedestrian tunnel, has
been constructed since 1952. The campus plan was developed by
a planning staff directed by Reginald Isaacs, now professor of
regional planning at Harvard University. Consultant for the plan
was Walter Gropius, one of the founders of the Bauhaus in
Germany and former dean of Harvard University's Graduate
School of Design.

With about 1,000 beds, Michael Reese is the city's largest
privately operated hospital. In addition to its clinical services, it
carries on distinguished research in medical fields.

When the trustees of Michael Reese Hospital decided on
developing Prairie Shores, they indicated in this way that they had
also decided to remain in the present location as an anchor for
the renewal area. The already successful—though
incomplete—Lake Meadows development may have
been a factor in both decisions.

Above, Prairie Shores.

139

Dunbar Vocational High School—
29th to 31st Street, along King Drive.
Architects: Holabird and Root (1960)

At the northern end of Lake Meadows, directly across King Drive, is the Dunbar Vocational High School, a single building stretching from 31st Street to 29th. This will probably serve as the model for other vocational schools, for it is a well-planned institutional building that seems to function with efficiency.

Prairie Courts—26th Street and King Drive.
Architects: George Fred and William Keck (1954)

Farther north on King Drive, spreading to 26th Street, is a public housing project called Prairie Courts, which plays an important role in the economic mixture of families in the area.

Mercy Hospital—2510 King Drive.
Architects: C. F. Murphy Associates;
Interior Designers: Mary Louise Schum
and Eileen Reilly Siemans (1968)

Just north of 26th Street, the new Mercy Hospital complex has been developed. Mercy was the first hospital in Illinois, having been granted its charter in 1851. Early patients included cholera victims and Chicagoans injured in the Great Fire of 1871. It now has a 355-bed hospital in a high-rise building just completed. This handsome 14-story structure of white concrete and bronzed glass has a unique design that is hard to describe, culminating in an unexpected change of style at the top floor—the convent for the hospital's sisters—which gives the impression of a very wide cornice. The building carries almost a suggestion of another culture; it might be a great Mayan temple if the shape were different!

The interior design, however, has repeated reminders of the religion that has inspired its services from the beginning. These decorations too are unique, the work of a Spanish artist, Nacio Bayarri, discovered by the interior designers (who were assigned their responsibility as soon as construction of the new hospital was started). On each floor, as you get off the elevator, you will see a strikingly modern piece of sculpture or

Opposite, Mercy Hospital.

140

another kind of contemporary decoration. In the chapel one wall is made up entirely of a colorful mosaic mural, and another is a window wall decorated the whole length with lacy, welded-iron patterns representing—in a most unusual fashion—scenes in the life of Christ.

Mercy Hospital and Michael Reese together, dominating the "new South Side" (south of the Adlai E. Stevenson Expressway), constitute a large medical center for the area.

South Commons—2901 South Michigan. Architects: Gordon and Levin and Associates (1968)

Walking west to Michigan Avenue and back south to 29th, you come to South Commons, another renewal project. It has already introduced 1,800 housing units, planned not only for racial integration but for economic integration as well, and for families and persons of all ages. It expects eventually to provide space for some 35,000 people with middle incomes—both lower-middle and upper-middle. High- and low-rise apartment buildings and townhouses are combined with open spaces and a community center. The excellent site plan gives a feeling of spaciousness in spite of the fairly high population density. The green spaces and malls make this a delightful urban setting.

⊡ Illinois Institute of Technology—3300 South Federal Street. Architects: Ludwig Mies van der Rohe and Ludwig Hilberseimer; Friedman, Alschuler, and Sincere; PACE Associates (Planners, Architects, Consulting Engineers) (1942-58); Skidmore, Owings, and Merrill (1963)

Michigan and 30th Street mark the beginning of the Illinois Institute of Technology, which—like Michael Reese to the east and Mercy Hospital to the north—has become an anchor important to the successful renewal of the area. IIT itself has grown with the community; it now consists of technical colleges; departments of architecture and of city and regional planning; the Institute of Design, which was established in 1937 by Laszlo Moholy-Nagi as the successor to Germany's famous Bauhaus; a graduate school; and an evening division at which students can earn degrees in engineering. It now includes also the John Crerar Library, referred to separately below.

142

The 100-acre campus of IIT replaces what at the end of World War II was one of the city's worst slums, cleared through the machinery of urban renewal. The campus plan was prepared by Ludwig Mies van der Rohe and Ludwig Hilberseimer, both of whom had left the Bauhaus in Nazi Germany to come to this country in 1938. Mies, serving as dean of IIT's School of Architecture, designed many of the educational, administrative, and residential buildings, all of them low structures of severely simple design. Crown Hall is an exceptionally fine example of his work. The steel girders above the roof eliminate the need for interior columns, thus allowing uninterrupted space inside, which has flexibility of use. The proportions of the building are classic in symmetry and scale. If you can imagine Doric columns in front, you can "see" a Greek temple! The many designs by Mies on this campus—in the Administration Building, classroom buildings, chapel, Commons Building, and residence halls—all attest to his philosophy, "Less Is More."

It seems appropriate to the purpose of this engineering institute that several architects have been involved in its construction. Skidmore, Owings, and Merrill—who planned recent additions such as the handsome Crerar Library, gymnasium, and the Student Union Building—have followed the general design and spirit of Mies van der Rohe.

John Crerar Library—35 West 33rd Street.
Architects: Skidmore, Owings, and Merrill (1963)

After functioning for more than 40 years in a building at the northwest corner of Randolph and Michigan (architects: Holabird and Roche, 1920) and several years before that in the upper floors of Marshall Field's store, this famous library of science, technology, and medicine moved its incredible number of books and journals to its new building on IIT's campus, which will doubtless be its permanent home. Crerar is a "public" library established by a bequest of $2 million from its namesake. Though none of the books or journals may leave the building, they are always available to the public for use within the library itself.

Interestingly, this last move of the Crerar Library fulfills a request in John Crerar's will that it be "located in the South Division of the city inasmuch as Newberry Library will be located in the North Division."[7]

Modular
Townhouses, 50th
St. & Blackstone
Ave.

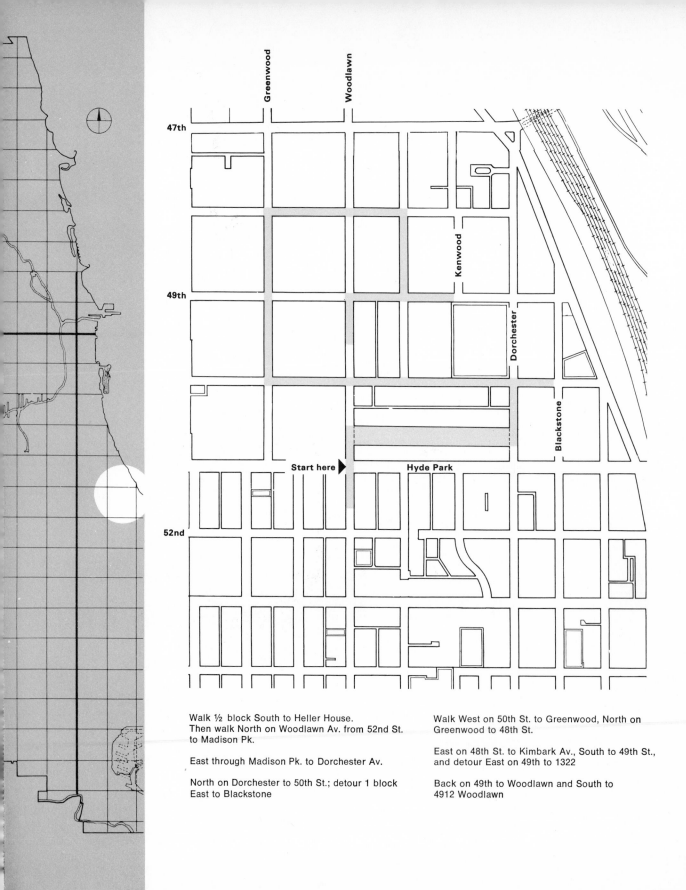

Greenwood

Woodlawn

Kenwood

Dorchester

Blackstone

47th

49th

52nd

Start here ▶   Hyde Park

Walk ½ block South to Heller House.
Then walk North on Woodlawn Av. from 52nd St.
to Madison Pk.

East through Madison Pk. to Dorchester Av.

North on Dorchester to 50th St.; detour 1 block
East to Blackstone

Walk West on 50th St. to Greenwood, North on
Greenwood to 48th St.

East on 48th St. to Kimbark Av., South to 49th St.,
and detour East on 49th to 1322

Back on 49th to Woodlawn and South to
4912 Woodlawn

Walk · 15

KENWOOD-MADISON PARK

WALKING TIME: At least 2 hours.   HOW TO GET THERE: Take a southbound CTA bus
No. 1 (Drexel-Hyde Park) on Michigan Avenue. Get off at Hyde Park Boulevard (5100 S) and
Woodlawn Avenue (1200 E).

You are now at the south end of Kenwood, which lies just north
of the Hyde Park area. Here are some of the finest old mansions,
wooded gardens, and boulevards in the city. Among the houses
called to your attention here are a number that are famous because
of the architects who built them; these of course will be
identified. On the whole, however, houses have been selected for
their individual architectural quality, whether or not a
name-architect designed them.

At the turn of the century, Kenwood was actually a suburb
of Chicago, where many of the wealthiest families built
their estates. Residents have carried some of Chicago's most
noted—and notorious—names: Julius Rosenwald, Max Adler, Ben
Heineman, Harold Swift, and the tragically doomed families of
Leopold and Loeb. As the depression of the 30's struck some
of the owners and later, when the return of prosperity only
increased the costs of domestic help, as well as the difficulty of
security it, the expenses of maintaining such mansions often
became too exorbitant to meet. Between much absentee
ownership and neglect of property by some who still lived there,
Kenwood was rapidly deteriorating. Houses were being sold
indiscriminately, and the usual flight of white residents at the
appearance of a few black families was threatening.

Citizens of Kenwood are to be thanked—and congratulated—
for saving the neighborhood. An interracial committee
of home-owners took the situation in hand. Dedicated to the
conviction that character and ability to maintain property, not
color of skin, determine whether or not a prospective purchaser
will be a desirable neighbor, they worked with real estate
dealers to establish a stable, well-integrated community. Naturally,

because of the kind of houses available, most Kenwood home-owners of both races have upper-middle or high incomes. For many years a local committee sponsored a "Kenwood Open House" weekend each spring, when outsiders were invited to call at a specified number of homes and witness the success of this undertaking.

In Kenwood, too, as in Hyde aPrk, urban renewal has been responsible for some effective rehabilitation and redevelopment. Two citizens organizations that cooperated actively with the city government in recent changes are the Hyde Park - Kenwood Community Conference and the South East Chicago Commission. Other groups interested in Kenwood's redevelopment are the Amalgamated Clothing Workers Union and the Lake Village Development Corporation, which are planning hundreds of new townhouses and apartments for middle-income, racially integrated tenants.

At Lake Park Avenue and Hyde Park Boulevard, the city is constructing a new *Kenwood High School* for the community, replacing the old inadequate building, which now uses a cluster of mobile vans for the additional classrooms needed. The new structure is scheduled for completion in 1969. (*Architects: Schmidt, Garden, and Erikson*)

◧ **Heller House**—5132 South Woodlawn Avenue. Architect: Frank Lloyd Wright (1897)

This 3-story brick house is an early example of Wright's work. It seems at first quite unlike the "Prairie House" that he designed 12 years later, for the compact upright lines of the first 2 stories contrast markedly with the widespreading horizontal lines of the Robie House (see Walk No. 16, Hyde Park - University of Chicago). Yet the widely projecting eaves and the openness of the third story suggest some of the later design.

Note the molded plaster frieze at the top of the building— by the sculptor Richard Bock.

Madison Park—Between Hyde Park Boulevard and 50th Street, running from Woodlawn to Dorchester.

Cross Woodlawn at Hyde Park Boulevard (51st Street), and walk north about half a block to the entrance of Madison Park.

Opposite, top, Heller House. Bottom, 1302 East Madison Park.

149

Madison Park is not a park in the usual sense of the word. It is, instead, a small residential section of Kenwood that seems to belong completely to itself. As you pass through the large iron gate that tells you the name and the fact that it is private, you see a long stretch of green, with trees and mounds, bordered on each side by a street with a continuing line of houses, occasionally an apartment building, in varying styles, most of them built probably 2 generations ago. The minute you are inside the gate, you are overwhelmed by the almost rural quiet of the place. Madison Park stretches from east to west 3 blocks with no north-south streets coming through, and east-west traffic from outside is minimal. The strip of park down the center is used only by the residents—usually a few children playing happily and perhaps an adult lounging on the grass reading. Despite the city-like rows of houses close together on each side, Madison Park does indeed have much of the small-village atmosphere about it. It is populated by families of many races and ethnic origins, who have cooperated to maintain the beauty and serenity of this delightful area.

1239-41-43 East Madison Park—Architect: Y. C. Wong (1967) At the west end of Madison Park, on the south side of the street, stop at 1239-41-43 and see 3 handsome new townhouses constructed in 1967, designed by Y. C. Wong. These are among the very few newly constructed buildings in the Park, but they seem to blend very well with their neighbors. A yellow brick wall shields lovely private gardens from the view of passersby. The horizontal lines of the stucco upper wall and glass windows give the north facade an appearance of strength. The south facade, which faces Hyde Park Boulevard, has garages conveniently located just below the living room terraces.

1302 East Madison Park (about 1925)—Across the street, at 1302, is a charmingly unconventional yellow brick apartment building. The pitched roof and garage below the main entrance suggest the style of many buildings in San Francisco. Other features that give this building individuality are stairs to the first-floor apartments on each side of the garage and attractive metal grillwork across the balcony of the main entrance.

1366-80 East Madison Park—Architect: Y. C. Wong (1961) Farther down on the same side, at 1366-80, you come to 8

150

stunning townhouses well known in the Chicago area—the architect Wong's "Atrium Houses." The exterior walls have no windows whatever, the outside light for all the rooms coming from an interior open court, or atrium. The complete privacy and quiet provided by this arrangement are considered a decided advantage in urban living. If you are fortunate, one of the owners may show you around his home.

Farmer's Field—50th to 49th Street and Dorchester to Kenwood Avenue. With the Atrium Houses you have reached the east end of Madison Park, which is Dorchester Avenue. Walk north on Dorchester to 50th Street. At the northeast corner, to your right, stands the Church of St. Paul and the Redeemer, 2 Episcopal churches recently merged, in a relatively new building constructed after the old St. Paul's was damaged by fire. To your left, at the northwest corner of Dorchester and 50th Street, you will see the sign "KENWOOD PARK." This stretch of plain green "pasture" covering an entire block has long been known to Chicagoans as "Farmer's Field." Although the history of Farmer's Field seems somewhat hazy, a house-owner on 50th Street says that a resident of days gone by told him a cow used to graze there every day as recently as the 1920's. A downtown bank is credited with having bought the property with the commendable intent of keeping it unchanged.

Modular Townhouses—
50th Street and Blackstone Avenue.

Walk one block east on 50th Street to Blackstone Avenue, to see the Chicago Dwellings Association's 6 demonstration *modular townhouses*. Set on land provided by the Department of Urban Renewal of the City of Chicago, these prefabricated 4-room, all-electric, air-conditioned houses were erected by the National Homes Corporation of Lafayette, Indiana. The extraordinary speed with which the land was prepared, houses erected, and full-grown trees planted in the landscaping was a dramatic sight for anyone who could get close enough to watch it. (Private cars were kept out of the area during the operation.) These houses are part of the city's program to experiment with 200 modular houses to be sold to moderate-income families for about $16,000 with low down payments and monthly carrying charges. The public reaction has been very receptive. A factory is to be constructed within the city for the purpose of using local labor and capital to construct many thousands more of these units. Guerdon Industries of Vicksburg, Mississippi, is likewise providing similar houses in other parts of the city.

1351-1203 East 50th Street—Now walk on 50th Street and note the row of townhouses extending from *1351 to 1319*. All are well-maintained houses about 75 years old. Farther on, at *1243 East 50th*, is an older house, built about 1875, a charming gray house with white trim, set in a garden. At *1220*, across the street, is an enormous red brick Georgian house with white door, shutters, and trim. The windows and entrance are in good scale. At *1229*, back on the south side of the street, is a gray frame house with very high ceilings, which has an appearance of great dignity and serenity. At *1207 and 1203* are 2 red brick, 2-story townhouses constructed as recently as 1965—designed by Grunsfeld and Associates. Set well back from the street, they blend perfectly with their older neighbors.

4940-4929 South Greenwood Avenue—Continue west to Greenwood and enjoy the beauty of the many old trees, fine shrubbery, and delightful front yards. These provide much of the charm of the area, and Kenwood home-owners are determined to keep it that way. The majority of the houses along Greenwood were built between 1910 and 1925.

Walk north on Greenwood and stop at *4940*, on the west side of the street. This is a 3-story, red brick mansion of collegiate Gothic design. Unusual Gothic ornamentation surrounds the front windows and doors. At the read are a tremendously large yard and garden, and a garage with living quarters above.

Be sure to note the mansion across the street at *4939 Greenwood*—an enormous red brick house with quoins at the corners and high-pitched roof. Doric pilasters adorn the entrance porch. This was the home built by Max Adler, of Adler Planetarium fame (see Walk No. 12, Burnham Park: Museums.)

Opposite, top left, 4935 Greenwood. *Top right*, Stained glass poppy detail in door of the Magerstadt House. *Bottom*, 4819 South Greenwood.

And a bit farther north, at *4935*, is a heavy, 3-story building with semicircular facade extending the entire height. Note the stone columns at the entrance porch and the ornament on the pediment at the roof line. At *4935½ South Greenwood*, to the

152

rear, is a 2-story coach house of similar design and material as 4935. Remodeled in 1963, it contains new kitchen, fireplace, and paneled study. It is typical of many of the old coach houses in the area.

At *4929 South Greenwood* is a well-proportioned red brick house of Georgian design. The white wood trim is in good scale with the rest of the facade.

◨ **Magerstadt House**—4930 South Greenwood. Architects: George W. Maher (1906); Arthur Myhrum (1968) The Magerstadt House, on the west side of the street, was designed by a former assistant of Frank Lloyd Wright and quite naturally reflects to some extent Wright's style—the long plan and side entrance, for instance, and the wide overhang. On the other hand, Wright would surely not have used the two unnecessary pillars that pretend to support the porch roof. And the building as a whole is more massive than most of Wright's. The present occupants of the house completed its rehabilitation in 1968. The interior lighting, bathrooms, and kitchen have been completely remodeled; the woodwork has been restored and repainted. In general, the interior has a new glow, making this a truly delightful home.

4920 and 4906 South Greenwood—The 3-story limestone, English Tudor house at *4920 Greenwood* is worth viewing. Take particular note of the enormous grounds and gardens, and of the iron picket fence.

At *4906 Greenwood* you will see a red brick symmetrical facade with a design similar to early Louis Sullivan.

1222 East 49th Street—Architects for remodeling: Crombie Taylor and Edward Noonan (1946) Walk 2 blocks east—for a short detour—to a very charming former coach house built originally in 1906 and remodeled 40 years later. Although the exterior remodeling is at a minimum, concentrated primarily in the west wall and the entrance, it is characteristic of the quality and style exhibited in the interior remodeling. The stunning, all-glass west wall of the living room was formerly the coach entrance.

4900 South Greenwood Avenue—Back in the mainstream of the walk, on Greenwood Avenue, you come to a 3-story neoclassic red brick mansion at 4900. The enormous, light gray limestone Doric columns give this structure an appearance of a large apartment building rather than a private residence. Constructed about 1900, it still dominates the corner of 49th and Greenwood.

4850 South Greewood Avenue—Architects: George Fred and William Keck (1967)   Here is a cluster of 3-story, red brick, freestanding townhouses, all with pitched roofs (one of them a mansard roof). They make a handsome addition to this section of Kenwood.

4819 South Greenwood Avenue—This stately Georgian mansion has red brick walls with quoins of the same material at the corners. The grand scale of the windows and the ceiling heights give the house an appearance of enormous dignity. The immense, well-landscaped grounds include a tennis court at the rear.

1126 East 48th Street—Architects for remodeling: James Eppenstein (1941); Arthur Myhrum (1963)   Walk north on Greenwood and then east on 48th Street until you come to 1126, a large gray brick house. Originally constructed in 1888, it has been remodeled twice, the major part taking place in 1963. By removing the original front staircase the architect was free to design a stunning 3-story entrance hall on the side of the building, facing a landscaped patio to the east. He set a library adjacent to the entrance hall, with a wall of grillwork between, and placed a large living room at the front of the building, facing 48th Street. Other alterations have provided this house with modernized kitchen, spacious rooms on the 2nd floor—including a spendid master bedroom, with "His" and "Her" separate dressing rooms, bathrooms, and studies—and guest rooms on both 2nd and 3rd floors.

1125 East 48th Street—Architect for remodeling: Ernest A. Grunsfeld (1938)   Across the street, at 1125, is a 2-story gray frame house, originally constructed about 1895 and remodeled more than 40 years later. The main house has an elegant entrance hall, dining room, and kitchen on the 1st floor, 4 bedrooms and 2 baths on the 2nd. The living room is in a 1-story east wing, with windows to the south, facing a large landscaped garden and play area.

155

1144-1158 East 48th Street—Architect: Y. C. Wong (1965)
Farther east on 48th Street you come to a row of 8 townhouses
that have been cited for architectural excellence—designed by the
same architect who planned the famous atrium houses in
Madison Park. The 9-foot walls that encompass the gardens
around these homes are characteristic of this architect's
emphasis on privacy for the home-owner.

1322 East 49th Street—Architect for the 1-story wing, Frank
Lloyd Wright (1895)   Now walk east on 48th Street to Kimbark
Avenue (1300 E), then south to 49th Street, and east again
on 49th until you reach 1322. Here you will see a 2-story garage
house with a 1-story wing designed by Frank Lloyd Wright in his
earlier days. The yellow Roman brick and wide overhang of
the roof indicate that Wright was already experimenting
at this early stage of his career—with quite handsome results.

4858 South Kenwood—Sometimes attributed to Frank Lloyd
Wright or Louis Sullivan (1890)   The yellow frame, neoclassic
house to the east, at the corner of 49th and Kenwood, has
no hint of either Frank Lloyd or Louis Sullivan, though both
have been given credit for designing it.

4915 and 4912 South Woodlawn Avenue—Now walk west
on 49th Street to Woodlawn, and then turn south for the last 2
stops on this walk. At *4915 Woodlawn* is another red brick
Georgian house, with an excellent formal facade. Two circular
bays extend from grade to roof. The white wood trim is in good
scale, and so are the slender white Ionic pilasters at the entrance.

Across the street, at *4912*, is a modern house in the heart of
this middle-aged group of homes—well set back from the sidewalk
and shielded by trees and shrubbery. (*Architect: John Johansen,
of New York, 1950*) Although constructed nearly 20 years ago,
the house looks surprisingly contemporary. The base is of
random-cut limestone and the overhanging balcony of wood.
Painted sections of the base—large rectangles in yellow, blue, and
green—give a splendid, light feeling to the house. The all-glass
stairwell contributes a special quality to this excellent design.

Although the proposed walk ends here, there are many more
homes in Kenwood that are beautiful and noteworthy, as those
who continue exploring will discover.

Henry Moore
Sculpture, "Nuclear
Energy."

158

HYDE PARK - UNIVERSITY OF CHICAGO

Hyde park and the University of Chicago are practically
inseparable. Faculty, university staff, married students, graduate
and undergraduate students, alumni, and friends of the University
are clustered about the campus in new and old houses,
townhouses, and apartments. And a large percentage of the
non-university residents of this interracial community
are business and professional people.

Hyde Park families are civic-minded to a high degree and guard
with real concern their parks, lakefront, and trees. They have
sometimes been very much concerned about individual houses
that were razed by recent urban renewal projects. At the same
time, they recognize too that urban renewal has made many
desirable changes in the neighborhood—removing some badly
deteriorated apartment buildings, restoring many fine old homes,
and constructing new buildings where land was cleared.

Because of the close relation between Hyde Park and the
University of Chicago, no attempt has been made in this walk
to separate arbitrarily University buildings from others in the area
(though of course each University building is identified as such).
For anyone interested in making a more thorough tour of the
University campus by itself, free 2-hour tours are conducted by
the U. of C. each Saturday, starting at 10:00 A.M. from Ida Noyes
Hall, 1212 East 59th Street. (For any further information on these
official tours call MIdway-3-0800, extension 4425 or 4429.)

It has seemed desirable, however, to divide No. 16 into 2 parts—
16A and 16B. These 2 walks must *not* be interpreted as a division
between "town and gown." They are suggested only as a possible
geographical division of an area that has no *logical* division,
in the hope that each walk will be more pleasurable and
less tiring than both together would be.

Since a purely arbitrary separation was necessary, it has
been made at the most obvious geographical dividing line—the
Midway Plaisance. Walk A will take you to Hyde Park -
University of Chicago buildings that lie definitely north of the
Midway; Walk B will take you to the Midway and the
buildings along both north and south sides of it.

Opposite, Harper Court.

159

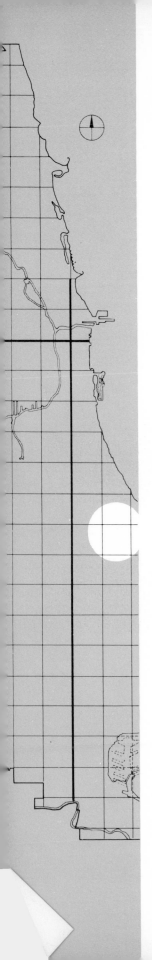

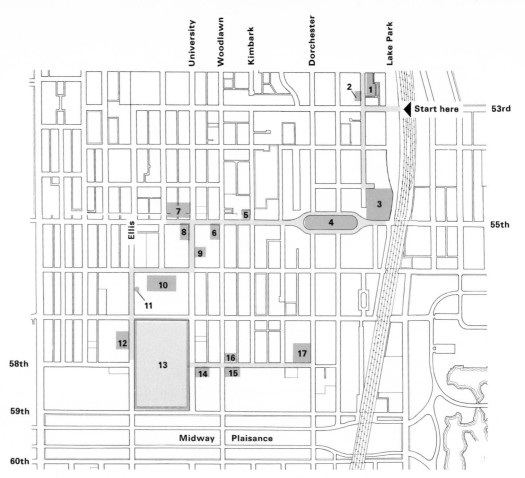

1. Harper Court
   52nd to 53rd, Harper to Lake Park Av.

2. Harper Theatre and Coffee House
   5238 Harper Av.

3. 55th St. Shopping Center
   54th Pl. to 55th, Harper to Lake Park Av.

4. University Apartments and Town House Complex
   1400-1450 E. 55th and surrounding area

5. St. Thomas Apostle Church
   5472 Kimbark Av.

6. Augustana Evangelical Lutheran Church
   5500 Woodlawn Av.

7. Lutheran School of Theology
   1100 E. 55th St.

8. Stanley R. Pierce Hall, U of C
   5514 University Av.

9. 5551 S. University Av. Bldg. (Apartments)

10. Regenstein Library, U of C
    1101 E. 56th St.

11. Henry Moore's "Nuclear Energy" Sculpture,
    near Regenstein Library

12. Geophysical Sciences Bldg., U of C
    58th St. and Ellis Av.

13. University of Chicago Quadrangle
    57th to 59th, Ellis to University

14. Oriental Institute, U of C
    1155 East 58th St.

15. Women's Residence Hall, U of C
    5825 Woodlawn Av.

16. Robie House (Inst. of International Affairs)
    5757 Woodlawn

17. Chicago Theological Seminary
    Faculty Quadrangle
    58th and Dorchester Av.

Walk · 16a

North of the Midway

WALKING TIME: 2 hours.   HOW TO GET THERE: Take an Illinois Central (I. C.)
suburban train at its Randolph and Michigan underground station, and get off at 53rd Street.
(All express trains and many of those marked ''Special'' stop at 53rd. Check before boarding
the train.) Or, if you go by car, take the Outer Drive south to 47th Street, turn west under
the I.C. railroad's viaduct, and then south on Lake Park Avenue (1400 E). Continue on
Lake Park to 53rd Street, where this walk begins.

Harper Court—Between 52nd and 53rd Streets,
Harper and Lake Park Avenues, 2 blocks west of
the Illinois Central's 53rd Street station.

The first stop on this walk is Harper Court. Originally designed
to provide space for Hyde Park artisans displaced by urban
renewal, Harper Court shows what can be done when city
government, university, and community organizations cooperate
in the clearance and rebuilding of a blighted area. The sunken
court has become the focal point of a group of art galleries, shops,
and restaurants that have added sparkle and zest to the
neighborhood. Shops selling dresses, fabrics, books, candles,
picture frames, and Scandinavian furniture have become
popular meeting places for Hyde Parkers.

Harper Theatre and Coffee House—5238 South Harper,
across the street from Harper Court.

The Harper Theatre is the anchor of Harper Court. Remodeled
in 1963 from an ordinary movie theatre—which in turn had
replaced an old-time vaudeville house—it is now an intimate
theatre showcase. Its coffee shop is furnished and decorated with
the tables, chairs, and classic pharmacist's materials once
adorning Finnegan's drugstore, which stood at the corner of 55th
and Woodlawn before redevelopment of the area. Pieces of
wrought-iron grillwork that decorate the Harper Theatre lobby
came from the balconies of the unusually distinguished fire
escapes of Theodore Starrett's Hyde Park Hotel, demolished
just before the Harper Theatre renovation.

161

University Apartments—1400-1450 East 55th Street. Architects: I. M. Pei; Harry M. Weese and Associates; and Loewenberg and Loewenberg (1959-1962)

Three blocks south of Harper Court, a major part of the Hyde Park renewal is evident in two 10-story apartment buildings in the middle of 55th Street, which has been widely extended on each side to allow a continuing flow of east and west traffic. Known as the University Apartments, these buildings constitute one of the first large-scale urban renewal projects of its kind. Citizens committees and governmental agencies cooperated to bring about these first-rate results. The South East Chicago Commission and the Hyde Park-Kenwood Community Conference did outstanding work.

Built in an extremely simple form, these twin apartment towers have a forceful horizontal rhythm, resulting largely from the long stretches of closely positioned windows. Although the buildings are set in the midst of city traffic, the landscaping—with trees, flowers, pool, and fountain—softens the effect. The many townhouses that surround University Apartments, to the north and the south of 55th Street, were designed by the same architects.

55th Street Shopping Center—To the east and north of University Apartments. The mall of the 55th Street Shopping Center is of special interest. Among the stores here the *Hyde Park Co-op Supermarket* is particularly significant as a neighborhood development. Starting as a small buying club in the early 1930's, it is now owned by more than 11,000 members and in 1967 reported an annual business of more than $6 million. It claims to be the largest cooperatively owned retail grocery store in the country. The building is light and airy, with many features that facilitate family shopping. Summer and winter the large entrance is wide open during store hours. Customers merely pass through a curtain of air that keeps the inside temperature cool in 90° weather and warm on the coldest winter days. (Architects: George Fred and William Keck, 1959)

St. Thomas Apostle Church—5472 South Kimbark. Architect: Barry Byrne (1922)

The influence of Frank Lloyd Wright on his former apprentice can be noted in the design of St. Thomas Apostle Church, at the

162

corner of 55th and Kimbark. The warmth of color in the building
material, the sculpture around the entrance, and the human scale
on which all seems to have been constructed give this church
an especially appealing effect. Inside, the fourteen Stations of the
Cross, carved in bas-relief by the Italian sculptor A. Faggi,
are justifiably famous for the sweep and rhythm of their design.

Lutheran School of Theology—1100 East 55th Street.
Architects: Perkins and Will Partnership (1968)

Two blocks west of St. Thomas, on the north side of a
boulevard-like reconstructed 55th Street, is the Lutheran School
of Theology, consisting of 3 stunning sections with transparent
enclosures of lightly tinted glass between sweeping curved
steel columns that rest on sturdy pins, much like
those in bridge construction.

Diagonally across 55th Street, at 5500 Woodlawn, is the new
Augustana Evangelical Lutheran Church of Hyde Park, in
low, spacious design—planned by Edward D. Dart, of Loebl,
Schlossman, Bennett, and Dart. Within the main entrance stands
an impressively unconventional bronze statue of Christ, the
work of Egon Weiner. The statue was cast in Norway.

Stanley R. Pierce Hall—
University of Chicago, 5514 University Avenue.
Architects: Harry M. Weese and Associates (1959-60)

On the south side of 55th Street, one block west of the Lutheran
church, is Pierce Hall, a University of Chicago residence for
undergraduate students. A high-rise tower, with an effective
2-story extension, this has become a distinguished addition to
the University campus. Tiers of bay windows—a feature restored
by this architect, after years of disuse—accentuate the vertical
lines of the structure. Actually the building houses 4 separate
residence halls—Henderson, Shorey, Thompson, and Tufts.

◘ **5551 South University Avenue Building**—
Architects: George Fred and William Keck (1937)

Now walk south on University and note the brick building on
the east side of the Street at 5551—one of the earliest modern
buildings in the area with cooperative apartments. The 2
architects themselves live in 2 of the 3 apartments, each of
which extends over an entire floor. Across the front of the
building at ground level are 3 garages, and the entrance is
placed inconspicuously at the side, far back from the street.
Contrast in the brick facade on the University Avenue side is
provided by dark metal louvres, 2 at each floor level—for the
2 wide windows—with a stretch of contrasting brick between

Opposite, Stanley R. Pierce Hall.

165

them. At the time this building was erected its design was considered quite extreme, though today it blends well with other architecture in the area and seems to meet naturally the needs of the city dweller. A plaque on the corner of the building reports its selection as an Architectural Landmark.

Regenstein Library—
University of Chicago, 1101 East 56th Street.
Architects: Skidmore, Owings, and Merrill (1969)

Continue south on University Avenue to 56th Street, then turn right and walk west 2 blocks to Ellis Avenue. At Ellis turn left (south again) to approach the University of Chicago campus. This area is now being rebuilt into a magnificent north campus addition. On the site of the old Stagg Field—famous alike for earlier football triumphs and the scientists' first nuclear chain reaction—stands the University's new Regenstein Library, a tremendously popular addition to the intellectual life of the campus. Of the same gray limestone as its Gothic neighbors, it has a modern design that is impressive in scale. Still under construction in 1969, this titanic library, costing well over $20 million, will have a capacity for more than 3 million volumes.

Bronze Sculpture, "Nuclear Energy"—
Ellis Avenue between 56th and 57th streets.
Sculptor: Henry Moore (1967)

Between Regenstein Library and Ellis Avenue, halfway down the block, is a great bronze sculpture—12 feet high, weighing 3 tons, which stands on a base of black polished granite. Entitled "Nuclear Energy," this extremely simple but impressive work of art by the sculptor Henry Moore commemorates man's achievement in completing the first atomic chain reaction— as explained in one of the 4 plaques mounted on a slab of marble in the grass across the sidewalk. Under a Stagg Field bleacher near this same spot, on December 2, 1942, Enrico Fermi and 41 other distinguished scientists accomplished the great breakthrough that introduced the Atomic Age. Speaking of the sculpture himself, Moore has explained that it relates both to the mushroom cloud of a nuclear explosion and to the shape of a human skull, with reminiscences of church architecture in the lower part.

Opposite, Geophysical Sciences building.

166

Geophysical Sciences Building—
University of Chicago, 58th and Ellis.
Architects: I. W. Colburn and Associates; J. Lee Jones
(associate architect) (1969)

One block farther south on Ellis, on the west side of the street,
is a building of startlingly unique architecture, the University's
Geophysical Sciences Building—the first in a science center that
will eventually occupy the entire block. Cross to the east side of

Ellis for a better view. Much of the design was determined by the demands of present-day research and teaching in the geophysical sciences. It seems at first to have no relation whatever with the neo-Gothic buildings of the original Quadrangle directly across from it, but it has actually made concessions to the earlier style. The brick walls, for instance, which carry the load, are covered with a thin layer of Indiana limestone, the material used in the older buildings, and the brick itself allowed to show only here and there. And the numerous towers, though of highly individual form, supposedly bring the entire building into greater harmony with the Gothic-towered structures of the old campus. Towers used for such requirements as air supply and stairs are supplemented by others less strictly functional, which place cooling equipment above elevator shafts.

University of Chicago Quadrangle—
57th to 59th, between Ellis and University.
Architects: Henry Ives Cobb; Shepley, Rutan, and Coolidge; Charles Klauder; and others
(1890 to the present)

Across the street from the new Geophysical Sciences Building is the original campus of the University of Chicago, called "The Quadrangle." Before entering the Quadrangle, however, look back across Ellis to note the University Press, the University Bookstore, and then the enormous complex of buildings that accommodate the biological sciences. Here are the biological research laboratories and the University's hospitals and medical school.

Occupying 4 solid blocks, the Quadrangle as a whole follows the original plan prepared by Henry Ives Cobb in 1890—a large central quadrangle flanked by 3 small quadrangles to the south and 3 more to the north, all surrounded by buildings of Indiana limestone in the late English Gothic style. Cobb himself designed all the buildings that were constructed before 1900, and later architects used the neo-Gothic style exclusively through the 1940's. This mass of Gothic structures comprises the architectural heritage to which subsequent architects generally deferred.

168

The student newspaper, the *Maroon* quoted Eero Saarinen from the *Architectural Record* of November 1960,[8] during the time when he was consulting architect to the University of Chicago:

> Wandering in the University of Chicago today, one is amazed at the beauty achieved by spaces surrounded by buildings all in one discipline and made out of a uniform material; where each building is being considerate of the next, and each building —through its common material—is aging in the same way. It is significant that on a small court on the University of Chicago campus [referring to the one used by Court Theatre] built between 1894 and 1930, three different architects—Henry I. Cobb; Shepley, Rutan, and Coolidge; and Charles Klauder— built the four different sides of the court. All are in the Gothic style, and the court gives us today a beautiful, harmonious visual picture.

The cohesiveness of the old quadrangles does not rest entirely on the use of the Gothic style. In fact, the Administration Building, which encloses the main Quadrangle on the west, defies this tradition, conforming only in the material used. In large part the harmonious effect comes from the fact that these architects all envisoned their buildings as contributions to a larger unity.

Oriental Institute—1155 East 58th Street. Architects: Mayer, Murray, and Phillip (1931)

Across the street from the eastern edge of the Quadrangle, on the east side of University Avenue, is the internationally famous Oriental Institute. It contains one of the world's major collections of art, religious, and daily life objects from the Ancient Near East: Egypt, Palestine, Syria, Anatolia, Mesopotamia, and Iran. The time range covered is from about 5000 B.C. to about 1000 A.D. Open daily 10:00 A.M. to 5:00 P.M.; closed Mondays and Thursdays, and from 12:00 noon to 1:00 P.M. Tuesdays and Wednesdays.

Women's Residence Hall—5825 Woodlawn. Architect: Eero Saarinen (1958)

A residence hall for women students, on the south side of 58th Street, is first-rate architecture, although it is not up to the very high standards of design established by Saarinen in the Law School Quadrangle. (See Walk 16b.)

Robie House.

⊡ Robie House—now Adlai Stevenson Institute of
International Affairs, 5757 Woodlawn.
Original Architect: Frank Lloyd Wright (1909)
Architects for restoration: Frank Lloyd Wright Office,
Wesley Peters (in charge), William Barnard, Jr.,
Contractor (Son of original contractor) 1964;
Skidmore, Owings, and Merrill (1967)

Declared a National Historic Landmark, 1964

On the east side of Woodlawn, at the corner of Woodlawn and
58th Street, is Frank Lloyd Wright's famous Robie House, which
was recently renovated from public subscriptions after it had
been donated to the University by William Zeckendorf. Built as

170

a private home, this is probably the most well-known example of Wright's "Prairie House." The Citation by the Architectural Landmarks Commission reads:

> In recognition of the creation of the Prairie House—a home organized around a great hearth where interior space, under wide sweeping roofs, opens to the outdoors. The bold interplay of horizontal planes about the chimney mass, and the structurally expressive piers and windows, established a new form of domestic design.

In 1967, after being restored and refurnished in its original style, the Robie House became the Adlai Stevenson Institute of International Affairs.

Chicago Theological Seminary Faculty Quadrangle—
corner of 58th and Dorchester.
Architect: Edward D. Dart, of Loebl, Schlossman, Bennett, and Dart (1963)

Now turn east on 58th Street, and stop at Dorchester to see a surprisingly unconventional group of recently constructed buildings—homes for Chicago Theological Seminary faculty. No attempt was made here to harmonize the architecture of the houses with that of the older buildings around them. On the contrary, they defy previously accepted patterns with refreshing individuality. Instead of following the lines of the street, for instance, as the endless rows of houses in Chicago—and most other cities—do, their sides face the street on a diagonal, as if set there deliberately somewhat askew. The roofs, instead of being flat or gabled, slope steeply from one side to the other with wide overhang. All 8 houses, harmonizing well with each other, are clustered around a central green that is elevated so that it can slope down to the sidewalk.

A plaque on the house at the corner reports an award for excellence in architecture.

This is the end of Walk 16a. To return to the Loop, walk north to 57th Street and then east 3 blocks to the elevated station (55th, 56th, 57th) of the Illinois Central suburban line that brought you out to Hyde Park.

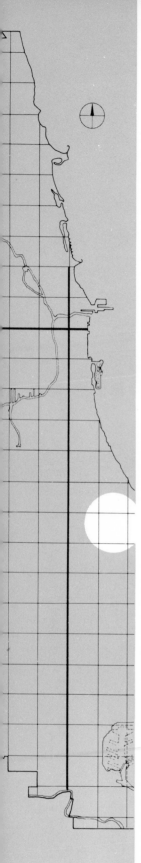

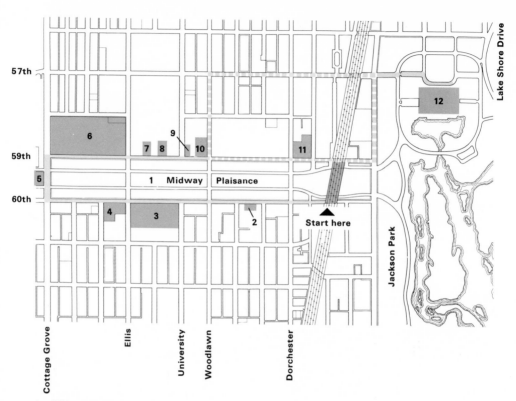

57th

59th

60th

5

1 Midway Plaisance

3

4

6

7 8

9

10

11

12

2

Start here

Cottage Grove

Ellis

University

Woodlawn

Dorchester

Lake Shore Drive

Jackson Park

1. Midway Plaisance
   59th to 60th St., Jackson Park to Washington Park

2. Center for Continuing Education
   1307 E. 60th St.

3. Laird Bell Law Quadrangle, U of C
   1111 E. 60th St.

4. School of Social Service Administration, U of C
   969 E. 60th St.

5. Lorado Taft's "Fountain of Time"
   W. end of the Midway

6. Hospital Complex, U of C
   950 E. 59th St.

7. Harper Memorial Library, U of C
   1116 E. 59th St.

8. Social Science Research Bldg., U of C
   1126 E. 59th St.

9. University President's House
   5855 University Av. (on 59th St.)

10. Rockefeller Memorial Chapel, U of C
    E. 59th St., corner of Woodlawn Av.

11. International House, U of C
    1414 E. 59th St.

12. Museum of Science and Industry
    E. 57th St. at S. Lake Shore Dr.

- - - - Alternate route

Walk · 16b

The Midway Plaisance and Its South and North Sides

WALKING TIME: 1½ hours.   HOW TO GET THERE: Instead of getting off the I.C.
suburban train at 53rd Street—as you did for Walk 16a—stay on until 59th Street, having made
sure in advance that your train will stop there! Or, if you go by car, follow the instructions
given for Walk 16a, continuing on Lake Park until you reach 59th Street.

Midway Plaisance, stretching from Jackson Park on the east to Washington Park on the west, between 59th and 60th streets.

Before coming down from the I. C. elevated platform, look west
for an overall view of the Midway Plaisance, a block wide and
some dozen blocks long, stretching all the way from Jackson
Park (just behind you) to Washington Park on the west—
all green lawns, trees, and sidewalks, with 4 highways for
east-west traffic.

This great green mall was constructed in 1890 as the formal
entrance to the 1893 Columbian Exposition, to be held in what
is now Jackson Park. The sunken parts of the Midway Pleasance
are a reminder that these were filled with water back in 1893—
impressive lagoons to be admired before you reached the
exposition proper.

Other reminders of that famous world fair are the enormous
gilded statue of the Republic, by Daniel Chester French, now
placed farther on in Jackson Park, where it is passed daily by
hundreds of commuters on their way to and from the Loop, and
the Museum of Science and Industry, which is the last stop on
this walk. (Though it stands 2 blocks north of the Midway, it
seems an appropriate ending for a Midway walk.) Another
legacy from the fair, the charming Japanese teahouse on an
island in a Jackson Park lagoon, which was the delight of Hyde
Parkers a generation ago, was first damaged by fire and then
completely abandoned.

Called merely "The Midway" by neighborhood residents, this
parkway is especially popular with University of Chicago

173

students, who use its long stretch of sunken lawns for sunning and studying in summer and for exercise in winter, when it is flooded for ice skating.

Statuary marks each end of the Midway. On the east stands a sturdy mailclad warrior on horseback, a tribute from Chicago's Czechoslovakians to their first president, Masaryk. The figure is supposedly one of the Blanik knights, who—according to legend—slept in a mountainous cave in Czechoslovakia until the time should come to arise and rescue their country. On the west is Lorado Taft's "Fountain of Time," which will be included in this walk.

Center for Continuing Education—
1307 East 60th Street.
Architect: Edward Stone (1963)

On the south side of the Midway, at 1307 East 60th, is the Center for Continuing Education, which is the University's conference and hotel center, made possible by funds from the W. K. Kellogg Foundation. Living quarters, conference rooms, restaurant, and cafeteria provide liberal facilities for out-of-town conferees. Restaurant and cafeteria are open to the public. (The structure is not considered one of Stone's best works.)

Laird Bell Law Quadrangle—The University of
Chicago Law School, 1111 East 60th Street.
Architect: Eero Saarinen (1960)

Turning west, you pass the Industrial Relations Center at 1225, also affiliated with the University, and come to the University Law School. This elegant low quadrangle is far and away the most successful building on the campus of the University. It blends well with the Gothic dormitories to the west and the American Bar Center to the east.

At the east end is a completely closed auditorium, which contrasts markedly with the enormous library west of it, for the library uses all-glass walls set at effective angles with each other. Inside the building, the auditorium is connected by wide corridors with lecture rooms and lounges that extend to the west. Actually, there are two auditoriums—one set over the other. One is used as a court room for demonstrations and the other for lectures. The stunning sculpture in the pool outside, called "Construction in Space in Third and Fourth Dimensions," is the work of Antoine Pevsner, who created it specifically for the Law School.

School of Social Service Administration Building—
969 East 60th Street.
Architect: Ludwig Mies van der Rohe (1965)

The Social Service Administration Building of the University, the last building to be noted on this side of the Midway, is a Mies van der Rohe creation. Black steel and glass and an open plan give the structure an imposing appearance. It seems not at

Opposite, Library building, Laird Bell Law Quadrangle.

175

all out of place or off tempo and fits well with the other buildings on 60th Street. The policy of inviting distinguished 20th century architects to design new buildings has been most rewarding to the campuses of Harvard, Yale and the University of Chicago.

Fountain of Time—west end of Midway Plaisance, at entrance to Washington Park.
Sculptor: Lorado Taft (1922)

After an interval of neglect, Lorado Taft's haunting sculpture called "The Fountain of Time" has fortunately been restored. A hooded, "craglike" figure of Time (to use Taft's own adjective in describing his mental image), with his back to the Midway, gazes across a pool at a long procession of human beings as they move through life. The Chicago sculptor said that his inspiration came from these lines in a poem by Austin Dobson:

> *Time goes, you say? Ah no!*
> *Alas, time stays; we go.*

Both the immobility of Time and the onward sweep of human life are well expressed in this unusual sculpture.

Be sure to walk all around the Fountain of Time, to view it from every angle. On what seems to be the back is another procession of people, including a figure of the sculptor himself and his Italian assistant.

Rockefeller Memorial Chapel—
1156-80 East 59th Street.
Architect: Bertram G. Goodhue, whose associates— after his death—supervised the construction according to the plans he had drawn up (1928)

Now back on the north side of the Midway, walk east on 59th past a series of U. of C. buildings—Billings Hospital at 950, Harper Memorial Library at 1160, the Social Science Research Building at 1126, and the president's house on the corner of University and 59th (official address, 5855 University). At 59th and Woodlawn stands Rockefeller Memorial Chapel, one of the most imposing buildings of the University's campus, donated by

Opposite, Rockefeller Memorial Chapel.

176

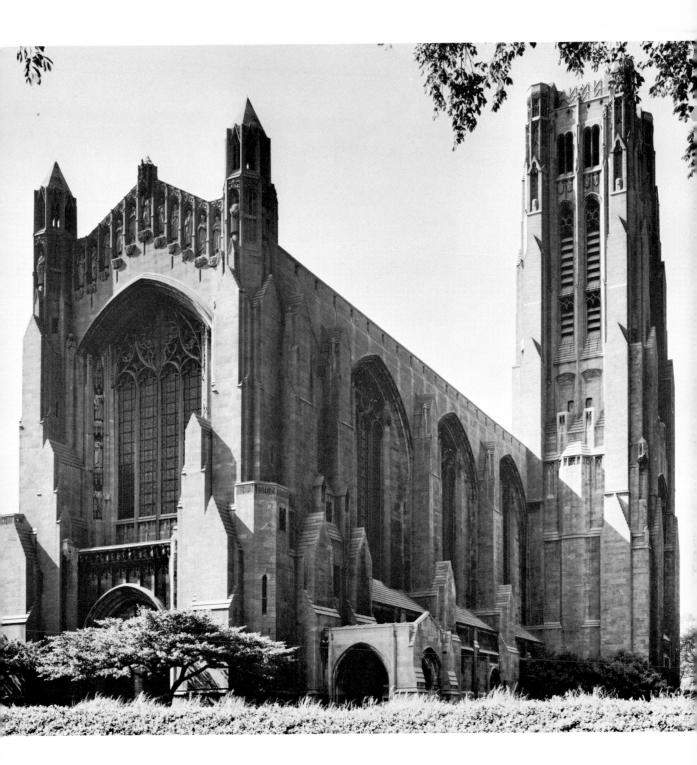

177

and named in honor of the University's founder. This is an excellent example of the late Gothic style by a prominent architect interested in the Gothic revival. The Carillon Tower bells (72 of them) are noteworthy for the excellence of the tones and the quality of the sound. They were given, a few years after the chapel was completed, by the same donor in memory of his mother, Laura Spelman Rockefeller.

The chapel is the scene of many University functions, such as concerts, pageantry, graduation ceremonies, and other convocations. And, to add a social note, the Rockefeller-Percy wedding was held here in 1968!

The colorful banners hanging inside Rockefeller Chapel come from a collection of 44 *liturgical* banners created by Norman Laliberte for the Vatican Pavilion at the World's Fair in New York that ended in 1965. The artist, a Canadian-American now living in Brewster, New York, is said to be a deeply religious man, who has been able to catch the simple appeal, even the humor, of medieval religious art work. Known officially as the Mary MacDonald Ludgin Collection, these banners were a gift to the University in 1966 from one of its trustees, Earle Ludgin, in memory of his wife.

As you stand outside Rockefeller Chapel on the corner of 59th and Woodlawn, look to the north for a glimpse of 2 other places

178

of worship—the beautifully executed red brick tower of the
U. of C. Theological Seminary's chapel one block north and one
block east, at 58th and University, and the exquisite spire of the
First Unitarian Church one block farther north, at 57th
and Woodlawn.

To proceed to the Museum of Science and Industry, the last stop
on this walk, you could walk north on Woodlawn from
Rockefeller Chapel, getting closer views of these two churches,
and turn east on 57th Street. Or you could continue down the
north side of the Midway, passing other U. of C. buildings—
Ida Noyes Hall, the laboratory school of the University, and
International House—before turning north to 57th Street.

Museum of Science and Industry—
East 57th Street at South Lake Shore Drive.
Architect: Charles B. Atwood, of D. H. Burnham and
Company (1893). Architects for restoration:
Graham, Anderson, Probst, and White for the exterior;
Shaw, Naess, and Murphy for the interior (1929-40)

Before climbing the stairs at 57th Street and Lake Park (where
you can get an Illinois Central suburban train back to the Loop
as frequently as at 59th Street) walk one block east into
Jackson Park for a good view of the Museum of Science and

Above, Museum of Science and Industry.

179

Industry. A visit inside, as with the museums around Burnham Park (see Walk No. 12), rates a separate trip. You could spend whole days here without completing the exhibits.

Just a view of this enormous building is an experience. Erected as the Palace of Fine Arts for the 1893 Columbian Exposition, it follows an elaborate Greek revivalist style—precisely duplicating various parts of temples on the Acropolis at Athens. Ionic columns, doorways, and the giant-sized caryatids (13 feet tall, weighing about 6 tons each) are copied from the Erectheum; the carving on the metope panels and frieze is reproduced from the Parthenon. Materials used, however, were not those of the Acropolis temples. For the original "temporary" building heavy brick walls were merely covered with plaster, and the Ionic columns were constructed of wood lattice frame, then covered with a plaster composition called staff.

Though widely admired as the showpiece of the Columbian Exposition, this building and others in the neoclassical style brought forth the bitter statement from the Chicago architect Louis Sullivan so often quoted: "The damage wrought by the World's Fair will last for half a century from its date." Whatever its influence on architecture, however, the "Palace of Fine Arts" has become a decidedly modern museum with chief emphasis on technology, a popular place visited by millions of people each year—3,160,429 in 1968.

The transformation was by no means simple or painless. The Palace of Fine Arts building was abandoned in 1920, when the Field Museum, which had been using space here, moved to its own building nearer the Loop. Not until several years later was it rescued from neglect. The extraordinary amount of money needed to restore both exterior and interior as a permanent building and to establish it as an industrial museum came largely from Julius Rosenwald, though his initial contribution of $3 million was apparently inspired by a bond issue of $5 million for this purpose passed by the voters of the South Park District. (Rosenwald's later contributions brought his total gift up to about $7.5 million dollars.)

In the current museum exhibits, you can see yourself on closed-circuit television, hear yourself on the phone, watch chickens being hatched, see how the human embryo develops from conception to birth, go down into a section of an actual coal mine, operate the extensive miniature railroad, or walk through the town of yesterday. The press of a button will put into motion principles of physics, electronics, or chemistry, dramatizing the basics of science and mathematics as nothing else ever did.

For this particular walk, however, just look at the building and ponder on the incongruity between the beautiful, Greek-temple exterior and the 20th century science and technology it houses!

Henry Clarke House

Wabash

Michigan

47th

◀ Start here

Walk · 17

MICHIGAN BOULEVARD GARDEN APARTMENTS—HENRY B. CLARKE HOUSE

WALKING TIME: ½ to 1 hour.   HOW TO GET THERE: Take a southbound CTA bus No. 6 (Garfield) on Michigan at Jackson (300 S), and get off at 47th Street. Walk west on 47th to the entrance of the garden of the Michigan Boulevard Garden Apartments. The boundaries are 47th Street, Wabash Avenue, 46th Street, and Michigan Avenue.

Michigan Boulevard Garden Apartments—
54 East 47th Street.
Architect: Ernest Grunsfeld (1934)

Two great pioneer merchants of Chicago, Marshall Field and Julius Rosenwald, were strong advocates of neighborhood conservation and adequate housing for all segments of the population. They believed that the construction of new housing in a run-down area might inspire the owners of adjacent properties to restore their buildings. With this aim in mind, Marshall Field built the Old Town Garden Apartments on the Near North Side (see Walk No. 18), and Julius Rosenwald the Michigan Boulevard Garden Apartments here on the South Side. This first-rate pilot housing project consists of 5-story buildings (containing 452 apartments) located along the periphery of a large rectangular inner garden. The buildings and grounds are well maintained, in contrast with those of the surrounding area. Trees and shrubbery are mature, and show excellent care and attention. The building walls are of beige-colored brick. Quoins mark the corners of each building and are carried horizontally around each at the 1st-floor level. The garden arches are strengthened by red terra-cotta moldings.

For those living in Michigan Boulevard Garden Apartments Mr. Rosenwald's dream of assisting middle-income Negroes to obtain better housing at reasonable rents has been fulfilled. The rest of his dream, unfortunately, has not materialized, for the community around his apartments has not been rehabilitated. So his Garden Apartments development remains somewhat isolated and apparently unrelated to its surroundings.

183

Recognizing the partial failure of such attempts at community improvement as those of Field and Rosenwald, the city of Chicago is now attempting a more comprehensive approach—on the thesis that the city operates as a network of interlocking systems. In the *Basic Policies for the Comprehensive Plan of Chicago*, for example, is a series of 12 diagrams showing how a run-down area would be restored. The policies were based on the need for a logical series of developments, with the ultimate goal that no one improvement be carried out independently of the other. Attention would be given simultaneously to improving the streets; improving public transit lines; locating industry in relation to rail and arterial roads; rehabilitating apartments; lessening residential density; replacing old dwelling units where necessary; and providing desired public facilities, including schools, business locations, and recreation areas; and improving nearby lakefront areas.

This concept of rehabilitation has been implemented in some parts of the city in recent years—most successfully, for example, in Hyde Park-Kenwood (see Walk No. 15); Lake Meadows, Prairie Shores, and South Commons, in the Illinois Institute of Technology area (Walk No. 14, The New South Side); and the Lincoln Park Conservation area (see Walk No. 21). For some years the availability of funds at low-interest rates through government sources has also encouraged individual property owners to rehabilitate their property.

Henry B. Clarke House—4526 South Wabash Avenue. Architect: Unknown (1836)

After strolling through the grounds of the Michigan Boulevard Garden Apartments (possibly even through the apartment of a hospitable tenant), walk west to Wabash Avenue and then north to 4526 Wabash. Here is the oldest building in Chicago—the Henry B. Clarke House. It is sometimes referred to as the Widow Clarke House, and she did indeed live in the mansion many more years than her husband, remaining after his death until 1872—one year after the Chicago Fire.

That this imposing frame house escaped that conflagration must have seemed providential, for at that time it stood at Michigan Avenue and 16th Street, hardly a dozen blocks from the fire's

Opposite, Henry B. Clarke House.

184

185

southern boundary. And the only other Chicago home that could equal it in grandeur, the William G. Ogden House, also built in 1836, was completely destroyed. In fact, the next owner may very well have decided on moving the house to its present location in 1872 both as a safety measure and a way to escape the view of the Fire's ruins to the north of its earlier site.

Note the extraordinarily high windows at the main-floor level, an indication of the equally high ceilings within. Some changes were made in the house at the time it was moved: an original porch and tall window shutters were removed, and the somewhat incongruous square turret added.

The Clarke House today is used as a community center, and a visitor is likely to be greeted by girl scouts or boy scouts attending a meeting or preparing for a special event. It is pleasant to imagine the Clarke ghosts looking on and enjoying these young and lively inhabitants of their fine old house!

Walk-18

An arched doorway
to Old Town
Gardens.

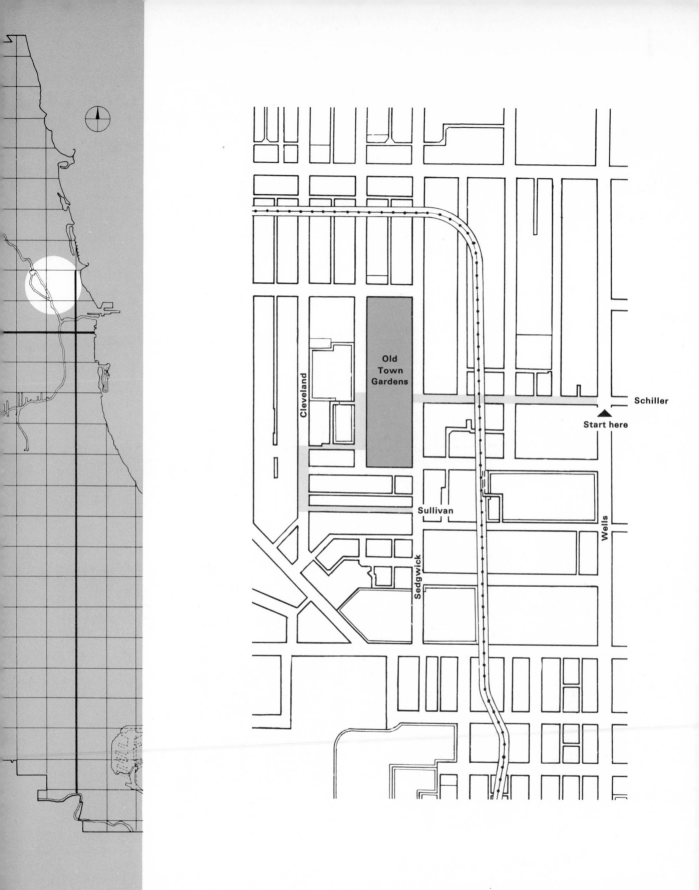

Cleveland

Old
Town
Gardens

Schiller

Start here

Sullivan

Wells

Sedgwick

Walk · 18

OLD TOWN GARDENS, FORMERLY MARSHALL FIELD GARDEN APARTMENTS

WALKING TIME: ½ hour.   HOW TO GET THERE: Walk west to Wells Street (4 blocks west of State), and take a northbound CTA bus No. 10 (Lincoln-Larrabee) on Wells. Get off at Schiller (1400 N). Then walk 2 blocks west to Sedgwick (400 W) and the apartments called Old Town Gardens at 1448 Sedgwick.

Old Town Gardens was one of the first privately financed housing developments in the United States—built by the Marshall Field Estate as the Marshall Field Garden Apartments *(architects: Andrew J. Thomas, of New York City, in association with Graham, Anderson, Probst, and White, of Chicago, 1929).* Besides affording good housing to young middle-income couples and families, the Marshall Field Estate hoped to create a new environment for a deteriorating neighborhood. The philosophy at that time was that modern new housing set in a garden would influence surrounding property owners to improve their property. Unfortunately, this did not prove true here, and the city is now endeavoring to rebuild some of the surrounding area.

Old Town Gardens consists of 628 dwelling units, 20 stores, a ramp garage for 163 cars, and a central heating plant with utility tunnels. The stores and dwelling units are located in 10 walk-up structures, each 5 stories high. These 10 buildings are situated in a 5.67-acre plot bounded by Sedgwick, Blackhawk, Hudson, and Evergreen streets. The garage and heating plant are across Sedgwick Street, opposite the dwelling units.

The construction of these buildings is fireproof—or reinforced concrete with steel columns and brick masonry walls. The 10 buildings form a periphery around gardens and a recreational inner court. As you stroll through the court, consider the fact that this development is 40 years old. Remodeling and modernization of the apartments is planned by the owners for completion in 1969.

This has been a one-stop walk, to see an old housing development of considerable interest. Before you leave the area, walk 2 blocks west to Cleveland Avenue (500 W), turn south on Cleveland, and then return to Sedgwick by walking east on Sullivan Street (1307 N), to see an incredible contrast with Old Town Gardens. This area obviously needs large-scale rehabilitation and restoration.

Row of townhouses
by Louis Sullivan at
1826-34 Lincoln
Park West.

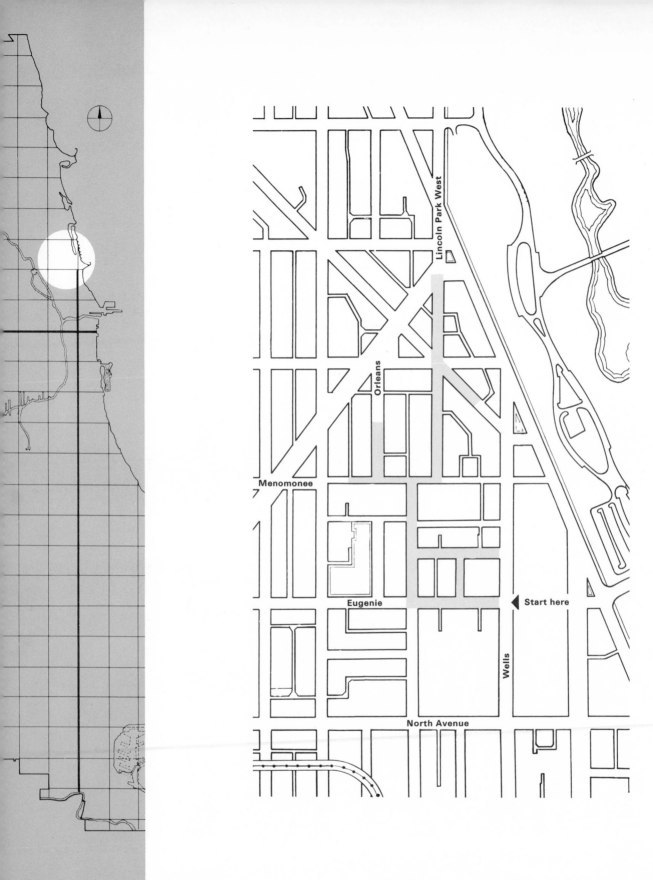

Menomonee

Orleans

Lincoln Park West

Eugenie

Wells

North Avenue

◀ Start here

Walk·19

OLD TOWN TRIANGLE

WALKING TIME: 1½ hours.   HOW TO GET THERE: Take a northbound CTA bus No. 10 (Lincoln-Larrabee) on Wells Street (4 blocks west of State). Get off at Wells and Eugenie (1700 N).

Start at Eugenie Avenue and walk west to *Crilly Court,* a famous bit of Chicago. At the end of World War II, this section of the city was overcrowded and rapidly deteriorating. The owner of several large walk-up apartment buildings decided to deconvert and rehabilitate his buildings, two of which were back to back, separated by an alley. By replacing old wooden porches with steel balconies and stairs, and transforming the yards into gardens and delightful play areas, he changed the entire character of the buildings. The city, taking cognizance of his fine work, named the short connecting street to the west Crilly Court after its innovator.

Crilly Court established the procedure for much fine conservation and rehabilitation work that characterizes the Old Town Triangle area. Many painters, sculptors, musicians, poets, authors, and architects have now made this area their home.

There are so many late 19th-century townhouses and walk-up apartment buildings here you may think that when you've seen one you've seen them all. Not so; each is a pleasant surprise, sometimes found tucked in between taller buildings or set back far from the street. The rich texture of the fine brickwork and stone ornament make an architectural "find" of many of the buildings.

Continue west on Eugenie to the west side of Crilly Court, where townhouses cover this entire side of the short thoroughfare. Crilly Court itself is a private road with characteristics that suggest a quiet side street in the west end of London about the time of Sherlock Holmes!

225 Eugenie—Walk across the street for a better view of this recently remodeled 3-story frame house, with a new stuco wall

and patio that make for privacy, and a charming entrance and facade.

235 Eugenie—Architects: Harry M. Weese and Associates (1958). A delightful contemporary structure of 7 maisonettes. These comprise 14 dwelling units of 2 stories each, the architect having placed 2 "layers" of 2-story townhouses in a row of 7.

1700 North Park Avenue—(300 W), New Orleans House. A modern structure in red brick and glass, 5 stories high, with the glass line slanted in from ceiling to floor. Parking is at grade, partially under the building. By adding high-density apartments to the area, this building detracts from the low-key atmosphere of the rest of the block.

1701, 1707, 1715, 1717 North Park Avenue (across the street)—Four-story walk-up apartments, well maintained; spacious, with high ceilings and fine-textured brickwork.

Old Town Players—1718 North Park. On the west side of the street again, you will see a charming old church building, tucked away behind trees, with a patterned brick walk. This structure has been remodeled into the home of the Old Town Players, a repertory theater group—oldest of many small theater groups in the city. The interior has been most successfully remodeled into a delightful arena for classical as well as modern drama. Performances weekends only. (For information phone 645-0145.)

Midwest Buddhist Church—1763 North Park.

At this point of the walk, stroll along *St. Paul (1732 N)*, to view the charming townhouses, trees, shrubbery, and vines there. Then return to North Park Avenue. Continue north past Willow (1746 N) and stop at the Midwest Buddhist Church, at 1763. Visitors are welcome.

This church, an important center for Buddhists in Chicago, sponsors two outdoor festivals each year—the brief Obon ceremony in July and the 3-day Ginza festival in August, at which classic Japanese dances and other Oriental activities are performed in lantern-decorated streets near the church.

Urban renewal plans call for the construction of a new Midwest Buddhist Church building in the Ogden Mall, just 3 blocks north. (See the last stop of this walk.)

Left top, Row of townhouses, Crilly Court. There are many attractive gardens in the rear. *Bottom,* Modern, double townhouses at 235 Eugenie.

316 and 334 Menomonee (1800 N)—Turn west on Menomonee to see a successful rehabilitation of an old apartment building at 316; and at 334 another example of successful rehabilitation, set behind a lovely garden.

1838 and 1835 Orleans Street (340 W)—At Orleans Street, walk north to 1838 and enjoy the ornate, red brick, high-ceilinged, mid-Victorian structure there. An excellent rehabilitation job. Note too, across the street at 1835, the charming old vine-covered townhouse and patio—well maintained.

1817 and 1801 Orleans—Now come back south on Orleans. Note the rehabilitated house at 1817, a 3-story, red brick, pre-Civil War structure. The Orleans apartment building, at 1801, is a rather poor facsimile of a New Orleans facade.

235 Menomonee—Farther east on Menomonee stands a daring rehabilitation of an apartment building: the 3rd story has been removed in order to give the 2nd-floor living room a ceiling 2 stories high. Excellent!

1802 Lincoln Park West (300 W)—Walk west again on Menomonee and turn north on Lincoln Park West. Stop at 1802—a charming, well-maintained mid-Victorian house, built about 1880. The brick wall and fine old trees make a delightful pattern.

1814 and 1816 Lincoln Park West—Farther north in the same block you come to 2 red brick, high-ceilinged houses in fine condition—surely the result of *tender, loving care!*

1826-34 Lincoln Park West—A row of 2-story, red brick townhouses set back from the building line. Designed by Louis Sullivan, these homes have a special charm, due partly to the terra-cotta ornamentation and good landscaping.

1836-38 Lincoln Park West—The showpiece in this group is the brick-and-frame Swiss-type house at 1838, which has unusually heavy wood ornament above the first floor. In a garden at the rear are 2 more brick houses, the one at 1836 having once been the home of Charles Wacker, first chairman of the Chicago Plan Commission—for whom Wacker Drive was named (see Walks No. 9 and No. 10). The 2-story frame house with a garden to the north is another example of how a well-maintained house can be kept livable and delightful.

1830-38 Lincoln Avenue—Turn to your right at Lincoln Avenue and walk southeast to see the 5 houses from 1830 to 1838. A walk in the alley to the rear is most rewarding, for they all have delightful rear patios. At the time of the Old Town Art Fair, held the second week in June each year, these patios are opened to the public.

1848 Lincoln Park West—Now return to Lincoln Park West, and continue north to 1848, to see another example of remarkable rehabilitation. The vertical brickwork at the center of the bay window carries all the way from grade to roof for a stunning effect.

1915 and 1917 Lincoln Park West—Still farther north, 2 fascinating rehabilitated townhouses. Although they were remodeled about 10 years ago, the work seems still fresh.

Ogden Mall—Named Ogden Mall as part of the Department of Urban Renewal's exciting new plan for the closing of Ogden Avenue, this new pedestrian mall is only partially completed. It is a diagonal thoroughfare, for which the portion to be closed extends from Clark Street on the east to North Avenue, about a mile to the southwest. When completed, it will be the major axis of a green belt connecting Lincoln Park to the residential community to the west.

Lincoln Park Tower—1960 Lincoln Park West. Architects: Dubin, Dubin, Black, and Moutoussamy (1967)

This apartment building has a first-rate design. It includes swimming pool and restaurant at the lobby level. It is well sited with respect to Lincoln Park and Ogden Mall.

Lincoln Park Tower.

Walk-20

The Farm-in-the-Zoo
on Lincoln Park's
South Pond.

1. Chicago Historical Society
2. Ira Couch Tomb
3. Farm in the Zoo
4. David Kennison Boulder
5. Chicago Academy of Science
6. Viking Ship
7. Children's Zoo
8. Francis W. Parker School
9. Main Zoo
10. Zoorookery
11. Lincoln Park Conservatory
12. Casting Pond
13. Alexander Hamilton Statue

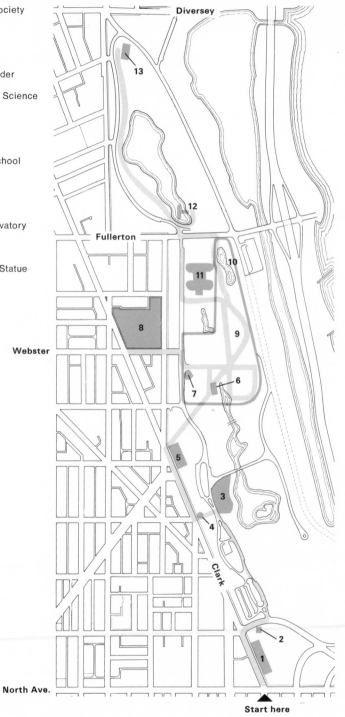

Diversey

Fullerton

Webster

Clark

North Ave.

Start here

Walk · 20

LINCOLN PARK : Museums, Zoos, Conservatory

WALKING TIME: 1½-2 hours (more if you want to enter the museums). HOW TO GET THERE: Take a northbound CTA bus No. 36 (Broadway) on Dearborn Street (1 block west of State Street), and get off at North Avenue (1600 N) and Clark Street.

Lincoln Park, like New York's Central Park, was designed by the landscape architect Frederick Law Olmsted. It is Chicago's largest park, covering some 1,000 acres of land just off the lake all the way from North Avenue (1600 N) to Hollywood (5700 N). This walk, however, will take you only through the southern part, no farther than Diversey Avenue (2800 N). In this section you are in the old Lincoln Park, as it was before the various northern extensions—on land redeemed from the lake—were added. And here you will find practically all of the park's special attractions.

At the southernmost border, where Dearborn Street ends at Lincoln Park, a rugged bronze figure of Abraham Lincoln stands to greet you, ignoring the very adequate bench behind him—despite its distinguished designer, Stanford White. This Lincoln statue, by Augustus St. Gaudens, is only one of nearly 30 large, miscellaneous statues in Lincoln Park—of such disparate personages as Garibaldi, Hans Christian Andersen, Beethoven, Shakespeare, John Peter Altgeld, and Emanuel Swedenborg. Perhaps the 2 most unexpected in this locale are the large nude figure of Goethe and the conventional equestrian statue of Ulysses S. Grant, though he appears not at all in *Grant* Park, where St. Gaudens' *seated Lincoln* is the main attraction (See Walk No. 1, Michigan Avenue: South).

Chicago Historical Society—
North Avenue and Clark Street.
Architects: Graham, Anderson, Probst, and White (1925)

Only a few steps away from the Lincoln statue is—appropriately —the Chicago Historical Society, especially famous for its

Lincoln and Civil War materials. It has occupied this building—a 2-story brick structure with a well-proportioned Georgian facade—less than 40 years, but the Society was organized well over a hundred years ago, in 1856. It is currently in the process of securing funds for much-needed extra space. In referring to the building addition, now scheduled for completion in 1970, Andrew McNally III, president of the Society, told the trustees:

> The planned addition to our building will provide space for our collections, space for new exhibits, space for handling school children, and space for us to conduct lively and exciting programs.

To anyone interested in this country's history, a visit to the museum is already a "lively and exciting" experience. The past comes vividly to life through dramatic displays, period rooms, costumes of famous Americans, and a collection of early autos and horsedrawn vehicles, as well as through the exhibits of manuscripts, paintings, prints, and maps. Seasonal contributions by the museum are an old-fashioned Christmas tree and an old-fashioned Fourth-of-July celebration with a reading of the Declaration of Independence, speech and band and fireworks. Old Hollywood films are sometimes shown Sunday afternoons.

Open daily 9:30 A.M. to 4:30 P.M.; Sundays and holidays 12:30 to 5:30 P.M. Children and teachers always free; other adults, 25¢ on Sundays and holidays.

Just north of the Chicago Historical Society, with its records of the city by the lake and of the people who made the records, is the tomb of one of those historic people—Ira Couch. Ironically, the rather small Couch Mausoleum is often overlooked, though its presence is proof that the Couch family won a lawsuit against the city to keep it here when the city cemetery was discontinued and the graves moved to private cemeteries. Ira Couch, originally a small tailor, became in 1836 one of Chicago's pioneer hotel owners—the proprietor of the Tremont House, then located at the northwest corner of Lake and Dearborn streets. The only other reminder of the park's earlier function is a boulder farther north, placed by the Sons and Daughters of the American Revolution over the grave of David Kennison, the last participant in the Boston Tea Party to die—in 1852, when he was 115 years old!

Lincoln Park Zoo, favorite haunt of thousands of Chicago's children, is actually 3 zoos—the Farm-in-the-Zoo and the Children's Zoo, as well as the century-old main zoo of the traditional kind. Children will be delighted to find the *Farm-in-the-Zoo* just a short walk from the Lincoln statue, through the underpass to the north. Although originated as a way of familiarizing city children with the farm animals they never see, it has proved equally fascinating to children coming in from the country. You will find here not only the smaller animals of farm life—chickens, ducks, and geese; pigs and sheep—but horses and cows as well. In the dairy barn are cows for milking and in another are beef cattle. In still a 3rd barn, recently added along with the beef cattle barn, horses are on display. The milking parlor in the dairy barn with all its modern equipment may not seem natural to a generation old enough to remember watching the "hired hand" squirt the milk from the cow into a big open pail (now considered unsanitary), occasionally aiming a stream into the mouth of a waiting cat beside him. But the present generation of course finds the farm machinery—milking machines and tractors and all the rest—more natural and more interesting.

In the main barn are many exhibits and demonstrations. There you can see samples of what is actually produced on a farm and learn how many ways they are used. You can also watch the process of manufacturing a number of things that are made from from products or especially needed on the farm—fertilizer, leather, or soap, for instance. Eventually, the Lincoln Park Zoological Society hopes, the Farm-in-the-Zoo will have 6 buildings.

Open daily 9:45 A.M. to 5:00 P.M. Free.

Across the road from the Farm In The Zoo is the *David Kennison Boulder* (already referred to), which marks the grave of the last survivor of the Boston Tea Party group, who—unexpectedly—died in Chicago.

Chicago Academy of Sciences—2001 North Clark.

The 2nd museum in Lincoln Park is the Chicago Academy of Sciences, a small natural history museum, which stands just one block north of the David Kennison Boulder, west of the farm. Founded in 1857, only one year after the founding of the Chicago Historical Society, this is the city's oldest museum, in fact the oldest *scientific* museum in the west. Here too Chicago's past is brought vividly to life—a past, however, long antedating anything you may have seen in the Chicago Historical Society's exhibits. For here you may walk through a section that reproduces Chicago of 350 million years ago—when it was only part of a coal forest! And a series called "Chicago Environs" presents dioramas showing animals and plants that flourished here when the area was still open prairie.

Officially the Matthew Laflin Memorial, this building is a real tribute to one of Chicago's early businessmen. Matthew Laflin came to Chicago in the 1830's, having sold out his business in the east to a man by the name of du Pont! He started one of the first stock yards in Chicago, near enough the hotel he had built to synchronize the 2 businesses. Another of his business ventures in Chicago was a bus line—which he later sold to somebody by the name of Parmelee! This restless innovator shared an ambition with many other early Chicago leaders—to rest at last in the city's cemetery with an imposing monument above him. Like many others he was distressed when the graves and monuments there were moved and Lincoln Park substituted. Unlike the others, however, he found a magnificent solution. Though he couldn't be *buried* where he had hoped to be, he *could* have an impressive monument there. That monument is the building of the Chicago Academy of Sciences, for which he provided $75,000—the Chicago Park District supplementing this with $25,000 from its own budget. The interior is currently being remodeled, but the Romanesque exterior still stands as a worthy memorial indeed for one of Chicago's earliest successful businessmen.

Viking Ship, Children's Zoo and Main Zoo.

Farther on, just west of South Pond's northern end is the *Viking Ship*, one of the historic carry-overs from the 1893 Columbian Exposition. This is the very boat—a copy of a 10th-century Viking ship—that was built by Norway at that time and sailed across the Atlantic with a crew of 12 men who brought official greetings from their country to the citizens of Chicago.

Toward the north end of South Pond during the summer months is the *Children's Zoo*, exhibiting all the baby

Opposite, Chicago Academy of Sciences.

204

205

animals that were born at the Zoo during the previous winter and spring. If you arrive at feeding time, you may see baby cubs drinking from bottles and perhaps some chimpanzees in high chairs eating with spoons!

Open daily 10:00 A.M. to 5:00 P.M.

The main *Lincoln Park Zoo* is the park's biggest exhibit. Now nearly a century old, it occupies 25 acres of the park's total acreage and is maintained by the Chicago Park District. The Zoo is said to have more than 2600 different kinds of animals, birds, and reptiles, representing a good cross-section of animal life. The schedule of feeding hours suggests some of the variety: starting at the monkey house at 1:00 P.M., or 11:00 A.M. in summer, it moves to the sea lions, then to the bird houses; on to the bears, wolves, and foxes; then to the small mammal house, and finally ends up at the lion house at 4:00 P.M., except Mondays. (The animal feeders can probably tell you when the reptiles are fed and why the lions are neglected on Mondays!)

In the *Zoorookery,* a specialty at the Lincoln Park Zoo, land and water birds make their home in a large attractive rock garden, and are free to come and go as they like.

Zoo hours: daily 9:00 A.M. to 5:00 P.M.; Saturdays, Sundays, and holidays 10:00 A.M. to 6:00 P.M.

Lincoln Park Conservatory—Just beyond the outdoor cages of the Zoo lies the Lincoln Park Conservatory, covering 3 acres of land. Its glass walls and roof protect a seemingly infinite collection of plants. The show houses, some of which date back to 1891, display a large collection of potted palms, a fernery, and a bit of real tropics where tropical fruit trees are propagated. (The Conservatory has 18 propagating houses, which may sometimes be seen by a visitor.) A Japanese garden comforts the old-timer—somewhat—for the loss of the outdoor Japanese garden that for years decorated a small island in Jackson Park, one of the reminders of the 1893 Columbian Exposition.

Four annual exhibits have become traditional: a show of azaleas in February and March, of lilies and spring plants in April, chrysanthemums of course in November, and poinsettias and Star of Bethlehem in December and January.

206

This is considered one of the finest conservatories in the country. Incidentally, most of the flowers that appear in Chicago's numerous parks are started in the greenhouses connected with this conservatory.

Open daily 9:00 A.M. to 5:00 P.M. Free.

Don't overlook the park's outdoor gardens near the conservatory—Grandmother's Garden, water-lily ponds, fountains, and formal gardens.

And did you remember to toss a coin—for luck—into one of the Conservatory's pools or little waterfalls?

Francis W. Parker School—330 Webster Avenue (2200 North). Architects: Holabird and Root (1962)

Before continuing in the park, cross Lincoln Park West at Webster Avenue (2200 N) to see the Francis W. Parker School. This U-shaped, 3-story, hard-burned red brick structure replaced an ancient 4-story half-timber Tudor Gothic building constructed in the early 1900's.

An outstanding independent private school (prekindergarten through 12th grade) this was one of the first progressive schools in the country, following the creative teaching concepts of John Dewey and Francis Parker. This is the school that brought a cow to graze in the front yard, so that city children could have some touch of experience with the country. (This was in the days before the Farm in the Zoo at Lincoln Park across the street.) Visitors sometimes question the wisdom of the overall architectural plan—placing the building on the Clark Street side of the property and leaving the side facing the park, which is some of the most valuable land in Chicago, for a play field. The school's board of trustees, however, who are as progressive as its policies, agreed to allow the green belt from the park to continue to Clark Street as its contribution to the community.

In a delightful courtyard facing south you will see a reflection pool, flower garden, and stainless steel sculpture by Abbott Pattison. This charming setting is often the background for school functions, such as plays, receptions, and other ceremonies. The brick wall separating the courtyard from the play field contains some original terra-cotta plaques from the razed Garrick Theatre

207

Building designed by Louis Sullivan—first known as the Schiller Building, which stood at 64 West Randolph until its demolition in 1961. (The Second City theater group also used stones from this building. See Walk Number 36.)

Lincoln Park's Casting Pond—Statues of Linné, Jefferson, and Altgeld.   Before you cross Fullerton Avenue, be sure to note the heroic-scale limestone statue of a male figure with 4 female figures at the 4 corners of the pedestal. The male figure is the 18th-century Swedish botanist Carl von Linné.

Farther north, along Stockton Drive just beyond Fullerton, lies Lincoln Park's North Pond, the *casting* pond for the use of anyone interested in developing that particular fisherman's skill. And just beyond the casting pond and ball-playing areas stands a golden statue of Alexander Hamilton, erected in 1952, designed by the architect Samuel Marx. (See also Walk No. 24.) This is the northernmost point in your walk. If you go over to the statue and up onto the plaza on which it is mounted, you will have a rewarding view—the Elks Memorial to the west (see Walk No. 24); To the north, the direction that Hamilton himself is facing, and slightly east, is a bronze figure of John Peter Altgeld, governor of Illinois not long after the Haymarket Riots (see Walk No. 32), who lost his political career but gained eternal fame for his courageous integrity in freeing the men he was convinced were unjustly charged with the bomb throwing on that dark day. To the east you will see the Diversey Yacht Club, and to the south (if you are willing to turn your back on the great gentleman!) a panoramic view of Chicago's always impressive skyline.

Pickwick Village
Apartments.

209

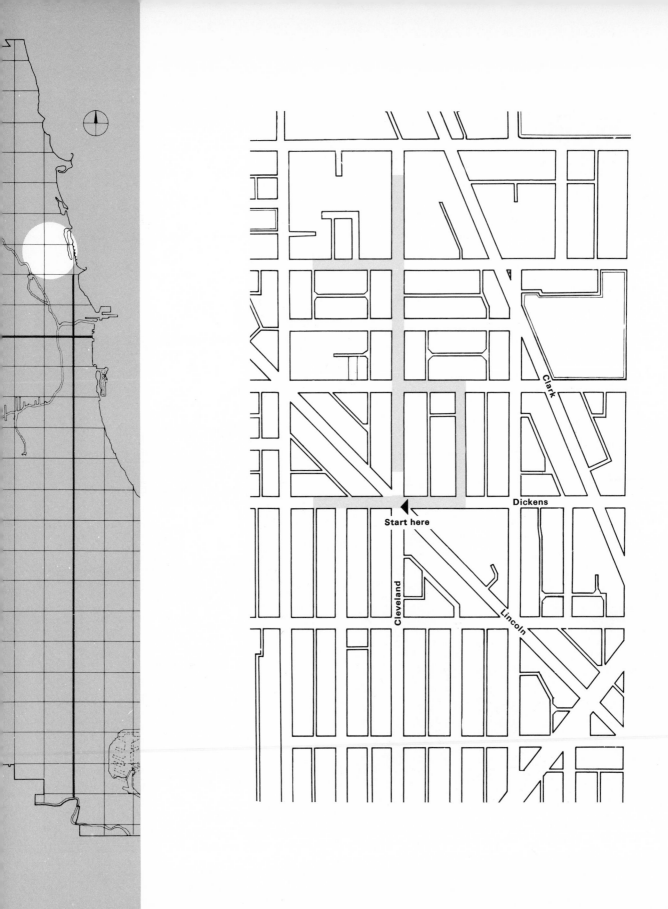

Clark

Dickens

Start here

Cleveland

Lincoln

Walk · 21

LINCOLN PARK CONSERVATION AREA :
Dickens, Hudson, Cleveland, and Belden Avenues

WALKING TIME: 1½ hours.   HOW TO GET THERE: Take a northbound CTA bus No. 10
(Lincoln-Larrabee) on Wells Street (4 blocks west of State). Get off at Dickens (2100 N)
and walk west on the south side of the street.

You are now in the heart of the Lincoln Park Conservation
area, where many improvements have been made and are still
taking place. The city through urban renewal *and* the citizens
through active participation in planning and cooperation with the
city have produced an outstanding program for the rehabilitation
of the entire 3-square-mile area. The little sign "LPCA" that
you see on windows or doors stands for Lincoln Park
Conservation Association and—being interpreted—means:
"We believe in the future of our area and are willing to work and
fight for it if necessary." (One of the ways the LPCA works for
the future of the area is by raising funds at a Puppetry Fair, held
annually the first weekend in October at the Francis W. Parker
School, 330 West Webster.)

Note first the new brick parkways and recently planted
trees, especially if you recall this area as it used to be—muddy
or dusty, where grass never grew.

The walk will take you around a number of streets in the area
where you can see interesting results of the conservation efforts.
Dickens, Hudson, Cleveland, and Belden avenues have been
selected, because along these streets—in close walking distance
of each other—are outstanding examples of architectural
rehabilitation. So many houses have been remodeled successfully
here that comment cannot possibly be made on each. What is
chiefly significant is that so much good remodeling *has been
done* and in the process has upgraded a whole area to the
point of enormous charm, grace, and vitality.

Pickwick Village—515-29 Dickens. Architect: Stanley Tigerman
(1965)   Stop first at a new structure called Pickwick Village on
the corner of Mohawk at 515-29 Dickens—a complex of eight

3-story townhouses on an open court with shrubbery and a piece of abstract sculpture. Each house has a rear patio screened off from neighbors and passersby. An off-street parking area is provided. This is a well-planned housing group, which blends with its older neighbors but still has the advantage of newer facilities.

Dickens Square—550-54 Dickens.   On the north side of the street, farther west, is an example of fine rehabilitation, not only of individual buildings but of a whole development. Six old structures, which had been in deplorable condition for years, were successfully restored to the original appearance of their exteriors and rehabilitated inside. *At 550* the center of the first 2 stories is effectively treated with glass from floor to ceiling. Gardens, patios, and open courts have been grouped around the buildings. The entire development is enclosed by a red brick wall with a series of arches, providing rhythm—as well as privacy—to this enclosure of 19th-century gentility.

540 Dickens—Architect: Arthur Carrarra (1959)   Now come back east to 540 Dickens. The exterior of this house (painted white) has been remodeled, with its entrance placed at grade instead of at the former 2nd-floor location. The style of General Grant's period has been retained outside, while the interior has been made contemporary with new lighting, new fixtures, and new central fireplace. Charming gardens can be viewed from the street over the old iron picket fence.

2100 Hudson (432 W)—Architects: Booth and Nagle (1968)   Now walk east to Lincoln Avenue at Cleveland, continue one block to Hudson, and head north. This is a quiet short block of charming, old, well-maintained houses owned by professional writers, painters, and sculptors. The contemporary character of one *new* group of 6 townhouses, at 2100, is shown by the trim, clean lines.

Policeman Bellinger's Cottage—2121 Hudson. Architect: William W. Boyington (before 1871)   On the east side of the street, a plaque on the building at 2121 states: "This is Policeman Bellinger's Cottage, saved by heroic effort from Chicago Fire of October 1871." It is clear that even heroic efforts could not save many houses, for the majority in this area were built after 1871. Note how well maintained the houses are at *2115-17* and at *2116-18* across the street. At *2127 and 2131* are examples of charming and successful rehabilitation.

2134-38 Hudson—On the west side of the street are some
restored and remodeled townhouses, grouped around a
well-landscaped courtyard, very well maintained.
Now return to Cleveland Avenue.

2111-21 Cleveland (500 W)—Walk west to Cleveland, then turn
south to see the group of 4-story red brick former townhouses at
2111-21, now successfully converted into apartment buildings.
The below-grade patio at 2111-15, with marble floors and stone
walls, adds charm to the exterior. The original entrance doors
and roof cornices have been refinished. New glass panels at the
below-grade apartment give the structure an air of modernity.

2114 and 2116 Cleveland—On the west side of the street, at
2114 and 2116, are 2 red brick townhouses constructed about
1880. Wooden bay, turret windows, and a mansard roof make
this remodeled apartment building very attractive.

2125 Cleveland—On the east side again, excellent rehabilitation
work in the facade at 2125—yellow brick at the first floor and
stained pinewood at the second floor, with a balcony and glass
panel doors that reach from floor to ceiling.

2124 Cleveland—Across the street, at 2124, is a red brick,
mid-Victorian house built about 1880, with delightfully slender
white Doric columns at the entrance and balcony overhead, and a
mansard roof, with fascinating iron picket work at the roof peak.
This building has been remodeled into apartments
with no loss of the original charm.

2129-31 Cleveland—Architect: Richard Barringer (1958)   Two
townhouses of red brick with bay windows and entrances at
grade, instead of at the second floor as they were before
remodeling. The exterior facades retain most of the original dour
appearance, but the interiors have been done over successfully.

2137-39-41 Cleveland—Still another series of old townhouses
successfully remodeled into apartments—3 ivy-covered houses
of brick and stone. Here too, new entrances at grade replace the
former 2nd-floor entrances; yet the charm and general character
of the old facades have been retained.

455 Grant Place (2232 N)—At the corner of Cleveland and Grant Place is a newly constructed 3-story apartment building of hard-burned brick, built around an open court. The court entrances are below grade in a patio facing Grant. This is a well-planned complex that blends with the surrounding, older structures.

2215 Cleveland—Architect: Bruce Graham (1969)   Here is a stunning example of a well-designed urban townhouse— two-story, monolithic concrete, including a walled-in garden that completely encloses the site. There are travertine marble walks, and a black steel bar gate.

2234-36 Cleveland—A 3-story frame duplex townhouse. The brick face on the grade level and wood siding at 2nd- and 3rd-floor levels are painted gray. Black and white trim around windows and white Corinthian columns at entrance complete this charming, very old structure, built around 1874.

515 Belden (2300 N)—At Belden turn west to 515, where there is a complex of about twenty 2-story townhouses built around an open court. Although fairly well designed, the density is much too high and can only result in noise, traffic, and neghborhood congestion in general.

534 Belden—On the other side of the street, farther west, are some red brick townhouses remodeled into apartments. From the white limestone and glass entrances to the new balcony at the former entrance, this is a most successful enterprise.

538-544 Belden—A marvelous old sandstone apartment building. The remodeling includes metal grillwork on the balcony, black trim around doors and windows, and a black cornice on the ornate roof—for a most attractive effect.

2325 Cleveland—Back on Cleveland Avenue, at 2325, you will see a 3-story house painted gray, set back from the street, with an iron picket fence. A square bay window and roof turret give this 1880 house a definite stamp of individuality.

In considering that changes that have been made in this area, it is well to note that certain basic ingredients are essential to the success of extensive rehabilitation in any given area:

1. The area involved should be near schools, transportation, and recreational facilities.
2. The physical work required for rehabilitation must be feasible and then done well.
3. There must be a market that will pay the inevitably higher rents.

The Lincoln Park Conservation area meets all 3 of these requirements. Both this fact and the determination and dedication of its residents have contributed to its conspicuous success.

2234-36 Cleveland.

Walk-22

Arthur J. Schmitt
Academic Center,
DePaul University.

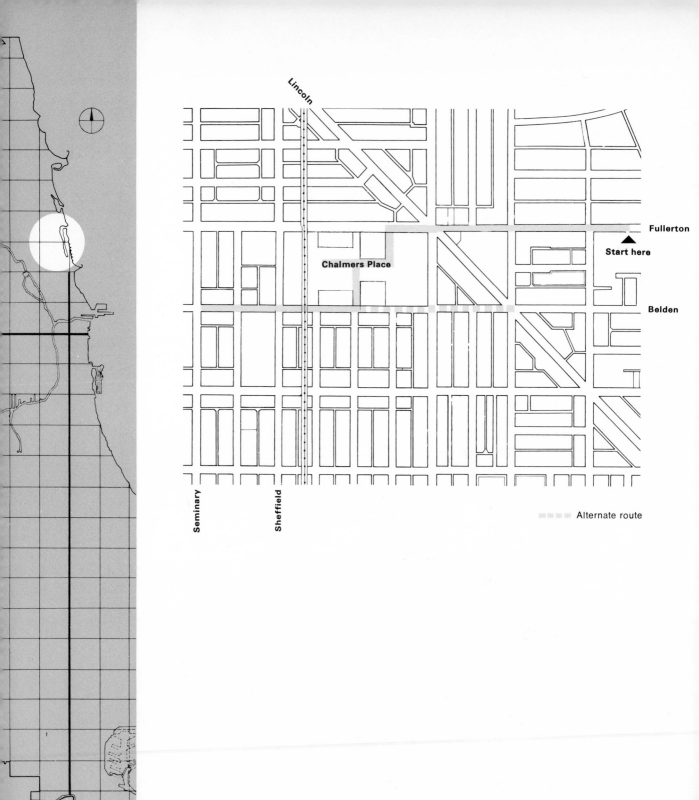

Lincoln

Fullerton

Start here

Chalmers Place

Belden

Seminary

Sheffield

▪ ▪ ▪ ▪ Alternate route

Walk · 22

FULLERTON AVENUE, McCORMICK SEMINARY, DePAUL UNIVERSITY

WALKING TIME: About 1½ hours.   HOW TO GET THERE: Take a northbound CTA bus
No. 22 (Clark Street) on Dearborn Street (1 block west of State). Get off at Fullerton Avenue
(2400 N). Walk west to Cleveland Avenue (500 W), where this walk starts.

The community you will enter now is most fortunate in having
several exceptionally fine institutions in its midst. A walk through
the area will quickly demonstrate the pride with which these
institutions and the people regard their community—a factor
essential to success in almost any community conservation effort.

This walk will take you primarily to institutions of learning
or healing, and through their campuses, but you will also
come to pleasant walking areas with many interesting
old townhouses en route.

Cenacle Retreat House—513 West Fullerton.

After the first 2 blocks on Fullerton, going west from Clark
Street (which are not the most exhilarating part of the walk), you
will come to a number of points of interest. You will pass a large
convent, the Cenacle Retreat House, constructed in 1965 of
hard-burned brick; it is an imposing, well-maintained
addition to the community.

St. Paul's Church and Parish House—
Of the Evangelical and Reformed Church (United
Church of Christ), 655 Fullerton.

The buildings at 655 Fullerton were erected in 1950, after a
large fire had destroyed the earlier church and parish house of
St. Paul's. The design is modified Spanish Romanesque, with red
brick and stone trim. The tall, well-proportioned spire, which is
well located, gives the church the proper, much-needed
height. The buildings relate well to each other,
for the site planning is good.

219

Children's Memorial Hospital—2300 Children's Plaza.
Architects: Schmidt, Garden, and Erikson (1961)

At 700 Fullerton is the nationally known Children's Memorial
Hospital—official address, 2300 Children's Plaza. This is one of
the various hospitals served by Northwestern University's
Medical School. (See Walk No. 7, Lake Shore Drive) The design
of the hospital building, which was developed at various
stages by the same architects, is strong but not too severe.

McCormick Theological Seminary—
800 West Belden.
Architects for recent additions:
Holabird and Root (1965, 1968)

Cross Halsted and continue west to the McCormick Theological
Seminary, on a completely enclosed 20-acre campus stretching
from Fullerton back south to Belden, and from Halsted on west
to Sheffield. This Presbyterean seminary has been educating
students for the ministry since 1859. Just walk west on Fullerton
to the first entrance gate with an opening for pedestrians,
and take a little time to enjoy this beautiful campus. Note
especially the new classroom building (1965) and the McGow
Memorial Library (1968), both designed by Holabird and Root.
The architecture of the McClure Memorial Chapel (1961), which
is Georgian, is in contrast of course with the contemporary
design of the 2 buildings just named, though it was also designed
by Holabird and Root. There is no jarring effect, however,
because the site planning is first-rate and the space is adequate.

Chalmers Place (900 W)—part of McCormick
Theological Seminary campus.

Now turn west and stroll around Chalmers Place, a private
square. In this pleasant green area, comparable to Louisburg
Square in Boston, are 3-story 19th-century townhouses facing
on the north and south sides of the Place. To the west is the
limestone Commons building of the Seminary, in collegiate
Gothic, with dining halls and conference rooms. And to the
west of the Commons is a second green space and square, with a
student dormitory, an apartment building for married students,
and a gymnasium. (To the east are the school buildings,
already described.)

DePaul University—Lincoln Park Campus, 2323 North Seminary.

Now return to the McCormick Seminary chapel; walk south to Belden, then west under the L tracks to DePaul University's Lincoln Park Campus—official address 2323 North Seminary (1100 W). (DePaul University also operates a downtown branch, at 25 East Jackson.)

The first building of interest here is *Alumni Hall, 1011 West Belden*, a huge limestone building with granite base, which houses the University's athletic center.

An outstanding structure on the University's newly expanded campus (DePaul is undergoing tremendous growth and expansion of facilities) is the *Arthur J. Schmitt Academic Center, at Belden and Seminary avenues (architects: C. F. Murphy and Associates, 1967)*. This is an imposing concrete building with 6 floors of classrooms, offices, and seminar rooms. By raising the entrance level well above the street, the architects have given this structure an imposing approach and the effect of great height. The cantilevering of the upper level will remind you of the Blue Cross - Blue Shield building, also designed by C. F. Murphy Associates. (See Walk No. 3, Dearborn Street.)

Some day, when the surrounding area is cleared for campus purposes, the Center will have an even more imposing appearance.

If you desire, a stroll eastward on Belden Avenue to Lincoln Avenue will be most rewarding. You will see several art galleries and unusual taverns along Lincoln Avenue. The famous John Barleycorn Tavern is well worth a visit. You will find there a most unusual decor, serious music, and color slides of great works of art.

Walk-23

North Side of
Fullerton Avenue.

Lakeview

Demming

Roslyn

Start here

Orchard

Fullerton

Clark

Walk · 23

DEMING PLACE AND NEARBY STREETS

WALKING TIME: 1 hour.   HOW TO GET THERE: Take a northbound CTA bus No. 76
(Diversey) on Wabash or a No. 153 (Wilson-Michigan) on State. Get off at Roslyn Place
(2500 N) at the edge of Lincoln Park, and walk 2 blocks north to Deming Place (2534 N). If you
are driving, you will find parking space available during the day.

Deming Place and the surrounding streets constitute one of
those pleasant surprises in the heart of a big city—an
area overwhelmingly residential with charming 19th- and early
20th-century townhouses set back from the street, with spacious
lawns and handsome old trees, on streets that curve and can be
really explored only on foot. Walking here is a delight!

Swedish Engineers Society of Chicago—
503 Wrightwood, formerly the Francis J. Dewes House. Architect: Cudell Herez (1964)

First of all, walk west on Deming past the *Columbus Hospital*
and parking lot, and then 1 block north to Wrightwood (2600 N).
There on the corner, at 503 Wrightwood, is the headquarters
of the Swedish Engineers Society of Chicago—a limestone
structure in baroque style, with enormous male and female figures
supporting the upper balcony of wrought iron, a departure from
the exclusively female caryatids of ancient Greek sculpture!
Heavy ornament surrounds the entrance and upper window. A
Mansard roof tops off the building. The annual celebration
December 13 for the crowning of Santa Lucia features superior
smorgasbord and special Swedish entertainment.

Townhouses, Apartment Buildings, and Churches

Although many of the comments that follow may sound
repetitious, you may be sure that the buildings referred to will
not *look* repetitious, for all have a most welcome individuality.

Deming Place

Come back south to Deming Place, passing a contemporary
6-story red brick building with Cor-Ten steel balconies. (For the

use of Cor-Ten steel in Chicago's Civic Center building, see Walk
No. 3, Dearborn Street.) Just west (on Deming) is a 4-story
high-ceilinged apartment building of the late 19th century. Across
the street is a row of 3-story, stone-front townhouses in Tudor
Gothic style, also of the late 19th century, well maintained.

St. Clement's Roman Catholic Church—642 Deming.

Cross Clark Street (which runs NW in this part of the city)
and continue west on Deming. Here the street starts to curve and
the buildings are set back farther from the street. The lawns
seem actually greener and the trees bigger and shadier! Continue
west to Orchard Street (700 W). At the corner of Deming and
Orchard stands St. Clement's Roman Catholic Church, just
beyond St. Clement's Convent, at 622. French Romanesque, with
limestone facade and a rose window over the entrance, this
church has a pleasant surprise awaiting visitors who go inside.
Above the spot where the apse and transept meet is a
dome with mosaic tile figures that give the viewer a
feeling of being in the 11th or 12th century.

Geneva Terrace (600 W)—Retrace your steps back east to
Geneva Terrace, and turn south. Here, unexpectedly, are again

Opposite, St. Clement's Church.
Left, Window detail, 2438 Orchard
Street.

227

some 19th-century townhouses with gardens and trees. *At 2461 Geneva* note the small house at the rear of the garden—built in pre-Civil War style.

Arlington Place (2440 N)—When you reach Arlington Place, walk east *to 525.* Note the pristine red-brick and stone facade with white wooden Ionic columns, all in good scale. This also reflects the style of the period before the Civil War.

Fullerton Avenue (2400 N)

Return to Geneva Terrace and continue south to Fullerton Avenue. West on Fullerton is an entire block of 19th-century townhouses. As you walk back east, note in particular these examples, all on the north side of the street:

646   A 3-story brick house.
638   A typically 19th-century house with bay window.
618   A 3-story house completely covered with ivy.

At the corner of this block you come to the *Lincoln Park Presbyterian Church,* a limestone structure in Romanesque style, old and well maintained. In the next block east on Fullerton are several more 19th-century townhouses, set back about 25 feet, with well-kept lawns and trees. *At 530 Fullerton* is the *Episcopal Church of Our Savior,* a charming structure of the late 19th century, in English Romanesque design.

Nordica Apartment Building—458 West Fullerton.   Still farther east, *at 458,* is a 4-story, high-ceilinged apartment building with a limestone facade and beautiful front lawn, all well maintained. This is a large building, extending half a block on Fullerton and half a block around the corner on Clark Street.

Lake View Avenue (400 W)—

2400 Lake View Avenue Building.
Architect: Ludwig Mies van der Rohe (1963)

As you cross Clark Street again, returning east, you come to the most famous building on this walk—at least the building planned by the most famous architect, Ludwig Mies van der Rohe. This is the apartment building at 2400 Lake View Avenue—a handsome structure sheathed in aluminum, with columns exposed at the base and the vertical lines carried by mullions.

Opposite, Swedish Engineer's Society.

228

The luxurious character of the apartments is indicated by the exterior plate glass and the marble walls of the lobby, to say nothing of the swimming pool adjoining the lobby.

Wrigley Mansion—2466 Lake View.

A the corner of Lake View and Arlington avenues, one block north, is the high-ceilinged Wrigley Mansion, a fine old building, well maintained. The exterior has limestone base and brick facade, with brick quoins at the 4 corners and abundant ornamentation at the 3rd-floor level.

Arlington Place

426 Arlington—Walk a few steps west on Arlington, to see another 19th-century townhouse, also well preserved. Observe the brick-and-limestone facade, with arches over the wooden bay windows.

431 Arlington—On the other side of the street, at 431, is a 3-story house with limestone facade and charming wooden bay windows.

438 Arlington—Back on the north side of the street is another 19th-century house, a 3-story Gothic revival in stone.

418 Arlington—And a little farther east, the last stop of this walk, a pleasant old brownstone, well maintained.

Walk-24

The Ryerson family mansion (Harris School).

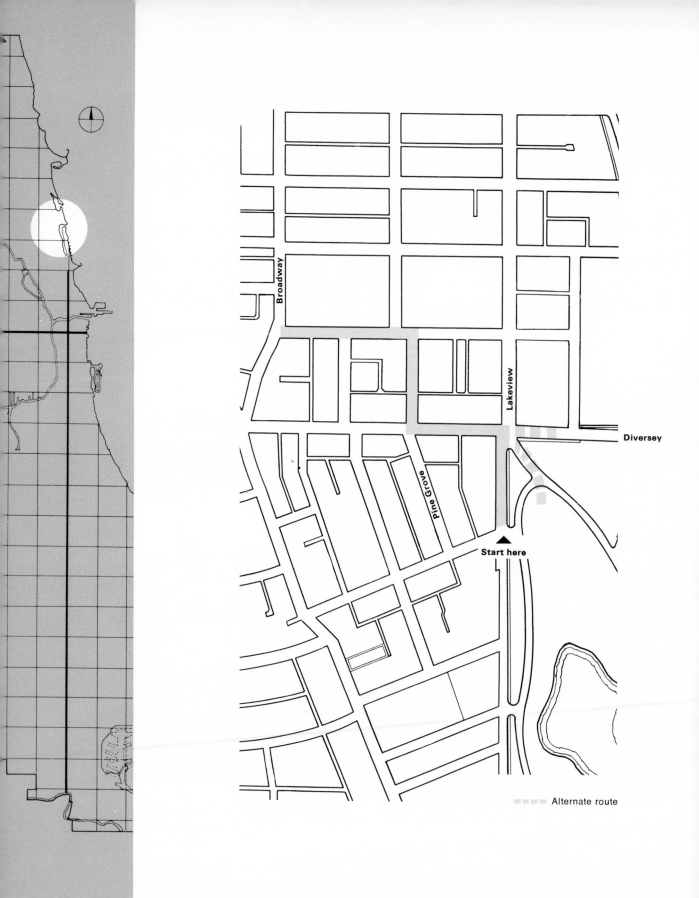

Broadway

Lakeview

Diversey

Pine Grove

▲
Start here

▰▰▰▰ Alternate route

Walk · 24

LAKE VIEW, DIVERSEY, SURF

WALKING TIME: 1 hour.   HOW TO GET THERE: Take a northbound CTA bus No. 76 (Diversey) on Wabash or No. 153 (Wilson-Michigan) on State, and get off at Wrightwood Avenue (2600 N).

Lake View Avenue (400 W)

Start this walk at the corner of Wrightwood and Lake View avenues, and walk north on Lake View.

2700 Lake View—*Architect: David Adler (1920)*   The handsome structure on the west side of Lake View, at 2700, is the former *Ryerson Family Mansion.* (The Ryersons also owned homes on Astor Street. See Walk No. 8, Gold Coast.) The house here on Lake View is said to be a replica of an 18th-century London townhouse. It is now occupied by the Harris School, a private elementary day school.

2704-2708-2710 Lake View—North of the Ryerson Mansion are 3 townhouses, all in the same style and tied together with a common roof and party walls—a characteristic seen in so many of our modern rows of townhouses. A stone base, dark red brick facade, wooden columns painted white, and slightly different ornamentation and details at each entrance give these houses an effect of special charm and grace. Note the delicate transom tracery over the doorways.

Elks National Memorial Building, 2750 Lake View—*Architects: for the main building, Egerton Swartout (1926); for the Magazine Building, Holabird and Root (1967).*   Next, on the same side of the street, is the monumental Elks National Memorial, originally constructed in memory of Elks who had died in World War I. The Memorial building consists of a great central rotunda—75 feet in diameter, 100 feet high—and 2 main wings. The base and columns support the huge dome, which is made up inside of pieces of marble from all over the world. The entrance is—of course!—adorned by 2 bronze elks. The Magazine Building is a recent addition, to provide a place for the many documents of the society. Indiana limestone is used throughout. The Elks Memorial main building is open to visitors daily from 10:00 A.M. to 5:00 P.M.

Diversey (2800 N)

Apartment Buildings—Diversey and Sheridan Road.
Architect: Ludwig Mies van der Rohe (1957)

At the northeast corner of Diversey and Sheridan Road, diagonally across from the Elks Memorial, are 2 aluminum-sheathed tower apartment buildings, designed by Mies van der Rohe and developed by the late Herbert Greenwald. The 2 towers are expertly sited so as to give each apartment a spectacular view. The columns are exposed at the ground level; mullions divide the windows and carry the vertical sweep upwards. The 2 structures have a sculptured, almost poetic quality.

Amalgamated Meat Cutters and Butchers Union Building—
2800 North Sheridan. Architects: E. F. Quinn and
Roy T. Christiansen (1951); (1950-64)

In a 3-story light gray limestone structure is the central office of a large and important trade union, the Amalgamated Meat Cutters and Butcher Workmen of North America. Two sculptured groupings are located on either side of the main entrance. The concept, suggested by the Union's executive director and carried out by the Chicago sculptor Egon Weiner, is made clear by the title—"Brotherhood in Bronze." Each group consists of 4 kneeling figures, representing the 4 races of mankind (often identified as African, American Indian, Asian, and European), all of whom are kneeling as a symbol of man's dependence on a higher power.

Other Sculpture on Diversey

At this end of Diversey Parkway are several other pieces of sculpture. At its eastern terminus in Lincoln Park is an allegorical bronze of Johann Wolfgang von Goethe—a male figure of heroic scale, dedicated in 1913 by the German people of Chicago.

About 100 yards south of the Goethe statue is a sculptured memorial to Alexander Hamilton, the first Secretary of the Treasury of the United States. The figure of Hamilton,

Opposite, Elks' Memorial building.

234

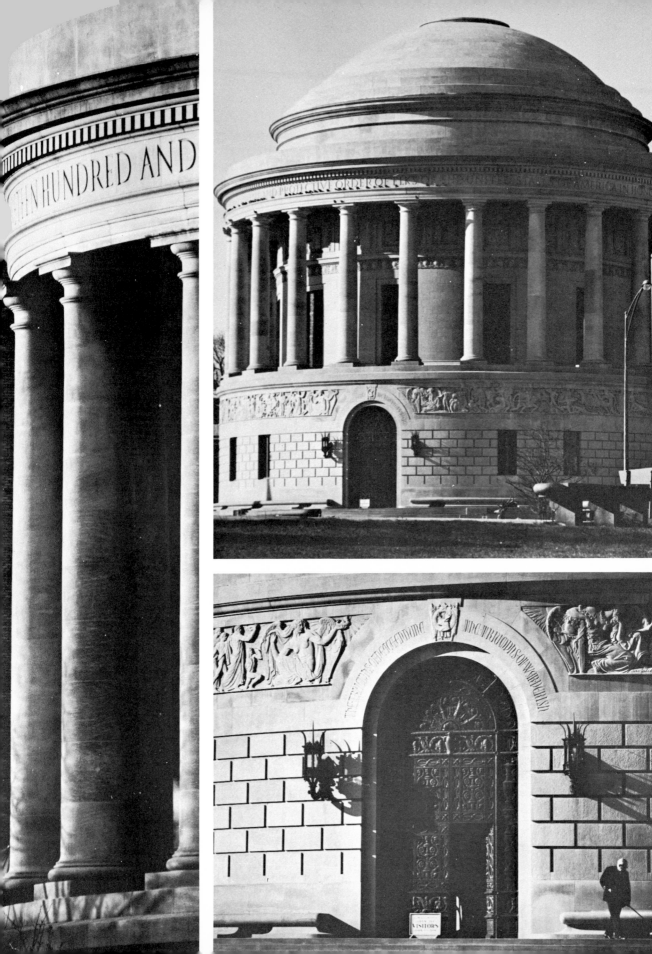

standing erect, though made of bronze is appropriately painted gold; it is mounted on a huge black granite structure, which makes a dramatic contrast. This monument was erected in 1952 from funds supplied in memory of Kate Sturgis Buckingham—the person who herself had left funds for the Buckingham Fountain in Grant Park in memory of her brother. (See Walk No. 1, Michigan Avenue: South.) The memorial was designed by Samuel Marx.

Brewster Apartments—500 West Diversey.
Architect: R. H. Turnock (1893)

Now walk west on Diversey to see a famous old apartment building at the corner of Diversey and Pine Grove (500 W)—the Brewster Apartments. Red polished marble appears at the entrance, and 4 columns at the 1st-floor windows. By all means obtain permission to go inside, for construction of the interior is far more inspiring than you would expect from the exterior. The light court, skylight, open grillwork, and stairways are all handled in a highly individual manner. It seems strange that this architect, who once worked with William LeBaron Jenney, should have produced so remarkable a building only once.

Somehow this 9-story structure, with its high ceilings and bay windows—rugged, rough-faced, built of dark gray granite—seems out of place on the Diversey Avenue of today, which is so crowded, busy, and commercial.

Surf Street (2900 N)

Britton I. Budd Apartments and Green Senior Center—500 Surf.

On Pine Grove, walk north to Surf. The Britton I. Budd Apartments and Green Senior Center, though no great architectural masterpiece, are worth noting because of their function. This remodeled structure, operated by the Chicago Housing Authority, is a mecca for many of the older citizens of the area.

Greenbriar Apartments—550 Surf, and
Commodore Apartments—559 Surf.

Walk west along Surf Street to the corner of Surf and Broadway. Here, on opposite sides of the street, stand 2 huge apartment buildings, which were constructed about 1890—the Greenbriar,

Opposite, Goethe statue opposite Mies van der Rohe apartments, Diversey & Sheridan.

237

at 550, and the Commodore, at 559. These dignified brick structures have open courts, high ceilings, and smooth brick walls. The design of each facade is modified Georgian. Entrances are from Broadway as well as from the courtyards facing Surf. When the sun is in the west, it shines through the lobbies into the courtyards. Both buildings are well maintained, affording tenants excellent living quarters.

This walk has shown you, among other things, quite a variety of apartment buildings—examples of modern architecture, from Mies van der Rohe's to the Chicago Housing Authority's, and 3 buildings dating back to the 1890's: the Brewster, Greenbriar, and Commodore.

3845 Alta Vista.

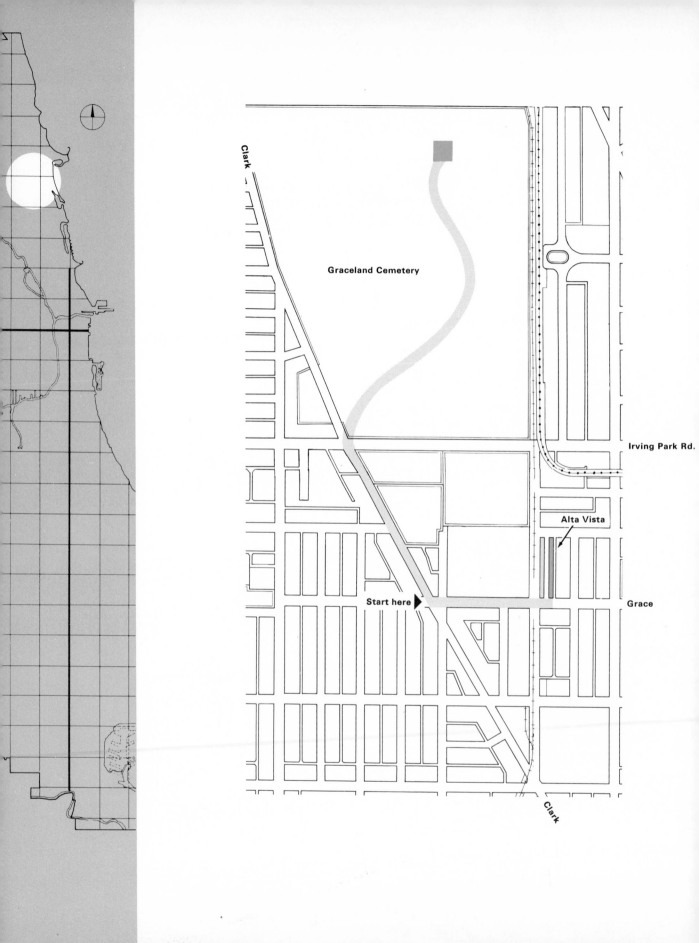

Clark

Graceland Cemetery

Irving Park Rd.

Alta Vista

Start here ▶

Grace

Clark

Walk · 25

ALTA VISTA - GETTY TOMB

WALKING TIME: 1 hour or less.   HOW TO GET THERE: Take a northbound CTA bus
No. 32 (Clark Street) on Dearborn Street. Get off at Grace Street (3800 N). Walk 2 blocks
east, past the House of Good Shepherd Convent, to Alta Vista (1054 W).

This short block has townhouses on both sides of a narrow street, which might be in Boston or Philadelphia or London. It seems to belong to a past century; it is definitely not a street of today. The well-maintained old houses—constructed at one time by one builder, who gave each house an individuality in design—are like an oasis in the surrounding desert of run-down housing. Most of the residents here are friendly and proud of their homes. Some are willing to show them to visitors.

3801—In this house, on the east side of the street, limestone columns surround a wooden entrance in a pleasant eclectic design.

3805—An attempt at classic detail in the facade makes this another eclectic design. Note the stained-glass transom.

3802—On the other side of the street, a classic Georgian facade. The large wooden cornice at the roof line and over the entrance relate well with the bay window of the living room. Good scale.

3812—Another stained-glass transom over the entrance doorway.

3814—A Greek revival facade, with Doric pilasters of wood at the entrance and windows. A wooden cornice at the roof level gives the facade a sense of good scale.

3819—On the east side again, still another stained-glass transom—clearly one of this architect's favorite features. Ionic wood columns at entrance and 2nd-floor windows. A bay window at the first-floor level.

3824—Back on the west side of the street, a limestone facade and bay window. A doorway in natural finish completes this interesting townhouse.

241

3826—An English half-timber facade gives variety to the facades here at the northern end of the street.

3830—An old brick facade of good scale and workmanship.

3845—On the east side again, the last house on this walk, with wooden cornice and red brick trim.

On your return to Grace Street, walk behind the houses on the west side of Alta Vista. You may catch a glimpse here and there of some attractive patios and gardens.

Above, 3824-3826 Alta Vista. *Opposite*, some of the various doorway treatments on Alta Vista.

242

□ **Getty Tomb**—Graceland Cemetery, 4001 North Clark.
Architect: Louis H. Sullivan (1890)

Upon your return to Clark Street, walk north to the Graceland
Cemetery, at 4001, to see the Getty Tomb—one of Sullivan's most
beautiful works. The lower half of this structure is plain,
unadorned stone. The ornamentation of the upper half and of
the bronze doors is exquisite, with the 2 designs well harmonized.
This was proclaimed an Architectural Landmark:

> In recognition of the design which here brings new beauty
> to an age-old form: the tomb. Stone and bronze stand
> transformed in rich yet delicate ornament, a requiem for the
> dead, an inspiration to the living.

You will find the Getty Tomb in the northeast section of the
cemetery, on the west side of the lake. Many famous Chicagoans
are buried in Graceland Cemetery, but the Getty Tomb
transcends in beauty all other monuments there.

Louis Sullivan's Getty Tomb.

244

Arcaded
townhouses,
Pullman.

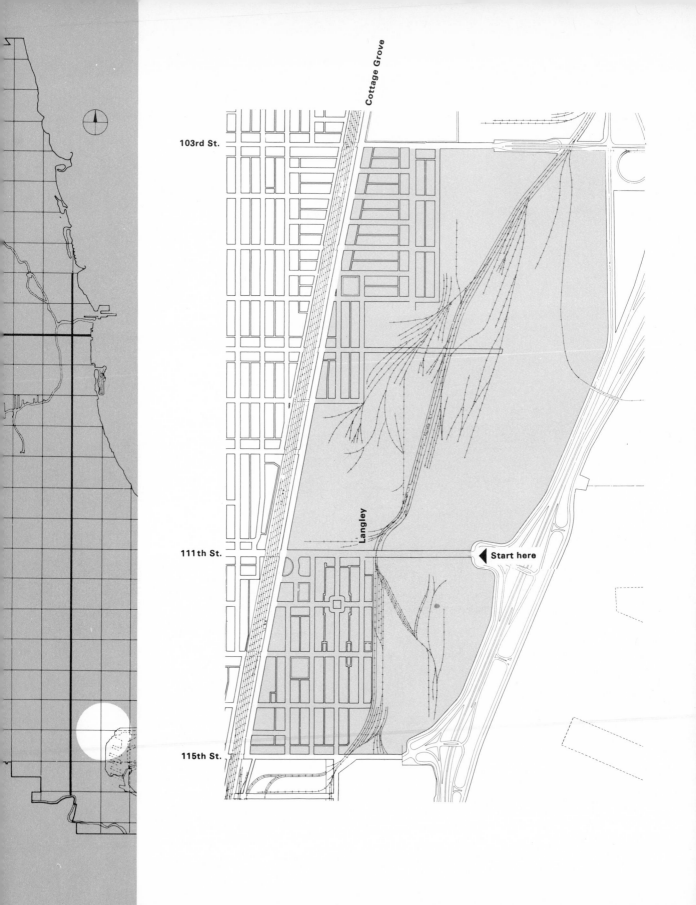

Cottage Grove

103rd St.

Langley

111th St.

◀ **Start here**

115th St.

Walk · 26

PULLMAN

WALKING TIME: 1 hour.   HOW TO GET THERE: Take an Illinois Central (I. C.) suburban
train at Randolph and Michigan (underground station) to Pullman. (Inquire about which train
you should take.) Time—about 30 minutes. If you drive, take the Dan Ryan Expressway-East
to 112th Street, Pullman.

The community of Pullman, near Lake Calumet on Chicago's
Far South Side, was built as a model industrial town by George M.
Pullman, an early Chicago engineer. The town and all its
buildings, one of the first developments in this part of Chicago,
were designed by the architect Solon S. Beman and the landscape
engineer Nathan F. Barrett. In the late 1870's Pullman selected
this site for his Pullman Palace Car Company, which
manufactured his recently devised Pullman railroad cars. (The
first sleeping car was built in 1858, and the Pullman Palace
Car Company, a partnership of George Pullman and Andrew
Carnegie, was formed in 1867.)

For his model company town Pullman bought a long, narrow
triangular tract of land bordering the western shore of
Lake Calumet. Boundaries of the land were 103rd and 115th
streets north and south, Langley and Cottage Grove east and west
—4500 acres of what was then undeveloped prairie in the Village
of Hyde Park (not yet a part of the City of Chicago). The land
was purchased by the Pullman Land Association and the
Pullman Palace Car Company.

The town, which would be served by the Illinois Central
Railroad, was to have all the community facilities near the IC
depot—a hotel, a church, a school, and an arcade building with
stores, offices, library, theatre, and bank—everything owned
of course by the Pullman company. Work began on the Pullman
plants and 1,750 housing units in 1880. Early the next year
the first residents began moving into the 2-story row houses and
the cheaper apartment buildings planned for lower-income
workers. The factories were located north of 111th Street, along
with related enterprises, such as the Pullman Car-Wheel

247

Pullman Works.

248

249

works, the Allen Paper Car-Wheel works, the Pullman Iron and Steel Company, and the Union Foundry.

A walk through Pullman today gives you the sense of visiting an unreal town, though the houses, hotel, and village square are much the same as they looked at the turn of the century—an excellent showcase of town planning principles of the late 19th century. This is not a deserted ghost town (though the Pullman ownership and domination have vanished), but it does seem more like a movie set than an actual part of Chicago. In viewing the Florence Hotel, for example, an elaborate 4-story building with many gables and turrets, you may wonder whether it seemed real even to the Pullman residents of that day and just how much Pullman's workers ever used it. Mr. Pullman himself doubtless entertained there many guests to whom he showed his village with pride.

In this "model town" project Pullman was doubtless motivated partly by philanthropy as understood in his day and partly by enlightened self-interest (though he wouldn't have called it that). He believed that his employees would be happier if they could live near their work, in houses or apartments more attractive than the usual workers' homes, surrounded by all the facilities needed for daily living.

But Pullman's model town failed to bring happiness to his workers. Unrest hit the community—in those days made up mostly of German, Irish, Scandinavian, Scotch, and English descent—because they couldn't own their own homes and they felt that rents and prices in the company-owned store were too high. By 1889, when petitions were filed for the annexation of Hyde Park to Chicago, feeling was so high among the Pullman workers that they voted for annexation over Mr. Pullman's opposition. Still the community remained very much an independent town within the city and for a while it prospered. As orders and production increased in the Pullman plants, more workers settled there, until the population by 1892 included more than 20 nationalities. Additional housing built north of 103rd Street became known as North Pullman.

Real trouble lay ahead, however. The decline of the company town began with the depression of 1893-94, following the great

250

boom Chicago had experienced with the Columbian Exposition of 1893. Unemployment rose and wages dropped, but rents and food prices remained pretty much the same. Mr. Pullman's refusal to restore his employees' wages to their previous figures and his prompt dismissal of several members of a committee that had called on him to discuss the matter precipitated a company-wide strike.

Since some of the workers belonged to the American Railway Union headed by Eugene V. Debs, the strike quickly became a nationwide issue, with an organization called the General Managers Association coming to the support of Pullman. After considerable violence and destruction of property, as well as the workers' refusal to run the trains, President Cleveland sent federal troops to take over—so that the mail could go through. Although at first the president's action caused even greater violence, it ultimately broke the strike. Eugene Debs was thrown in jail and his union weakened to the point of ruin. And Pullman's bitter, defeated workers returned to their jobs on his terms, not theirs. The only victory they won was a decision by the Illinois Supreme Court not long afterward that the Pullman Company's charter did *not* give it the right to own and manage a town. So ended Mr. Pullman's Utopian dream of a perfect village for his workers!

Yet the buildings remain. After 1900 a greater number of Polish, Italian, and Greek immigrants came to Pullman, and older residents began to move out. From 1920 to 1940 the Pullman area remained fairly stable, merely becoming an older community. Residential growth extended into North Pullman as the industry continued to expand, but south of 103rd Street it has been negligible since about 1930. A number of industrial plants have developed in the Pullman area, and the Dan Ryan Expressway now defines the old community's eastern boundary.

Mrs. Thomas H.
Gale house, 6
Elizabeth Court,
Oak Park.

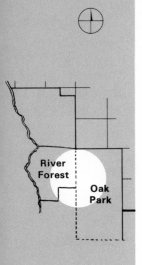

River Forest

Oak Park

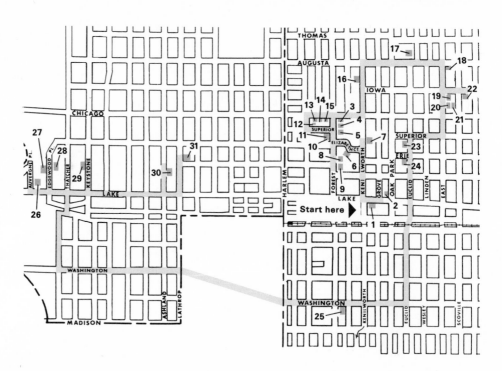

OAK PARK

1. Oak Park Unity Church
   and Parish House
   Lake St. and Kenilworth Av.

2. Memorial Fountain
   on Lake St. near Grove Av.

3. Frank Lloyd Wright House
   428 Forest Av.

4. Dr. W. H. Copeland House
   400 Forest Av.

5. Arthur Heurtley House
   318 Forest Av.

6. Mrs. Thomas H. Gale House
   6 Elizabeth Court

7. H. P. Young House
   334 N. Kenilworth

8. P. A. Beachy House
   238 Forest Av.

9. Frank Thomas House
   210 Forest Av.

10. E. R. Hills House
    313 Forest Av.

11. Nathan G. Moore
    House & Stable
    333 Forest Av.

12. Francis Wooley House
    1030 Superior St.

13. Walter Gale House
    1031 Chicago Av.

14. R. P. Parker House
    1027 Chicago Av.

15. Thomas H. Gale House
    1019 Chicago Av.

16. O. B. Balch House
    611 N. Kenilworth Av.

17. Harry S. Adams House
    170 Augusta Blvd.

18. W. E. Martin House
    636 N. East Avenue

19. H. C. Goodrich House
    534 N. East Av.

20. Edwin H. Cheney House
    520 N. East Av.

21. Rollin Furbeck House
    515 Fair Oaks Av.

22. William G. Fricke House
    540 Fair Oaks Av.

23. Charles E. Roberts Stable
    317 N. Euclid Av.

24. George Furbeck House
    223 N. Euclid Av.

25. George W. Smith House
    404 Home Av.

RIVER FOREST

26. William H. Winslow
    House & Stable
    515 Auvergne Pl.

27. Chauncey L. Williams House
    530 Edgewood Pl.

28. Isabel Roberts House
    603 Edgewood Pl.

29. J. Kibber Ingalls House
    562 Keystone Av.

30. E. Arthur Davenport House
    559 Ashland Av.

31. River Forest Tennis Club
    615 Lathrop Av.

Walk · 27

FRANK LLOYD WRIGHT IN
OAK PARK AND RIVER FOREST

WALKING TIME: 2 hours.   HOW TO GET THERE: Take a Lake Street CTA elevated train
headed for Oak Park at any of the Loop L stations, and get off at Oak Park Avenue. Walk 1 block
west to Lake Street and Kenilworth Avenue, where this walk starts. If you drive, take the
Eisenhower Expressway, turn off at Harlem Avenue, go north about 1 mile to Lake Street, then
4 blocks east to Kenilworth Avenue.

We are indebted to the Oak Park Public Library and W. R.
Hasbrouck for most of the information and descriptions given for
this walk. The order chosen for viewing Wright's works follow
that given in a booklet issued by the Oak Park Library, *A Guide
to the Architecture of Frank Lloyd Wright in Oak Park and
River Forest, Illinois.* Since the booklet includes pictures of all
the buildings referred to, it would be an especially
appropriate souvenir of your walk. Stop at the Oak Park Library
if you would like to secure one. Copies are available for $1.00
each. Library hours are 9:00 A.M. to 9:00 P.M. Monday through
Friday; 9:00 A.M. to 5:00 P.M. Saturday.

Frank Lloyd Wright was one of 3 great Chicago architects who
turned their backs on the accepted style of classic design and
created new forms for people of the late 19th and early 20th
centuries. The 2 others, who preceded him and doubtless
influenced him in his earlier years, were Henry Hobson
Richardson and Louis H. Sullivan. All were men of great talent
and originality. Among these, Wright gave the most attention to
domestic architecture and over the years developed a quite new
style of home, now known worldwide as the "Prairie House."
The Robie House in Chicago (1909) (see Walk No. 16, Hyde
Park - University of Chicago) is probably the most familiar
example of the Prairie House design.

The Chicago area is incredibly fortunate in having a practically
complete record of Wright's progress toward the Prairie House—
in more than 20 houses that he built in the suburb of Oak Park
and 7 additional houses in nearby River Forest. The buildings

255

listed for this walk cover a period of only about 20 years in Wright's life. But the impact of the type of house he had developed by the end of that period continues to be felt today in house designs all over the world. Low roof lines, wide eaves, open planes, casement windows, and car ports—all are characteristics of the Prairie House.

You will be surprised at the designs of some of Wright's earlier products, especially those before 1900; steep gables and dormer windows have little resemblance to the style now associated with his name. If you could choose a chronological order—which is obviously impractical!—instead of the geographical order that must be followed, you would more easily observe the record of changes in Wright's style.

Unless otherwise indicated, the buildings listed here are *not* open to the public.

Unity Temple (a Universalist church) and Parish House—Lake Street and Kenilworth (1906)

The Unity Temple is Wright's only *public* building in Oak Park— except for the Memorial Fountain just across the street to the north, on Lake near Grove Avenue (1903). The Temple is an esteemed international architectural landmark. Building a church in cubic form, without a steeple, was a revolutionary step, but the symbolism of light from above (through skylight and windows under the eaves) is surely no less valid for worshiping human beings than the centuries-old symbolism of the church spire for human aspiration.

With this church Wright effectively paved the way for modern use of concrete poured into wooden forms. The church's washed pebble surface, which gives the concrete a granite-like appearance, was also an innovation of Wright's, which in modified forms is still used by many top-ranking architects. A common entrance unites the church and parish house, although each is independent for its separate uses. The auditorium inside the Temple is in a sense an actual revival of temple architecture. With the pulpit in front center, Wright located seats on 3 sides, so that minister and congregation are close to each other. (Years later Wright used a similar plan for the Greek Orthodox church in Milwaukee.) Koeper, referring to the design of Unity Temple,

Opposite, Unity Temple.

257

has paid special tribute to Wright in these words: "Like the music of Bach, the architecture of Wright develops magnificent variations on simple themes."[9]

Unity Temple may be visited from Wednesday to Sunday between 11:00 A.M. and 5:00 P.M. Entrance fee is $1.50.

Frank Lloyd Wright House—428 Forest Avenue, and
Frank Lloyd Wright Studio—951 Chicago Avenue.
(House, 1889; Studio, 1895)

Next is the Frank Lloyd Wright House, adjoining his Studio, which faces the street around the corner, at 951 Chicago Avenue. Wood shingles, brick and stone were used. Both buildings were remodeled by Wright into apartments (1911).

The house and studio of Frank Lloyd Wright may also be visited from Wednesday to Sunday from 11:00 A.M. to 5:00 P.M. Entrance fee here is $1.25.

Dr. W. H. Copeland House—400 Forest Avenue. (Remodeled, 1909)—The remodeling of this house was not entirely according to Wright's plans and was not done under his supervision.

Arthur Heurtley House—318 Forest Avenue. (1902)—Roman brick. Remodeled later into 2 apartments—all at ground level.

Mrs. Thomas H. Gale House—6 Elizabeth Court. (1909; renovated, 1962)—Elizabeth Court is half a block farther south. The facade of this house is stucco with wood trim. Roofs are flat, in the Prairie House style, and the various planes give this small house tremendous architectural interest.

H. P. Young House—334 North Kenilworth (1895)—This is an 1895 remodeling; it retains the old farmhouse (around which Wright built the newer home) as the kitchen area.

P. A. Beachy House—238 Forest Avenue (1906)—This also incorporates an earlier house. It is built of brick, stucco, and wood trim.

Frank Thomas House—210 Forest Avenue (1901)—Built of stucco on wood frame, this house has been resurfaced with wooden siding. All rooms are above grade, with no basement. Here you can see some resemblances to the later Prairie House.

Opposite, Frank Lloyd Wright home and studio.

258

E. R. Hills House—313 Forest Avenue (Remodeled by Wright, 1902)—Stucco exterior with wood trim.

Nathan G. Moore House and Stable—333 Forest Avenue (1895, rebuilt 1924)—Roman brick, stucco, and wood trim exterior. The rebuilding in 1924 was necessary because of a fire that had destroyed the upper floor.

Francis Wooley House—1030 Superior Street (1893)—This house has been resurfaced with imitation brick siding.

Walter Gale House—1031 Chicago Avenue (1892)— Clapboard exterior.

R. P. Parker House—1027 Chicago Avenue (1892)—Another clapboard exterior. Note the high-peaked circular roofs, both in this and in the next house, so different from Wright's later style.

Thomas H. Gale House—1019 Chicago Avenue (1892)— Again, a clapboard exterior and high-peaked roofs.

O. E. Balch House—611 North Kenilworth (1911)—Stucco exterior with wood trim.

Harry S. Adams House—710 Augusta Boulevard (1913)— Brick and stucco exterior.

W. E. Martin House—636 North East Avenue (1903)—Stucco exterior with wood trim. This house has been converted into apartments.

H. C. Goodrich House—534 North East Avenue (1896)— Here we have another exterior of clapboards.

Edwin H. Cheney House—520 North East Avenue (1904)— This one-story brick house, set within gardens enclosed by brick walls, has a contemporary appearance, though it was built more than half a century ago. There are striking resemblances to the Robie House, which Wright built in Chicago 5 years later.

Rollin Furbeck House—515 Fair Oaks Avenue (1898)—The house here was expanded some years after its original constructions along with interior changes.

260

William G. Fricke House—540 Fair Oaks Avenue (1902; remodeled, 1907)—Stucco exterior with wood trim. A garage was added at the time of the remodeling.

Charles E. Roberts Stable—317 North Euclid Avenue (1896)—Originally built as a stable, this has now been converted into a house.

George Furbeck House—223 North Euclid (1897)—Brick with wood trim.

Above, Chauncey L. Williams House.

261

George W. Smith House—404 Home Avenue (1898)—Exterior of wood shingle. The high-peaked roofs are a sign of its early date.

The George W. Smith House is the last of the Oak Park houses by Wright that you are viewing on this walk. You go now to River Forest by walking West.

William H. Winslow House and Stable—515 Auvergne Place (1893)—The exterior is Roman brick and stone, with terra-cotta frieze above. Here you see many of the characteristics that will be incorporated in Wright houses of a later date—wide eaves, low roofs, a single chimney, and plain surfaces contrasting with ornamented sections.

Chauncey L. Williams House—530 Edgewood Place (1895)—Roman brick below the window sills and stucco above.

Isabel Roberts House—603 Edgewood Place (1908; rebuilt, 1955)—This house, built in the form of a cross, is especially distinguished by a 2-story living room.

J. Kibben Ingalls House—562 Keystone Avenue (1909)—Stucco and painted wood trim.

E. Arthur Davenport House—559 Ashland Avenue (1901)—The building materials here are stained wood horizontal board and battened sheathing. This is the last of the homes to be viewed in River Forest.

River Forest Tennis Club—615 Lathrop Avenue (at Quick Street) (1906)—Here too the exterior is of stained wood and battened sheathing. Charles E. White, Jr., and Vernon S. Watson were associate architects.

This walk has taken you from Oak Park's Unity Temple to River Forest's Tennis Club. Between the 2 you have seen many examples of Wright's chief contribution to American architecture —buildings planned as individual homes, from some of his earliest to those of a later period in which he was working out various forms of the Prairie House.

Eye level walks

Walk-28

Subway entrance, under the Chicago Civic Center building.

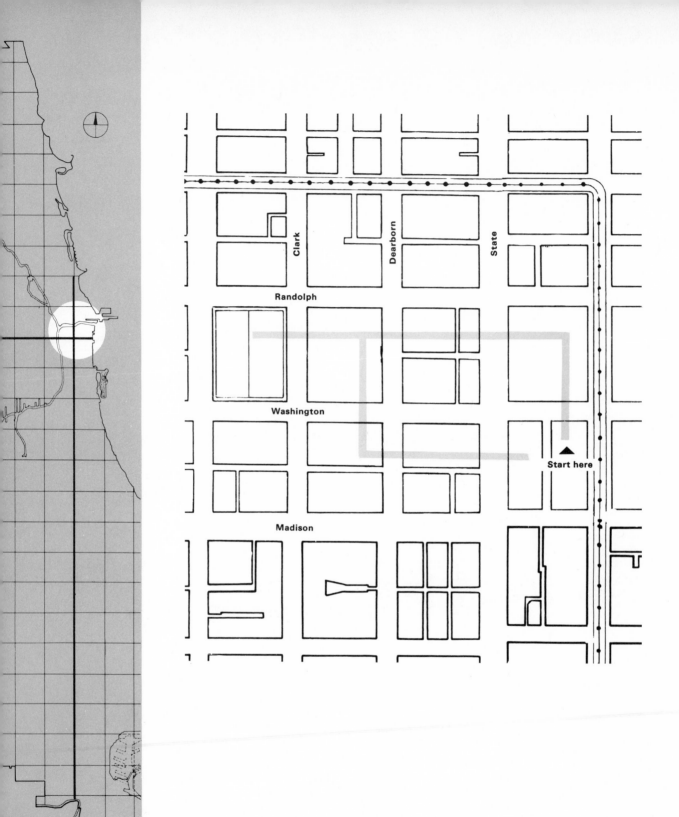

Clark

Dearborn

State

Randolph

Washington

Madison

Start here

Walk · 28

UNDERGROUND WALKWAYS

WALKING TIME: ½ hour (if you don't stop along the way to shop).   HOW TO GET THERE:
From Michigan and Randolph walk 1 block south and 1 block west to the southwest corner of
Wabash Avenue and Washington Street.

An all-weather walkway system underground, which is being
planned for Chicago's Loop, is partially completed and available
for a walking tour. When finished, the walkways will connect
the majority of the Loop buildings. Mail will be delivered by
postmen with pushcarts starting from the underground section
at the new loop post office, which will be in the Federal Center
(see Walk No. 3, Dearborn Street). Because of the outdoor
connotation of the term "walking tour," this suggestion for a
subterranean walk may seem odd. Yet one of Chicago's
fascinations is this underground walkway system, on a scale
that is rare today even in great urban centers like ours.

For a good sample walk, start in the basement of Marshall Field's
Men's Store, at Wabash and Washington. Walk north in the
basement through the tunnel under Washington Street that
connects this with Marshall Field's main store. You will know
you are on the other side of Washington when you come to
furniture and rugs in the Budget Basement of the main store.
Keep on walking in the same direction for about 6 aisles (through
the section for junior girls' clothing); then turn left (which will
be west) and walk on beyond the cafeteria (called "Budget
Dinette"). Just beyond the cafeteria turn right (north) and walk
past elevators and escalator, watching for a green light overhead
announcing "SUBWAY." When you see that sign, pointing to
your left, you can be sure you are on the right path. If you lose
your way *before* you reach this point, just ask an employee
how to get to the subway!

At the "SUBWAY" sign turn left—as it directs you—to reach
the entrance to the CTA subway. You will now be walking west.
The 2nd stretch of your underground walking begins at the

subway entrance and—continuing west—takes you through the State Street subway's Randolph-Washington station, past its ticket window and exits. Keep going west, following the large signs on the wall that read, "To Dearborn Street," but instead of stopping when you reach the Dearborn Street subway's Randolph-Washington station (for which the signs are primarily intended) continue walking west until you reach the lighted sign: "Chicago Civic Center." Here you will be entering the lower concourse of the Civic Center Building.

Now, instead of continuing west to the City Hall and County Building, as you could easily do, turn left (south) and walk by the offices of the Chicago Data Center. Through the glass walls, designed expressly to give sightseers the best possible view, you can see a number of modern machines with rows of tiny colored lights, flashing off and on constantly with a frantic sort of speed as they process data of various kinds for the city of Chicago. The *people* that you see working in these offices— there are not many of them—appear extraordinarily relaxed, whatever they happen to be doing, in comparison with the incessant, nervous-looking activity of the machines!

As you continue south now into the Brunswick Building (69 West Washington) you will be walking in a tunnel under Washington Street again, this time 2 blocks west of the first Washington tunnel. The Brunswick lower concourse is a complete shopping center. The first thing you will see—to the left as you enter the building is a barber shop impressively labeled "The Red Plush." Its window advertises "Continental, Sculptured Haircutting, Styling, and Shaping." "Maestro Gerhard," however, whose name accompanies this impressive offering, has had to come to terms with reality, for a recently printed placard in the lower part of the window announces: "Due to the large demand and for convenience of the people in the house it has become necessary for us to do *Conventional Haircutting* at standard prices."

Opposite, at the foot of this stairway in the Brunswick building is one of several maps of the underground walkway.

Unless you want to stop for services from Maestro Gerhard, walk by the other shops. You will find also a beauty shop, gift shops, both men's and women's clothing shops, drug store, stationery store, and several restaurants, the most noticeable

268

being the Handlebar, a Crane restaurant. (Don't overlook the metal map in the wall here near the Crane restaurant and at the other corners of the building, each of which marks the spot where you are at the moment.) When you finally come to a travel agency, you have reached the steps leading down to the Dearborn-Washington subway station and are headed east. Pass through the station and follow the tunnel into the State-Madison Building's lower concourse. Here you will pass a Stouffer's restaurant, several small shops, and a Walgreen's cafeteria. As you leave the building, you enter the State-Washington subway station. Beyond the ticket window you can go into the basement of Wieboldt's department store and take an escalator to the main floor, to go out onto State Street or Madison Street. Or you can end this subterranean trip by going instead into the basement of Stevens' women's specialty store. After taking the escalator there, you will exit on State Street.

Walk-29

Van Buren and
South Federal
Street.

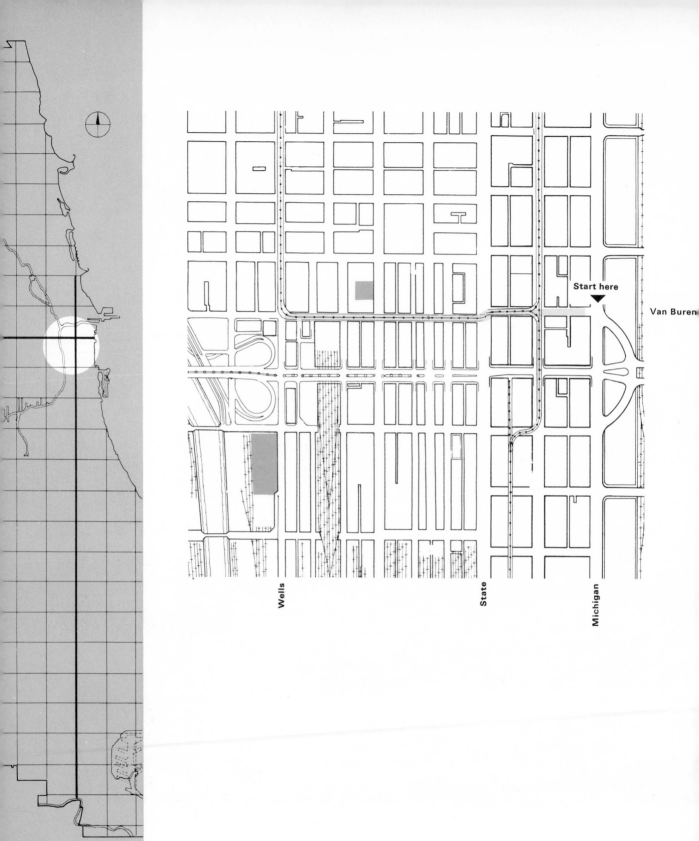

Start here

Van Buren

Wells

State

Michigan

Walk · 29

VAN BUREN STREET UNDER THE L

WALKING TIME: ½-1 hour.   HOW TO GET THERE: Take any southbound CTA bus on Michigan Avenue and get off at Van Buren (400 S).

Van Buren Street in Chicago's Loop resembles the old Third Avenue in New York City during the days of author John McNulty, who recorded the atmosphere of that eastern city's bistro-lined street for posterity in his writings. When the elevated rail line was torn down from above New York's Third Avenue, it left Van Buren the only street of its kind in the country. And the atmosphere here may not exist for too many years, because Chicago plans to replace the L with a Loop subway downtown. When that actually happens, Van Buren Street will go the way of Third Avenue.

Van Buren is one of 4 streets in Chicago that make up the "Loop" of the L's downtown route, and the L of course also adds its screeching and clanging to the scene along the other 3—Wabash Avenue, Lake Street, and Wells Street. But not even Wabash (which most closely resembles it) sustains the character of Van Buren Street, with its own variety of stores and other facilities, and its day and night habitués.

Only 6 blocks long, this dimly lit strip of Van Buren abounds in small stores, discount houses, taverns, tobacco shops, bakeries, small hotels (several "For Men Only"), liquor stores, and specialty stores—in addition to a major department store, Sears Roebuck (see Walk No. 2, State Street), and a commuter railroad station at La Salle.

The frequenters of Van Buren under the L range from Skid Row types to sophisticated shoppers, from suburban commuters and kingpins of La Salle's nearby financial district to those who seek the special amusement of the burlesque house.

A walk on Van Buren from Michigan Avenue west to Wells Street and back will give you the sounds, smells, and sights of a

Left, Looking East on Van Buren.
Right, "L" station at Van Buren
and State Streets.

busy big-city street that—for all its deterioration—is the result
of a vital link in Chicago's present transportation system. The
hustle and bustle and congestion, accentuated by the L traffic
above, create a special atmosphere rapidly disappearing from
the business districts of America's big cities.

274

Grand Central Station—
South Wells and West Harrison.
Architect: S. S. Beman (1890)

At Wells, look south 2 blocks to the old Grand Central Station. Though its name is no longer functionally appropriate—since the building of the much larger Union Station (see Walk No. 10) —Grand Central Station represents an important era in architectural progress. The design is a version of Italian Romanesque, with an especially noteworthy clock tower 222 feet high. In Chicago's soft soil the problem of preventing uneven settling of the tower was crucial, as Adler and Sullivan had recognized in building the Auditorium a few years earlier. Beman solved the problem in his own way—by driving piles down more than 50 feet to the firmer clay foundation below, making this the first building (by no means the last) to be constructed in this way. The enormous train shed attached to the waiting room, which allows plenty of open space, is a good example of the glass-and-iron construction of that period. "In appearance and function," says Koeper, "Grand Central Station is one of the most distinguished railroad stations in the country."[10]

Atlantic Hotel—316 South Clark Street, formerly the Kaiserhof. Architects: Max Teich (1892); Marshall and Fox (1915)

If you want to add to Van Buren's atmosphere of antiquity, stroll half a block north on Clark Street, and walk through the lobby and tavern of the old Atlantic Hotel, all the way through to La Salle Street. Known as the Kaiserhof in its early days at the beginning of this century, the hotel dropped that name, for obvious reasons, at the time of the first World War. The elaborate baroque style of both the facade and the interior was of course considered most elegant when the building was constructed. The old-style Victorian decoration in the main dining room (originally the "Ladies' Cafe")—frequent extra-large pillars, some round and some octagonal, mounted with fantastic plant-and-animal sculpture designs, with observant little owls at the top—is, sadly, a thing of the past already. The new management has torn it out for its 1968 redecorating.

275

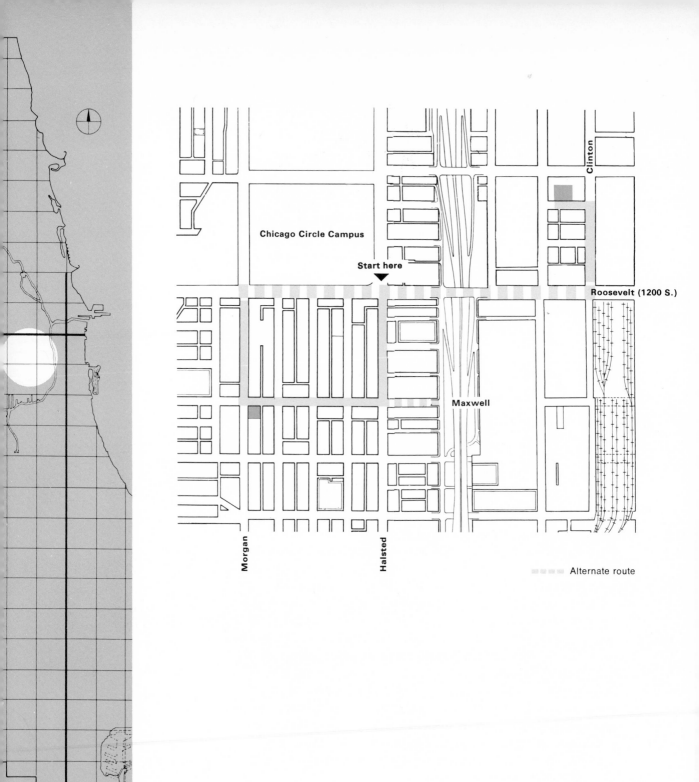

Chicago Circle Campus

Start here

Roosevelt (1200 S.)

Clinton

Maxwell

Morgan

Halsted

▬▬ ▬▬ Alternate route

Walk · 30

MAXWELL STREET MARKET, MAXWELL POLICE STATION, AND CHICAGO FIRE ACADEMY

WALKING TIME: 1 hour (unless you want to browse—and "negotiate" for purchases in the market).   HOW TO GET THERE: Take a westbound CTA bus No. 20 (Madison Street) at State and Madison to Halsted Street (800 W); transfer to a southbound bus No. 8 (Halsted Street), which will take you to Maxwell Street (1330 S). If you go by car, you will need to find a parking space some blocks away—perhaps in the U. of I. Circle Campus parking lots.

The best time to visit the Maxwell Street Market is Sunday morning any time of the year, for that is the time for the biggest turnout of customers and visitors—who themselves are part of the show! If a Sunday morning is impossible, however, any day of the week will do. Be sure to take this walk soon, for the Market is scheduled for clearance by urban renewal; it may be relocated or disbanded any time, depending upon the city's final plan.

Walking through the Maxwell Street Market is an experience in sound and smell as well as sight. Although the market has been reduced in size somewhat since the Dan Ryan Expressway was built in 1960, it had previously been expanded westward of its original boundaries by commercially minded immigrants from all parts of the world. (This area for many years has been a melting pot for thousands of Europeans, Latin Americans, and —more recently—southern Negroes.) Despite all changes in extent, the Market has retained much of its original flavor. Sidewalk vendors of many backgrounds promote their sales in many languages from pushcarts, wooden stands, and even the sidewalk, as well as from old store fronts and shops. Everything from articles of clothing to crowbars, both new and used (the source of the used being always somewhat dubious), are sold at "negotiated" prices, every sale being subject to debate in the true Old World style. And no passerby should expect to escape being accosted—perhaps literally buttonholed—as a potential buyer. This is all part of the sightseeing game on Maxwell Street. But you must be prepared to resist if you're really not interested in the special bargains they offer.

277

Maxwell Street Police Station—
Maxwell Street and Morgan (1000 W). (About 1870)

At the west end of the Market, at Morgan Street, stands the Maxwell Street Police Station, whose construction date (about 1870) makes it the oldest existing police station in Chicago. Every kind of violation of the law gets swept into this station house—burglary, prostitution, narcotics peddling, murder, rape, to name but a few. (Fortunately, because of the Market, you will be taking a daylight tour of the area!)

Chicago Fire Academy—
558 West DeKoven Street (1100 S).
Architects: Loebl, Schlossman, and Bennett (1960)

Walk 2 blocks north to Roosevelt Road where you may board a bus going east one mile to Canal Street, where you then walk 2 blocks to DeKoven and the Fire Academy. In front of the red brick Academy stands a large bronze sculptured flame, by the Chicagoan Egon Weiner, expressing the fury of the Fire of 1871, which supposedly started on this very spot. The Fire Academy was built on the site of the old house and barn of the O'Leary family, whose famous cow is alleged to have kicked over a lantern and thus set off the whole catastrophe.

A 30-minute introduction to how our present-day fire fighters are trained for service in the Chicago Fire Department is available in a tour of the Academy—an experience that always has a fascination for everyone, especially young people whether fire buffs or not. Tours by appointment: 9:00 A.M. to 3:00 P.M. Telephone: 744-4000.

While you are at the Academy, don't miss the exhibit of photographs in the main lobby or the ancient (1835) hand-pumper fire engine.

Chinese City Hall.

279

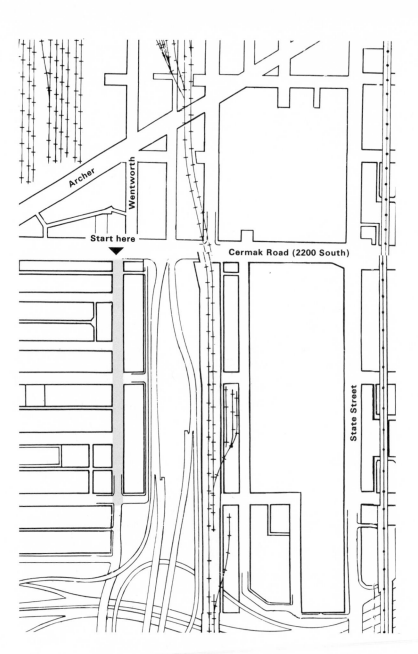

Follow your own interests, as you walk along
Wentworth Avenue between Cermak Rd. (22nd St.)
and 23rd St., noting side streets as you go.

Walk · 31

CHINATOWN

WALKING TIME: About 1 hour—exclusive of shopping or eating time. HOW TO GET THERE: Take a southbound CTA bus No. 22A (Wentworth) on Clark Street (2 blocks west of State). Get off at Cermak Road (22nd Street) and Wentworth Avenue (200 W) in the heart of Chinatown.

For the non-Oriental a walk in Chinatown is like a trip to another country—a small country, to be sure, of only about 9 square blocks. For a recently arrived Oriental it can hardly seem like his native country, but many native characteristics do persist. Chinese is the language you hear most in the streets, and— despite the neighborhood's catering to the tourist trade— Chinese is often the language printed on restaurant menus, sometimes, it is true, along with English translation. There's a newspaper in Chinese, a Chinese press, and churches that still use the Chinese language whether they are Buddhist or Christian.

No step-by-step directions are being given for this walk; you won't need them. Just follow whatever interests you most along 22nd Street and then along Wentworth Avenue, especially to the south of 22nd, with a glance at the side streets to be sure you aren't missing something especially interesting.

First-class Chinese restaurants, "snack bars," and grocery stores are too numerous to list. Gift shops with an eye to the touring customer are almost as frequent as the restaurants, selling beautiful authentic Chinese imports—often along with hundreds of cheaper souvenirs that may or may not come from China. You won't be able to miss the House of Buddha, on the east side of Wentworth or the "Ling Long Art Museum and Chinese Gift Shop" on the west side. Also on the west side is the On Leong Chinese Merchants Association, with its Buddhist shrine and the large auditorium long known as the Chinese City Hall— where matters of concern to the community were once discussed and handled by the local Chinese leaders themselves. Both the Buddhist shrine and the Chinese City Hall, however, are becoming more traditional than active, even for Chinatown's own residents, their chief significance now being as showplaces for the ever-present tourist.

The natural pride of Chinatown's residents in their Oriental background—as well as their very practical recognition that tourists find the old ways more interesting than the new!—has been somewhat diluted by their determination to become more adapted to the Occidental way of life. The very name of the *Chiam* Restaurant—always appearing in letters slightly resembling Chinese characters, followed by the explanation "(Meaning Chinese American)"—suggests the blending of the 2 cultures. And the organization called the Chinese American Civic Council of Chicago explains its origin with the remark:

> Many Chinese Americans have long realized the obligation of all Chinese in America to become better American citizens, to take a more active part in the American way of life and to contribute their special knowledge and talent to the enrichment of American culture.[11]

Commendable as this attitude may be, the tourist can only regret those trends that are changing Chinatown to "Chiam Town"! It is refreshing to find that as recently as 1966 the Council's bulletin called *CAP (Chinese American Progress),* a publication that carries both Chinese and English articles, devoted 3 pages to a reprint of "Chinatown's Restaurants," by Edward Robert Brooke (identified as "Food Spirits and Restaurant Editor" of *Omnibus*), which emphasized the attractions of the specifically Chinese qualities that are preserved here.

You might contact the Chinese American Civic Council, at 2249 South Wentworth (phone: CA-5-0234), about a *guided* tour of the area. In any case, try to see the fantastically designed figure called the 1000-arm Kwan Yin at the House of Buddha, 2235 South Wentworth. This gilded goddess, seated on a lotus petal, is more than 6 feet high and weighs 1,500 pounds—the culmination of some 20,000 man hours of work by skilled craftsmen.

It should be noted that the population of Chinatown, estimated at about 2,500, is by no means *exclusively* Chinese. This is an integrated neighborhood, with a substantial number of Negroes and people of Italian and Spanish extraction living together with the Chinese. It will surprise many people that only about 60 per cent of Chinatown's residents are of Chinese descent and that less than 20 per cent of all the Chinese living in Chicago have their homes here. It is still true, nevertheless, that those Chinese Americans living in other parts of the city generally have strong ties with Chinatown—through friends and relatives who do live here and through membership in "family associations" and civic organizations with headquarters in Chinatown. And it is in Chinatown that the exclusively Chinese celebrations are most evident—parades and weeklong celebrations for the Chinese New Year, for instance, which falls on a different Western date each year (early in February or late in January), and a parade on October 10, the day that China became a republic. The appearance of the famous Chinese dragon and those superior Chinese fireworks make these activities unique.

Before leaving Wentworth Avenue, be sure to go into some of the grocery stores, for these represent the one business in Chinatown geared more to its own residents than to outsiders. And don't fail to explore some of the side streets. Though most of the restaurants and gift shops are located on Wentworth or 22nd, you will find some interesting spots just off the thoroughfare.

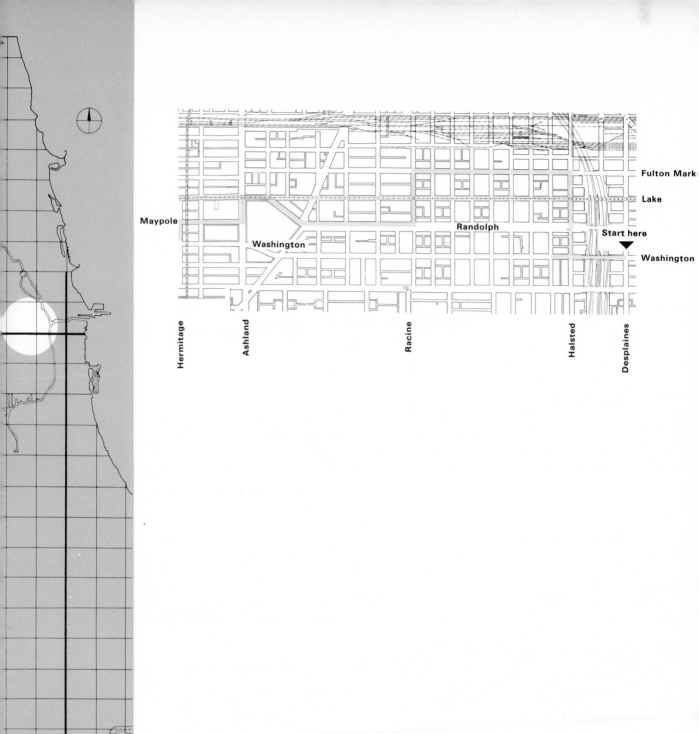

Fulton Mark

Lake

Maypole

Randolph

Start here

Washington

Washington

Hermitage

Ashland

Racine

Halsted

Desplaines

Walk · 32

HAYMARKET SQUARE; Wholesale Produce and Meat Markets; Hermitage Housing Development

WALKING TIME: 1½ hours.   HOW TO GET THERE: Take a westbound CTA bus No. 58 (Ogden-Downtown) on Randolph Street west of State Street. Get off at Desplaines Avenue (700 W). (For the sake of the bus driver, be sure to give Desplaines its proper midwest pronunciation—"*Dess*-plains"—not its French variant.) When you return, take the same bus, but you will need to come by way of *Washington Street,* since Randolph Street is westbound only.

This is an off-beat walk, rewarding to those who respond favorably to the sights, smells, and sounds of the marketplace but not recommended for those with overdelicate senses! It takes you through the part of Chicago where wholesale and retail handlers of meat and produce do uproarious business with each other daily—to supply the hotels, restaurants, groceries, and homes of the city.

This should be a *morning* walk, and the sooner you get there the better, for action in the markets starts even before dawn and is largely over, or at least thinned out considerably, by noon.

Haymarket Square

Before proceeding to the market sections, however, stop a few minutes at Haymarket Square, just half a block beyond the corner where you get off the bus—between Desplaines and Halsted. On this ill-fated spot stands a monument of a single policeman with his hand lifted, and carved in the stone below him are the words: "In the name of the people of Illinois I command peace." These are supposedly the words spoken to a group of workingmen by the police captain who came to Haymarket Square with about 175 policemen on May 4, 1886. During a period of great labor dissatisfaction, some 2,000 workers had met to protest police treatment the previous day of strikers at the McCormick Harvester works. In response to the police captain's words, the leader who was then haranguing the group declared, "We are peaceable." But at that very moment someone

IN THE NAME OF THE PEOPLE
OF ILLINOIS
I COMMAND
PEACE

from the crowd threw a bomb, which killed several policemen and injured many more.

Somehow this monument seems a sadly inadequate reminder of that tragic incident in Chicago's history and the equally tragic aftermath of panic in which 4 "anarchists" among the workers were tried, found guilty of murder, and executed, and 3 more were sentenced to life imprisonment.

Haymarket Square had many victims among both the police and the workers. Perhaps its only "hero" is John Peter Altgeld, who as governor of Illinois in 1893 studied the entire record of the Haymarket Square bombing trial and—convinced that these men were *not* guilty of murder as convicted, whatever their political beliefs may have been—had the courage to pardon the 3 "anarchists" still alive and serving their terms in jail. Altgeld's career in politics was ruined by this decision—as he well knew it would be, since feeling still ran high against all who participated in the Haymarket meeting—but his name in history has been honored for it.

Randolph Street Produce Market—
Randolph and Halsted (800 W)

To reach the Randolph Street produce market, cross over the Kennedy Expressway to Halsted Street, which is the center of the market. Don't expect an outdoor market like those in so many southern cities; Chicago's weather wouldn't make one feasible. But the many dealers do spread their wares from the inside of the huge brick buildings out onto sidewalk stands, so that fresh vegetables and fruits in season are visible everywhere.

If one of Chicago's numerous street peddlers supplies you with your fruit and vegetables, he quite probably was here (or at the South Water Market farther south) around dawn, dickering and bickering with the wholesale men and his competitors among the buyers, hoping to get the best produce at the lowest price. A noisy, exciting beginning he has for the quieter routine he follows later!

Barney's Market Club—741 West Randolph.

You can't overlook Barney's Market Club, the restaurant at the southeast corner of Randolph and Halsted with the large sign

Haymarket Square Monument.

287

that greets all customers with the traditional words, "Yes, Sir, Senator!"—a carryover from the days when Barney's restaurant was located near the railroad stations and catered largely to politicians traveling through Chicago. (Barney had obviously learned that none of these men objected to being called Senator, whether or not he actually rated the title.)

Fulton Meat Market (300 N)

Now walk north 2 blocks on Halsted, under the Lake Street L tracks, to Fulton Market, where wholesale dealers in meat, fish, and poultry hold forth. You can't miss it, for even the street signs say, "Fulton Market" (not just "Fulton"). Unless you are deterred at the sight of meat that obviously was not long ago a slaughtered animal, turn west and follow Fulton Market along its 8 blocks to Racine (1200 W). Here you will see block after block of delivery trucks from all parts of Chicago backed up and loading. Out to the trucks come huge carcasses of beef, weighed inside and rolled out on dollies; or clusters of whole lamb legs bunched together like bananas; or any of the other kinds of meat you generally see in smaller portions. And all around, weighing and hauling out the meat, are the wholesale dealers, clad in the white blood-spattered coats of the butcher's trade.

The poultry and fish deliveries, being in more familiar form, are less spectacular to the ordinary sightseer. And the really familiar-looking stores selling butter, eggs, and milk will be a welcome sight to anyone who has found the wholesale meat at all disturbing—especially the store carrying a sign reading "The Little Red Hen"!

The Hermitage Housing Development—
Washington-Hermitage Urban Renewal Area. Architect: Stanley Tigerman (1968)

When you reach Racine, turn back south (to your left) to Randolph Street. If you are tired of walking, take a westbound No. 58 bus again and get off at Ogden (1544 W). Or walk west on Randolph until you reach Ogden, a few blocks away. Just beyond Ogden, you will pass Union Park (which will be to your left) with its park house, tennis courts, ball field, swimming pool, and tots' playlot. Then at Ashland and Lake (one block north of

Randolph) walk south and then west on Maypole by the Mary
Thompson Hospital to your right and the Jesse Spalding Public
School to your left, to reach a housing development called The
Hermitage—a 108-townhouse project on a 3-acre site in the
Washington-Hermitage urban renewal area. These houses were
planned to accommodate moderate-income families in a park-like
environment. Each townhouse has a full basement and from
2 to 4 bedrooms, with modern gas facilities for heating, hot water,
and cooking. The simple, direct design is well executed. Note
the open space and play lots, also the 100 per cent off-street parking
and the community recreational facilities.

The Hermitage is not public housing, although many of the
home owners here are former tenants of the Chicago Housing
Authority. The houses, insured and financed through FHA
(Federal Housing Administration), are being sold through the
Foundation for Cooperative Housing. Purchasers are being
trained in housekeeping and in maintenance of building
and grounds.

Prices of these townhouses range from $17,000 to $20,000, and
the required down payment for a family with an annual income
under $11,000 is only $250.00. Several houses have been
especially designed to accommodate families with physically
handicapped children attending the Spalding School across
the street.

Developer of The Hermitage was the Chicago Dwellings
Association, nonprofit corporation of the city. To the west
is an enormous public housing complex of the Chicago
Housing Authority.

Carter H. Harrison Monument—
Washington Boulevard, this side of Ashland.

As you are looking for a bus stop for your return downtown, you
might stop a few minutes at the now wholly green statue of
Carter H. Harrison, with an excerpt from his address on being
elected mayor of Chicago. The monument was erected by the
Carter H. Harrison Memorial Association.

Walk-33

Fountains & statues
at Wells and Ohio.

Walk · 33

ANTIQUE SHOP ROW ON WELLS STREET

WALKING TIME: 1 hour.   HOW TO GET THERE: Take a northbound CTA bus No. 10
(Lincoln-Larrabee) on Wells Street. Get off at Wells and Hubbard (440 N), one block beyond
the Merchandise Mart, on the north side of the Chicago River.

Don't postpone this walk! Too many of the fascinating antique
shops that have lined Wells Street on both sides for a mile-long
stretch are already beginning to move or disappear altogether.
Signs of urban renewal can be seen, and the area is undeniably
due for such clearance. Except for the antique shops, there are
indications of inevitable decay. One large old commercial
building, for instance, has been long empty, to judge from the
layers of dust on the rumpled, drawn window shades. Here and
there are taverns of the old style; and then nearby the inevitable
tenant of a rundown neighborhood, a gospel mission church with
"JESUS SAVES" in large letters above the door. A veritable
Hansel-and-Gretel type of cottage in these unlikely surroundings,
from which you could once buy delicate metal flowers, now stands
empty, with a large parking lot beside it on the corner and new
construction going on across the street. Such "progress" is
needed, but with it will disappear a part of Chicago well worth
becoming familiar with, whether or not you are an antique buff.

Window-shopping along this stretch of North Wells is like
traveling through a museum. Not all the shops have adopted such
attention-luring names as Rummage Round, Fly by Nite, and
Dand D Antiques, Inc., but all have interesting wares. In these
windows you may see almost anything—old hobby horses,
Tiffany lamps, ship's lamps, Pennsylvania Dutch weather vanes,
Russian samovars, chunks of stone carvings from old buildings,
and large stained-glass or mosaic tile pictures, as well as the
expected assortment of furniture, clocks, and bric-a-brac.

So many of the shops carry signs declaring them "Open to the
Trade Only" that some courage is required for going inside,
though a real interest in buying is probably all that is needed to

293

Still life in store window and statuary yard along Wells Street.

make you welcome. In any case, going inside isn't really necessary unless you actually want to buy. The generally cluttered window displays are generous if not artistically arranged, and here and there a shop has set *outside* the door an especially tempting item, like a little old wooden icebox, a Franklin stove, or a hand-carved wooden settee.

If you are looking for stage properties to make your theatrical production authentic, this is the place to come. Several shops specialize in the rental of theatrical props.

While walking along Wells, you can't possibly miss a statuary shop on the west side of the street and its outdoor showplace on the other side. In the outdoor display at the corner is almost anything you could think of for enlivening your lawn—lions, watchdogs, eagles, and many demure maidens waiting to pour water from their vases into your fountain, as well as a copy of the little boy that Scandinavians consider a natural for a fountain but Americans sometimes consider improper!

You may have seen the greatest variety of antiques in what seem like completely unplanned window displays. But now and then you will be pleased to find a store of more than usual dignity. Don't miss 2 of this kind just off Wells Street on Erie (660 N). Though neither is open to the public, they are using buildings worth seeing, which have been restored in appropriately antique style, with such details as lanterns out front and old-style, dark wood Venetian blinds at the windows.

Whether you're genuinely interested in buying antiques, finding props for your stage production, or just aimlessly window-shopping, you'll be glad you took this walk. The walk ends at Chicago Avenue, 800 North.

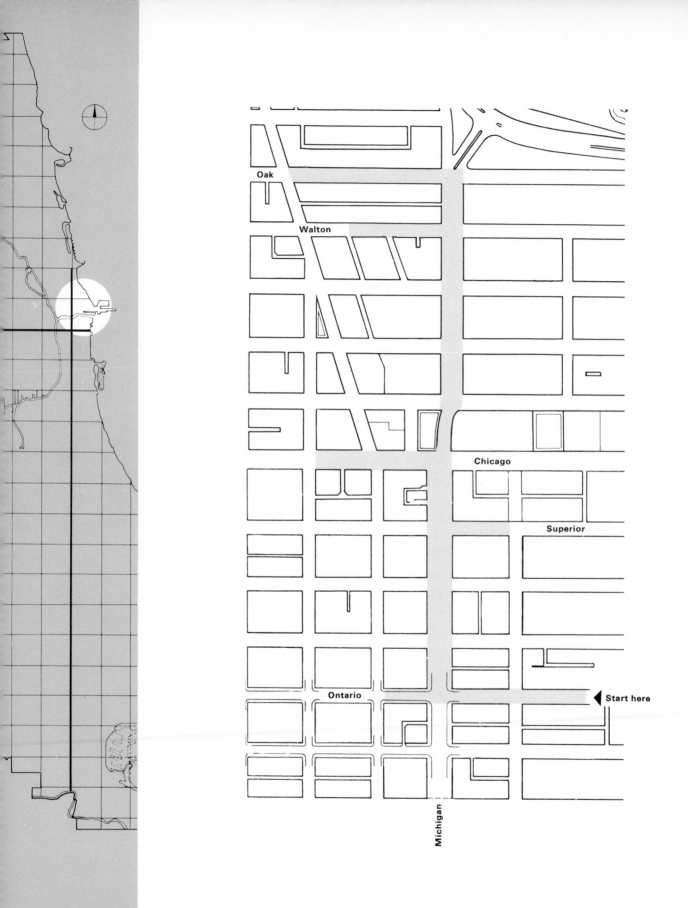

Oak

Walton

Chicago

Superior

Ontario

Michigan

◀ Start here

Walk · 34

NEAR NORTH SIDE ART GALLERIES

WALKING TIME: 2 hours.   HOW TO GET THERE: Take any of the following northbound
CTA buses—No. 151 (Sheridan) on Michigan; 152 (Addison) or 153 (Wilson-Michigan) on
State; or 76 (Diversey) on Wabash. (Or walk north on Michigan to the first bus sign beyond
Lake Street, where all of these buses stop.) Get off at Michigan and Ontario, (628 N)
and walk 2 blocks east to the Museum of Contemporary Art, where this walk starts.
If you are driving, turn off the Outer Drive *onto the Inner Drive* at Ohio Street (600 N);
continue north just 1 block, to Ontario, then drive west to 237, the Museum of Contemporary Art.

Chicagoans quite justly take pride in the fact that some of the
country's best private art collections are located here, often
available for public viewing at the various galleries and museums
in the city. Chicago's considerable interest in art (one of the
many characteristics that go contrary to a popular misconception
that Chicago lacks "culture") supports numerous galleries in
many parts of the city. The area of their greatest concentration
lies on Ontario and Oak streets and on Michigan Avenue in
between. Walk Number 12 has been chosen to cover this section
of the city because of the great cluster of high-quality galleries
within the one-mile stretch that is covered.

A substantial number of Chicago artists find their livelihood in
painting and sculpture. They would seem to have a ready market
through displaying their work in these various galleries.
Unfortunately for them, the majority of the art galleries in
Chicago, while generally interested in contemporary painting
and sculpture, apparently prefer showing the works of artists
of international stature and fame. Some, however, like the Conrad
Gallery and the Distelheim Galleries are especially interested in
Chicago and other midwest artists. And on occasion Chicago
artists are given prominent attention—as, for example, in the
joint venture November 2, 1968, of the galleries listed here
called "Response to Violence in Our Society," an especially
bitter attack by Chicago artists on the official handling of
demonstrators at the time of the 1968 Democratic nominating
convention in Chicago.

297

The 25 places listed for this walk do not include all the art galleries in the area; you may find others as you go along that have equal interest for you. Yet even these are obviously more than you can *visit* in the 2-hour period suggested, especially since many of them are on the 2nd or 3rd floor. Just discovering where all of these are, however, will be worth while, so that you may return to them later one by one. And even on this walk you might have time to browse a little in a few that attract you most.

You can generally visit the galleries weekdays from 10:00 A.M. to 5:00 P.M., some of them opening earlier, some later. Most of them are closed Sundays, a few both Sundays and Mondays. But of course their schedules are always subject to change. Instead of quoting precise hours, therefore, we recommend that whenever you count on visiting any given art gallery you check about its hours in advance.

Museum of Contemporary Art—237 East Ontario. Architects for remodeling: Brenner, Danforth, and Rockwell (1967)

In October 1967 the Museum of Contemporary Art opened in a building previously used by Playboy Magazine, remodeled for its present purpose. The building gains considerable distinction and strength from the sculpture attached to the facade, the last work of the late Zoltan Kemeny of Zurich, Switzerland. This red copper bas-relief, 50 feet long and 8 feet high, called "Interior Geography 2," was given to the museum by Mr. and Mrs. Maurice A. Lipschultz. It is the museum's only permanent work of art.

The Museum offers new shows every few weeks, frequently of an experimental kind—like its opening show in October 1967, called "Pictures To Be Read—Poems To Be Seen," and a late summer show in 1968 called "Options," referred to as "participatory art" because the museum visitor *had to take part* in most of the exhibit pieces before he could see what they were all about; directions with each "work of art" told him whether he was to pull levers, push buttons, or just walk into an enclosed space and shout to see the light go on at the sound of his voice! If you are one of those who think that art consists

Opposite, top, Sculpture by Zoltan Kemeny. *Bottom,* Museum of Contemporary Art. The painting on the wall just beyond the museum is "Pop Tart" by Claes Oldenburg.

299

only of oil paintings on canvas or representational statuary, you may find this museum disturbing. But you can't fail to find it exciting, and you shouldn't miss it.

Arts Club of Chicago—109 East Ontario, 2nd floor. Architect for the Club's interior: Ludwig Mies van der Rohe (1955)

The only other indispensable *inside* visit for this walk is the Arts Club of Chicago. Quite aside from any exhibit there, the interior of the Club is worth seeing, since it was designed by Mies van der Rohe. Though private, the Club opens all its exhibits to the public. And over the years it has a history of most distinguished exhibits, many of them the first in Chicago—or even in the country—of works by artists later recognized as of world importance. Rodin, Picasso, Toulouse-Lautrec, Vlaminck, Utrillo, and Brancusi, for instance, were given early one-man showings by the Arts Club of Chicago.

Other art galleries of the area, in order, are listed here. (Remember: For Ontario and Oak streets, the even numbers are on the north side of the street, odd numbers on the south. For Michigan Avenue, even numbers are on the west side of the street, odd numbers on the east.)

East Ontario (east to west)

Rosner Gallery, 235—next door to the Museum of Contemporary Art, specializing in student paintings, sculpture, photography and prints.

Richard Feigen Gallery, 226—advertises that this gallery specializes in showing "modern and old masters". The space is well designed and planned. Feigen also maintains a New York Gallery.

B. C. Holland Gallery, 224 (formerly at 155)—generally open to the public with no changing exhibitions. Interesting paintings of late 19th- and 20th-century artists are always on exhibit. This gallery, constructed in 1968, is the work of Stanley Tigerman, architect, and Bruce Greegre, Interior designer.

Lo Guidice Gallery, 157—an exceptionally well-designed space that shows many American and European contemporary painters and sculptors. Kinetic sculpture is often on exhibit.

300

Pro-Grafica Art, 155—specializing in the graphic arts—lithographs, etchings, prints, and posters.

Galleria Roma, 155, 2nd floor—Many of the best Italian contemporary painters and sculptors are represented here.

Vincent Price Art Gallery (Sears), 140, 2nd floor—showing paintings, sculpture, and prints as part of a chain operation intended to reach the vast middle-income buyers market.

Arts Club of Chicago, 109—already described in the opening paragraphs.

Fairweather-Hardin Gallery, 101—In the male-dominated gallery world, two women, Mrs. Fairweather and Mrs. Hardin, hold their own with splendid showings of contemporary art.

North Michigan Avenue (south to north)

Allan Frumkin Gallery, 620, 2nd floor—Mr. Frumkin, who maintains a New York gallery in addition to this one, often exhibits avant-garde sculpture and paintings to large and enthusiastic audiences.

Richard Gray Gallery, 620, 3rd floor—concentrates on showing works of 20th-century masters and emerging younger talents. These include paintings, drawings, sculpture, and graphics. Mr. Gray is an architect, though not active as such.

Kazimir Gallery, also 620, 3rd floor—featuring contemporary European painters and sculptors, especially constructionists.

Main Street-Joseph Faulkner Galleries, 642-646—cover a wide range of styles; with an enviable record of first-rate European and American contemporary painting and sculpture shows.

Stuart Brent Books and Records, 672—selling old and new prints and lithographs at moderate prices.

Welna Gallery, 936, 2nd floor—selling chiefly American painting and sculpture.

Kovler Gallery, 952, 2nd floor—(use the easternmost entrance on the Oak Street side of the building), offering first-rate shows of contemporary graphic artists and photographers, as well as painters and sculptors.

Oak Street (1000 N), east to west

Distelheim Galleries, 113—offering contemporary painting and sculpture with emphasis on Chicago artists.

Frank J. Oehlschlaeger, 107—showing contemporary painting, sculpture, and prints.

Gilman Galleries, 103—with 2 stories of avant garde art in all media and a small outdoor patio in the rear with sculpture on display.

Florentine Gallery, 49—offering principally French and Italian impressionist paintings.

Oak Street Book Store, 58—excellent lithographs and prints.

Other east-west streets, between Ontario and Oak

Jacques Baruch Gallery, 154 East Superior Street (732 N), 5th floor—a gallery in an apartment, for which appointments are necessary; run by a Polish-born architect, with a large stock of European and American oil paintings and sculpture, and such unusual items as icons and el fresco paintings.

Conrad Gallery, 46 East Chicago Avenue (800 N)—owned by Conrad Buck (whose parents were artists), featuring Illinois and other midwest artists, also offering art for rental and displaying sculpture in an outside court when the weather is favorable.

Nationwide Art Center, 70 East Walton (932 N)—carrying a large assortment of paintings and reproductions at moderate prices.

Arts International—Le Garage, 58 East Walton—with an enormous stock of paintings and reproductions at moderate prices.

Walk-35

Newberry Library.

Division

Oak

Dearborn

State

Rush

Start here

Chicago

Walk · 35

RUSH STREET

WALKING TIME: 1½ hours.   HOW TO GET THERE: Take any of the following northbound
CTA buses—No. 151 (Sheridan) on Michigan; No. 152 (Addison), or No. 153 (Wilson-Michigan)
on State Street; or a No. 76 (Diversey) on Wabash. Get off at Michigan and Chestnut (860 N).
Walk one block west to Rush Street. If you are driving, turn off the Outer Drive *onto the Inner
Drive* at Ohio Street (600 N); continue north 5 blocks to Chicago Avenue (800 N), then drive
west on Chicago to Rush Street (1 block west of Michigan), and follow Rush (which starts
to run NW at this point) 2 blocks farther to Chestnut Street (860 N).

A walk up Rush Street, from Chestnut to Division (1200 N), with
a side trip here and there, offers considerable diversion. This is
the "Glitter Gulch" of Chicago, characterized by its own type of
night clubs, restaurants, shops, and people. Watching the people
is no small part of the diversion. Your starting place is the little
park at Chestnut Street, where pigeons gather and the greatest
concentration of night clubs begins.

Chicago City Parking Facility No. 5—
875 North Rush Street.
Architects: Loebl, Schlossman, and Bennett (1955)

If you have driven into this area, you may have left your car
at a distinguished parking garage, known merely as City
Parking Facility No. 5. This first-rate structure is composed of
red brick and vertical concrete strips—the strips indicating the
location of the parking areas and the red brick portion the
mechanical elevator areas.

Most of the shops on Rush Street, even the beauty shops, are
open at night. And there's everything to see or buy—from
avant-garde clothing and accessories to camera equipment and
component parts for hi-fi sets. The stops you make along the way
will be determined not only by your taste but by your curiosity
as well. You may be attracted by the names, if nothing else—
such names, for example, as the Scotch Mist and the Rat Fink
on Wabash, one block west; Your Father's Mustache on State,
2 blocks west, where old-time movies with beer and peanuts

305

are always available; The Red Garter on Pearson Street; or Barnaby's (remember that ingratiating but short-lived cartoon strip?) on West Tooker Place, with peanuts again and dancing and general fun.

Walton (932 N) offers the first side trip of the walk, with an even greater variety of shops and restaurants than Rush itself. Running south from Walton, at 100 East, is a little back street called Ernst Court, with a series of shops and a well-known, off-beat restaurant bar.

Newberry Library—60 West Walton. Architect: Henry Ives Cobb (1892)

For a side trip of another type, go farther west to the Newberry Library, at 60 *West* Walton. This library of splendid Spanish Romanesque architecture stands on the site of the Mahlon Ogden house, a wooden mansion that miraculously escaped the Great Fire of 1871 but was later razed to make way for this building. Newberry Library—created by a bequest from Walter Loomis Newberry, an early Chicago businessman—owns another building just to the north at Oak Street (1000 N) and east at State (which, as you doubtless know, is the dividing line between east and west numbers). This is a fine old 4-story red brick structure on a private park, called the Irving Apartments, which were built about the same time as the Library itself.

The Newberry Library houses outstanding collections of reference materials—both books and unbound matter—that are used by scholars working on advanced research projects in the humanities. Over the years it has purchased entire libraries of individuals in this country and in Europe who had collected books and manuscripts in the fields of history, literature, and music. Several collections of Americana are particularly famous, including such unusual materials as grammars in Indian languages and extensive genealogical records.

Note the small park that the Newberry Library faces—old *Washington Square, once known as "Bughouse Square"* because it served as a forum, back in the 20's, for any radical or freakish speaker who chose to address his oratory to the crowds that were gathered each night in anticipation.

306

Another reminder of the past is *Tooker Place* to the east (863 N), site of the historic *Dill Pickle Club,* where beer drinking and ardent discussions were always the order of the night.

Oak Street (1000 N), like Walton, offers a side trip with a great variety of stores, shops, galleries, and cafes of its own. The *Esquire Theatre (architects: William and Hal Pereira, 1937) at 58 East Oak* was among the first of the art theatres in this country, serving coffee and displaying art in the lobby. Back on Rush Street, at 1026, is the more recently built *Carnegie Theatre (architects: Fridstein, Fitch and Associates, 1967*—who also designed *Mister Kelly's* supper club next door).

The Fortnightly of Chicago (Lathrop House)—
120 East Bellevue.
Architects: McKim, Mead, and White (1892)

At Bellevue (1031 N), take another side trip, to see the building at 120 East Bellevue, now occupied by The Fortnightly of Chicago, an exclusive private club. This imposing 3-story mansion —3 windows wide at the center with wide bays on each side— was originally the home of the Lathrop family. The symmetry of the facade, which is in keeping with its 18th-century classic style, is pleasantly relieved by having the entrance set in the left, not the center, of the 3 central arches.

And now return to Rush. On North State Street, where State joins Rush at Cedar, is a bar with jukebox music for dancing on each of 2 floors. This bar is so popular with young people, who gather here to get acquainted, that you can often see lines of them out on the sidewalk waiting to get in!

The walk ends on Division Street, where just *west* of State are 2 popular night clubs—an appropriate conclusion for the Rush Street walk!

Second City theatre
with Louis Sullivan
ornamentation from
the Garrick Theatre
building.

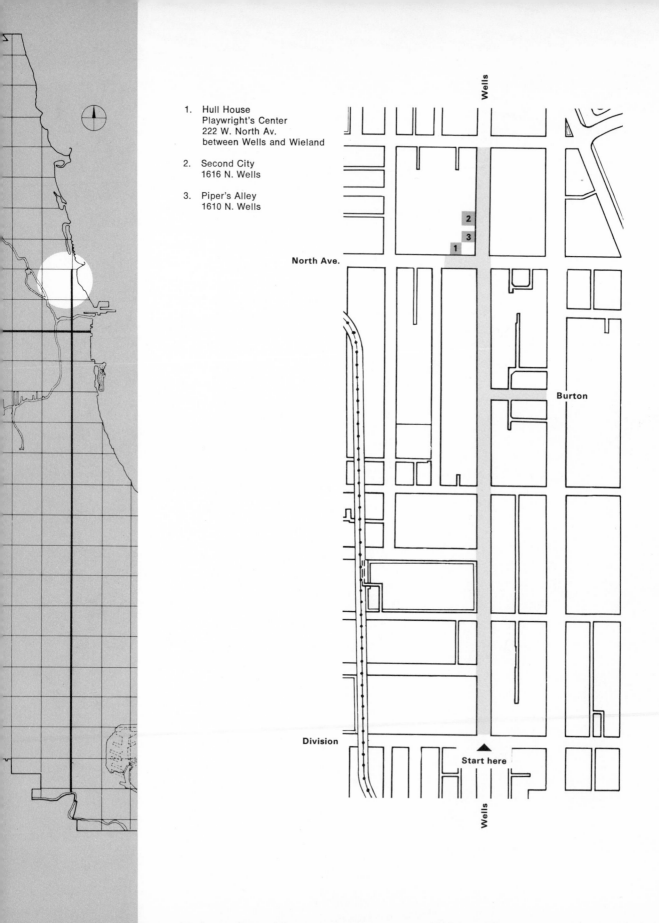

1. Hull House
   Playwright's Center
   222 W. North Av.
   between Wells and Wieland

2. Second City
   1616 N. Wells

3. Piper's Alley
   1610 N. Wells

Wells

North Ave.

Burton

Division

Start here

Wells

Walk · 36

OLD TOWN—THE WELLS STREET STRIP

WALKING TIME: 1½ hours (if you don't go Friday or Saturday night, when the streets are always jammed).   HOW TO GET THERE: Take a northbound CTA bus No. 11 (Lincoln-Wabash) on Wabash Avenue, and get off at Division Street (1200 N).

It's quite a sight, the Wells Street strip of Chicago's Old Town. It's the midwest equivalent of San Francisco's North Beach and New York's Greenwich Village. All the way from the first restaurants near Goethe and Wells, north to the multicolored row houses at the tip of Old Town Triangle (see Walk No. 19) it's a sight worth seeing!

Along this stretch of Wells Street is an amazing variety of stores and gift shops; restaurants, cafes, and night clubs; with an occasional art gallery or museum interspersed. You can buy anything here—from king-size candles to a corned beef sandwich, from the best in tableware to Japanese saki, from Oriental rugs to hand-blown glass figures. Or you can merely follow the lead of many young people—stash a bicycle in the rear of an ale house and sip a stein full. Whether you walk here day or night, you are sure to see rather amusing, odd-looking young people— "hippies" perhaps or just youngsters trying to look like hippies— as well as older visitors who have come by the dozens to look on. In any event the strip will give you many sights besides the shops and restaurants.

The architecture of this part of Old Town, if such it can be called, varies widely. Some of it is first-rate design, as in Soup's On (1246), the Scandinavian home furnishings store called Crate and Barrel (1510), and Antonio's Steak House (1528). Most of the facades, however, have been constructed exclusively to attract attention—in the same inevitably artificial way that the shops' names have been chosen, to vie with each other for novelty. You'll find, for example, Horse of Another Color, for a women's shop; Volume I, for a bookstore; Granny Goodfox, for a toy store; and for restaurants, such names as Quiet Knight (with folk music), Little Pleasures, the Hungry Eye, the Mad Greek, Pickle Barrel, and Chances R. Interestingly enough, a

311

bookstore with a more subdued name—Barbara's Book-Shop—seems to be a favorite gathering place for the serious young intellectuals of the area. And don't overlook the Volume I bookstore either.

One of the oldest establishments on these 6 blocks of Wells Street, dates all the way back to 1961! (The number that come and go with disturbing rapidity is a characteristic of the area.) At this restaurant it first became fashionable for customers to eat peanuts with their hamburgers and throw the shells on the floor. Along with such typically North American foods as hamburgers and peanuts, Old Town offers those of many other nationalities. By a recent count the various restaurants here were offering specialties in French, Spanish and North African, Mexican, Greek, Italian, Japanese, and East Indian and Pakistani foods, as well as Jewish dishes.

Music is frequent, of course, especially for dancing, though there is less variety than in the restaurants' menus. Mostly it is provided by folk singers, jazz bands, or jukebox.

These—and the magic name "Old Town"—are the attractions that crowd the street with customers and sightseers each weekend, as well as evenings in between. But the street has other attractions, such as 2 museums that fit perfectly in this environment: (1) the Royal London Wax Museum (1419) with life-size figures by Josephine Tussard of London—nearly a hundred of them (this is one way you can see such diverse "celebrities" as Elizabeth Taylor, Richard Burton, John F. Kennedy, Al Capone, and those involved in the St. Valentine Day massacre); and (2) Ripley's Believe-It-or-Not Museum (1500), the contents of which you can guess. Rumor has it that another museum, of ancient cars, called Cars of Yester Year, is also opening on Wells Street, at 1517. It may already be there.

Or, on a somewhat higher cultural level, you can hear new plays read or performed at Hull House Playwright's Center (22 West North Avenue, just off the north end of this walk); and any night but Monday you can attend really superior dramatic performances at Second City (1616 North Wells), where after each show the cast will improvise on topics suggested by the audience—except Fridays and Saturdays, when time is

Opposite, Piper's Alley with Its diversity of shops.

312

unavailable because of so many regular performances. Second City, a night club, more precisely a theatre-restaurant, has won well-deserved renown for its satirical revues and improvisation. In the brick facade of its building are embedded faces from Louis Sullivan's ornamentation of his famous Schiller Building (1892), later known as the Garrick Theatre Building (which stood at 64 West Randolph until it was demolished in 1961, only 2 years after Second City had been organized).

If you're a cat lover you will not have overlooked Feline Inn (1445) whether or not you feel that your own precious pet rates all the luxury provided the boarders there. Feline Inn also has exotic kittens and cats for sale.

Don't overlook Burton Place at 1500, a small side street tucked away to the east of Wells, one of Old Town's early residential streets. This one-block thoroughfare connects the Wells Street strip with Carl Sandburg Village, a glistening product of urban renewal, which has replaced an area of blighted buildings between LaSalle and Clark streets (see Walk No. 8, "The Gold Coast"). Unique and imaginative remodeling and rehabilitation make Burton Place fascinating. Tile mosaic, glass block, marble, terra-cotta, and old brick are some of the materials used in what is obviously self-help work without benefit of architect. Behind the brick walls you will find patios with marble walks, fountains, sculptured figures, flowers, and trees. A plaque on the wall at 155 Burton Place states that this building was restored in 1927 by Sol Kogen. (Mrs. Sol Kogen still lives there.)

Noteworthy examples of commercial renovation of old buildings are Gas Light Court (1407), an excellent example of what initiative and good design can accomplish; Maiden Lane (1521); and Piper's Alley (1610), named for a former owner, who is reputed to have baked fine bread. In Piper's Alley you are sure to see plenty of people as well as merchandise, for it is a veritable covered shopping center. It is by far the best.

(The recent urban development called Carl Sandburg Village runs parallel to this strip of Wells Street, from Division to North just one block to the east. It has been included in Walk No. 8, "The Gold Coast." Including it in this walk is not recommended if you want to savor a while the Old Town atmosphere!)

Notes—Index

Notes

WALK NUMBER 2

1. Giedion, Sigfried, *Space, Time, and Architecture, Sixth Edition.*
   (Cambridge: The Harvard University Press, 1946), p. 311.
2. Frederick Koeper, *Illinois Architecture.* (Chicago: The University of
   Chicago Press, 1968), p. 64.
3. Giedion, op. cit., p. 310.

WALK NUMBER 10

4. Kogan, Herman, and Lloyd Wendt, *Chicago: A Pictorial History.*
   (New York: E. P. Dutton and Company, 1958), p. 203.

WALK NUMBER 13

5. Kogan and Wendt, op. cit., p. 177.
6. Ibid.

WALK NUMBER 14

7. Graham, Jory, *Chicago: An Extraordinary Guide.* (Chicago: Rand
   McNally and Company, 1968), p. 343, note quoting part of John Crerar's
   will.

WALK NUMBER 16

8. Saarinen, Eero, "Campus Planning: The Unique World of the
   University," *Architectural Record,* November 1960, p.

WALK NUMBER 27

9. Koeper, op. cit., p. 204.

WALK NUMBER 29

10. Koeper, op. cit., p. 54.

WALK NUMBER 31

11. From the statement "How Chinese American Civic Council Was
    Started . . ." given on the inside front cover of the Council's
    publication *CAP (Chinese American Progress).*

Index

328

IRA BACH knows Chicago intimately. His unquenchable curiosity has led him through miles of walks in the city and its suburbs. He has acquired a deep familiarity with everything from the small details on the facade of the Rookery to Pullman's extraordinary "company town" on the far south side. As the Executive Director of the Chicago Dwellings Association, he reorganized that agency to develop and expand middle income housing in Chicago. Earlier he served the city as Commissioner of City Planning and Secretary of the Chicago Plan Commission, and before that as Executive Director of the Chicago Land Clearance Commission, in which capacity he was in charge of the slum clearance and redevelopment programs that resulted in Lake Meadows, Michael Reese, Prairie Shores, and Hyde Park-Kenwood. He has lectured at a number of universities throughout the country, and from 1958 to 1963 was visiting critic in City Planning at Yale University. In 1969 he resigned his position with the Chicago Dwellings Association to become president of Urban Associates, Inc. CHICAGO ON FOOT is his view, as planner, architect and citizen of the city he knows so well.